WEAPONS AND EQUIPMENT OF COUNTER-TERRORISM

WEAPONS AND EQUIPMENT OF COUNTER-TERRORISM

SECOND EDITION

MICHAEL DEWAR

ARMS AND
ARMOUR

Left: The Glover Transac
APC (see page 44) with security
forces deployed for action.

Arms and Armour Press
A Cassell Imprint
Wellington House, 125 Strand,
London WC2R 0BB

Distributed in the USA by
Sterling Publishing Co. Inc.,
387 Park Avenue South,
New York, NY 10016-8810.

Distributed in Australia by
Capricorn Link
(Australia) Pty. Ltd, 2/13 Carrington Road,
Castle Hill, NSW 2154.

British Library Cataloguing-in-Publication Data:
a catalogue record for this book is available from
the British Library

ISBN 1-85409-160-3

Designed and edited by DAG Publications Ltd.
Designed by David Gibbons; layout by Anthony
A. Evans; edited by Philip Jarrett; printed and
bound in Great Britain.

Acknowledgements.
The author is grateful to the many manufacturers
and institutions mentioned in the pages of this
book who have generously supplied information
and illustrations; the photographs are reproduced
by courtesy of the firms involved.

Michael Dewar, 1994

Contents

Glossary

AA	Anti-Aircraft
AP	Armour piercing
ADP	Automatic Data Processing
AFV	Armoured Fighting Vehicle
APC	Armoured Personnel Carrier
AM	Amplitude Modulation
ATO	Ammunition Technical Officer
CAM	Computerized Alert Monitor
CCTV	Closed Circuit Television
CLASSIC	Covert Local Area Sensor System for Intrusion Classification
CN	Riot control gas; tear gas precursor to CS
COR	Carrier Operated Relay
CRS	Compagnie Républicaine de Sécurité
CS	Riot control gas causing tears, salivation and painful breathing
CTW	Counter Terrorist Warfare
CWIED	Command Wire Improvised
DF	Direction Finding
DOV	Discreet Operational Vehicle
ECM	Electronic Counter Measures
EOD	Explosive Ordnance Disposal
EOR	Explosive Ordnance Reconnaissance
FM	Frequency Modulation
GPMG	General Purpose Machine-Gun
GRP	Glass Reinforced Plastic
GSG 9	Grenzschutzgruppe 9 (West German CTW unit)
HF	High Frequency
HOT	Haut subsonique Optiquement Téléguidé tiré d'un Tube
IED	Improvised Explosive Device
II	Image Intensification
IR	Infra-Red
IRA	Irish Republican Army
IS	Internal Security
LASS	Local Area Sensor System
LSI	Large Scale Integration
MG	Machine-Gun
MOD	Ministry of Defence (UK)
MPCM	Multi-Purpose Central Mount
MTBF	Mean Time Between Failures
NOD	Night Observation Device
OP	Observation Post
PLO	Popular Front for the Liberation of Palestine
RAG	Ring Airfoil Grenade
RCIED	Radio Controlled Improvised Explosive Device
RDF	Radio Direction Finding
RF	Radio Frequency
RX	Radio Receiver
SA	Small-Arms
SMG	Submachine-Gun
SWAT	Special Warfare Action Team
TI	Thermal Imaging
TOW	Tube-launched Optically-tracked Wire-guided
TX	Radio Transmitter
UHF	Ultra-High Frequency
VCP	Vehicle Check Point
VHF	Very High Frequency

Introduction

This book first appeared in 1987. It clearly met a need, since it sold widely around the world. Terrorist threats, civil disturbance and revolutionary warfare have not lessened in the past six years. It seems, therefore, that there is still a requirement for a volume such as this, which aims to provide a guide for those involved in the procurement of counter-terrorist weapons and equipment, for those military, paramilitary, police and Special Forces operatives actually engaged in the war against terrorism, and for the layman who wishes to be more aware of the ways and means available to protect our democratic way of life.

Despite the resolution of the hostage crisis in the Lebanon, and despite the end of the Cold War and consequently of such regimes as the Honecker regime in the former DDR, which harboured terrorists and instigated terrorism throughout Europe, terrorism remains the chosen tool of desperate minority groups across the world. In the Indian Subcontinent various ethnic groups use bombs and murder as their main instruments of coercion. In the Middle East, the defeat of Saddam Hussein has left most terrorist groups without a backer and without a cause. Nevertheless, fundamentalist Islamic groupings went on record after the resolution of the hostage crisis in late 1991/early 1992 as being determined to continue the struggle against Israel 'by other means'. Hesbollah and various other Palestinian organisations based in Lebanon and Iraq are unlikely to retire into obscurity, whatever the outcome of the peace process. Also, whilst Colonel Muammar Gadaffi publicly disassociated himself in December 1991 from state-sponsored terrorism in an attempt to extricate himself from the conse-

quences of the Lockerbie bombing, he and other leaders in the region are unpredictable and inconsistent. The further involvement of such regimes in terrorism cannot be entirely ruled out. Military rule in Algeria suppresses protest, but violence bubbles under the surface.

In South and Central America, revolutionary warfare, terrorism and narco-terrorism continue unabated. Although the Contras effectively ceased operations in Nicaragua in 1989, unrest persists in Guatemala, where an over-powerful army maintains a reign of terror over the Guatemalan Indian population. A truce between Government forces and the Farabundo Marti Liberation Nacionale (FMLN) in El Salvador remains in place at the time of writing; Panama is volatile and unpredictable. In Peru, the Sendero Luminoso (The Shining Path), a Marxist-Leninist revolutionary organisation, threatens the country. This determined and vicious terrorist group has advanced its revolution against a demoralised Peruvian government and military to the point where the international community could still be faced with a long-term emergency. Sendero Luminoso is not just another Latin American revolutionary movement that will, eventually, be defeated. It is a Maoist revolution based on China's Cultural Revolution. Insurgency experts have consistently underestimated the Sendero Luminoso for the past twelve years or so. Its Marxist indoctrination of young people, its extraordinary patience and its capacity for cruel Mafia-style intimidation makes its sudden defeat unlikely, despite the capture of its leader in September 1992. In Columbia, gang warfare and narco-terrorism flourish. Social conditions in urban areas of

Left: American SWAT team officer ready for action.

Above: British troops patrolling the streets of Londonderry.

Brazil seem likely to breed unrest and dissatisfaction. Left-wing terrorist organisations also exist in Chile and Bolivia.

In Africa, the Civil War in the Sudan continues, with no likely solution in sight. The Sudanese People's Liberation Army (SPLA) maintains control over some of the Christian and African south, and manages to outwit and usually outfight the Islamic Fundamentalist Arab regime in Khartoum. Somalia remains in a state of instability despite UN intervention. Liberia, Togo, Chad, Zaire, Nigeria and Western Sahara all have unresolved internal problems. Black-versus-black violence refuses to go away in the townships in South Africa. Much of this violence cannot be classified as terrorism *per se*, but ethnic and tribal disagreements are often the bedfellows of terrorism. The one breeds the other.

In Continental Europe the Red Brigades and the Bader-Meinhof groups seem to have been defeated, but everywhere fascism and racism and Far Right activities are on the increase. In Italy, Spain and the south of

France, immigration from the Maghreb is leading to a widespread racist backlash. In 1993, Monsieur le Pen of the French Far Right ominously claimed 15 per cent support across the country. In Germany neo-Nazi groups are re-emerging, condemning the flood of *Gastarbeiter* from Turkey, Rumania and Poland. Equally unattractive organisations are coming out of the woodwork in Belgium, and simultaneously the Walloons and Flemish speaking halves of Belgium are at each other's throats. In Spain, Basque separatists under the ETA banner stubbornly refuse to abandon their claim to a separate identity. Corsican and Breton nationalism is not entirely dead. Mafia-inspired terrorism in Italy became more prevalent in 1992-93.

In the Balkans, Central Europe and within the former Soviet Empire the potential for instability, civil war, violence and terrorism is immense. The Yugoslav Civil War of 1991-94, the fighting in many former Soviet republics and the ethnic tensions in Hungary, Rumania, Moldavia and elsewhere in the region do not bode well for the future.

In the United Kingdom, the situation in Northern Ireland changed radically in autumn 1994 with the declaration of a cease-fire. The Irish Republican Army (IRA) had until that time continued to bomb and murder in the name of Irish nationalism, while their counterparts in the Ulster Volunteer Force (UVF) and Ulster Freedom Fighters (UFF) did the same in the name of Loyalism. It must be hoped that the ceasefire will hold. In mainland Britain terrorism has even manifested itself in the shape of the Animal Liberation Front protesting against the use of live animals for experiments.

While rallies and marches in the streets are a legitimate form of protest in a liberal democracy, they clearly cannot be allowed to get out of hand. Whether it be French farmers protesting about the import of British lamb in the streets of Paris, Japanese stu-dents objecting to political corruption in Tokyo or South Korean citizens demanding more democracy, legitimate governments must maintain the means of keeping order in the streets. In this context, this book, as well as cataloguing anti-terrorist weapons and equipment also includes coverage of anti-riot equipment, as well as cataloguing anti-terrorist weapons and equipment. This does not imply that terrorism and rioting are synonymous; merely that the same forces are often employed to counter both.

One man's 'Freedom Fighter' is of course another man's Revolutionary. This book does not attempt to categorise revolutionary and terrorist organisations. Nor does it attempt to analyse, list or describe the many terrorist groupings that have terrorised the Western world since the 1960s, nor those extant today. Other books are available

Below: A vehicle checkpoint in Northern Ireland.

which attempt this task. Rather, this book seeks to demonstrate the extent of the civil and military counter-terrorist infrastructure, its techniques, and the panoply of sophisticated equipment available to combat terrorism successfully in whatever form it manifests itself. It is hoped that *Weapons and Equipment of Counter-Terrorism* will encourage the fainthearted and justify the resolve of all those who condemn terrorism.

There can be little doubt that terrorist organisations have become more sophisticated since the first version of this book was published, in 1987. The IRA in particular perfected the 'cell' system, first developed by communist guerrilla organisations in the 1950s and 1960s. The technique employed is to form small groups of four to six members, probably only one of which will be aware of the identity of any other member of the IRA outside his own cell. Even the leader of the cell is only likely to be in contact with an individual whose real name and identity is hidden from him. Thus, if an 'active service unit' or ASU, as the IRA calls its cells, is compromised, the damage is limited to that cell alone. In the past, ASU members may have been trained in the Middle East, probably in Libya, though today they will have received their training exclusively in Eire or Ulster and they will have been equipped with the necessary funds, weapons and explosives.

Certain types of plastic explosive are extremely hard to detect with the conventional weapon/metal detector, and may even escape detection by X-ray equipment, particularly if secreted on the person. However, increasingly sophisticated 'sniffing' equipment, which is able to detect such sub-

Below: British special forces in training.

stances, is now coming on to the market. Similarly, terrorists have become more audacious in their attacks on military installations. Thus surveillance and perimeter protection equipment, fencing and road barriers have all had to be improved to meet the increased threat. Quite rightly, indiscriminate riot control equipment is no longer always acceptable. While the use of tear gas may be acceptable in some circumstances, more discriminating equipment is increasingly required. Whereas in the former Soviet Union it was acceptable to use tanks to quell urban disturbances, there are very few places where such a blatant use of naked force would any longer be acceptable in a riot, or even in a counterinsurgency situation. In other words, there is a greater requirement for purpose-designed counterinsurgency and anti-terrorist equipment. The cheap option of deploying equipment originally designed for conventional warfare is becoming less

acceptable and, more to the point, inefficient.

Great advances have been made in the control of terrorism. Many of the terrorists of the 1970s are now dead or serving long prison sentences. Computer systems store vital data on known terrorists, suspects, terrorist organisations, their techniques and their capabilities, to the extent that there is even the possibility of predicting future actions. More efficient surveillance and intelligence infrastructures in the UK have frustrated many recent IRA attacks and uncovered spectacular illegal explosives and weapons hauls. The intelligence operation against the IRA was taken over by MI5 in 1992, a move that has already paid dividends. The disintegration of the former Soviet Union has meant that terrorists are no longer assured a safe haven in, for instance, the former GDR, which is known to have harboured terrorists. Semtex explosive, manufactured in the Czech Republic, is no longer

Right: A Lazy Tongs portable road block device – a simple way of disabling wheeled vehicles.

Below: American SWAT team in training.

so freely available for purchase by terrorist organisations. More effective airport security has reduced the likelihood of a renewal of the aircraft hijacking campaign, and at the same time frustrated attempts to introduce explosives on to aircraft. Many more innovations have changed the security climate.

These methods can, of course, counteract those known or potential terrorists who display a recognisable pattern of behaviour and who belong to a recognised group. What they cannot do entirely is control the pure 'symbolic' act with no previous pattern of violence. It is generally accepted by most security organisations that the lone assassin or a suicide squad can breach the most effective systems. The latest methods and equipment are unlikely to stop the revolutionary who poisons Israeli oranges, as an Arab recently claimed to have done, or an individual who implants poison in a well-known brand of headache cure, as happened in the United States in early 1986. It is impossible to guard all the areas of risk in a modern Western society. And the United States, which is already suffering terror by crime rather than as a result of politically motivated actions, became a target for terrorists when the World Trade Center was bombed.

Whether in a rural or an urban environment, operations short of conventional limited warfare are generally known as 'Low Intensity' or 'Internal Security' (IS) operations. In a rural environment it has usually been possible to use soldiers and to adapt conventional military equipment to meet any threat to the security of the state. In an urban environment, however, most governments have found it to be both militarily advantageous and politically expedient to train specialist IS forces and to develop or purchase special-purpose IS equipment. It is therefore largely in the urban sense that the term 'Internal Security' is used in this book. In their widest sense, IS operations include all operations undertaken by government forces against indigenous or infiltrated armed groups that constitute a threat to the stability of the state.

In some countries the army is automatically called upon to deal with a terrorist threat. Elsewhere, the police or specialist elements of the police are used. In the United States various SWAT teams are trained and equipped to deal with terrorist situations, and élite police squads, such as D11 of London's Metropolitan Police, have special expertise with firearms. In many countries a so-called 'third force', designed to deal with riots and other IS situations, has been created. These are paramilitary organisations, as exemplified by the CRS (Compagnie Républicaine de Sécurité) in France, the Bundesgrenzchutze or Federal Border Guard in Germany, and the Guardia Civil in Spain. There are also various 'élite' units. Britain's Special Air Service, a regiment of the Regular Army, enjoys an awesome reputation worldwide; West Germany has formed GSG 9, a paramilitary unit armed with small-arms, machine-guns, helicopters and APCs, although its members have the status of policemen; and in the United States there are a number of such organisations, including Delta Force. Every modern police force and army, to a greater or lesser degree, retains some sort of specialist anti-terrorist capability.

In Western countries, industry has become increasingly involved in the business of countering terrorism. Many companies offer a complete range of counter-terrorist equipment, some or all of which they manufacture themselves. Although many countries, particularly in Europe, now manufacture counter-terrorist weapons and equipment, the majority of the most successful companies can still be found in the United Kingdom and the USA. In the case of the UK this was partly a function of its large defence industry base, but was also a result of its need to develop sophisticated counter-terrorist equipment as early as 1969 because of the situation in Northern Ireland. This having been said, Germany, Switzerland, Italy, France, the Netherlands, Belgium, Spain and Israel all produce significant amounts of counter-terrorist and Internal Security equipment. The bias in this book is towards equipment manufactured in the UK, as this reflects the author's experience.

Coverage in this book cannot possibly be comprehensive. That would require a work stretching to many volumes, which would be highly repetitive and probably very boring. Such is the speed of development of IS equipment, and the rate of expansion of the IS industry, that this book can only hope to illustrate a representative range of different categories of equipment from all over the world. Nor does the book aim to illustrate just the latest equipment. Rather, it presents a representative cross-section of both the latest technology and well-tried equipment that has been in service for some time. No other book to date has brought together such a range of IS equipment.

The developed world, as this book demonstrates, is well armed and well prepared to deal with the continued onslaught of terrorism. Security forces are becoming better trained, better equipped and more experienced. Civilian companies now provide not only equipment but guards, expertise and complete training packages. More and more automobile companies are producing overt and covert IS vehicles, and police forces are

being equipped with sophisticated anti-riot and anti-terrorist equipment. Bomb disposal teams now have a wide range of advanced equipment to detect, disrupt and disarm every sort of explosive device. Scientists are working on still more sensitive explosives detection equipment for airports. Perimeter protection is becoming big business as security forces, public utilities and industry invest in safeguarding their assets. Perhaps the most interesting area of all is that of communications, where highly sophisticated surveillance, monitoring, jamming and interception equipment is constantly being refined. The terrorist faces an increasingly effective and sophisticated armoury of equipment. The effort must, and should, continue. If, as seems likely, propaganda by the deed becomes the principal means of revolutionary violence, it is the developed world that will suffer the brunt of the attack. The assault will be directed not so much against institutions or individuals, but against affluence and the Western way of life.

Below: American SWAT team preparing to assault.

Left: The classic image of special forces operatives in action.

Below: British soldiers prepare a robot bomb disposal vehicle.

1
Internal Security Vehicles

Today, most armoured personnel carriers tend to be tracked in order to perform their primary cross-country role in general war as efficiently as possible. However, tracked vehicles are not best suited to the IS role for a number of reasons. They are often difficult and expensive to operate and maintain; they are noisier than wheeled vehicles; they can cause damage to road surfaces; and, most important of all, they are classed as 'tanks' by the layman and the media. The use of 'tanks' in an IS situation is often politically unacceptable. In most IS situations, vehicles are required to operate mainly on roads and in an urban environment, so wheels are most suitable in every respect. Thus many purpose-designed IS vehicles are now manufactured to meet this new requirement.

Most IS armoured vehicles are 4 x 4 wheeled vehicles affording protection from small-arms fire up to and including 7.62mm. Some of the heavier IS vehicles afford protection against attack by 7.62mm armour- piercing weapons. They must be provided with observation blocks, so that the crew can see what is happening around them. In a conventional rural environment, when a vehicle is likely to be operating in wide open spaces in conjunction with many other vehicles and infantry on the ground, it is not so vital that a vehicle crew has a comprehensive all-round view of the ground. However, in an urban environment, to prevent a petrol bomber, for instance, approaching an armoured vehicle from a blind spot, an ideal IS vehicle must allow good all-round vision. Similarly, firing ports should be provided so that the crew can, if required, use their small-arms from within the vehicle.

Vulnerable points on the vehicle, such as the fuel tank and radiator, should be given special protection, particularly from petrol bomb attack. The other main threat is from attack by anti-tank grenade. In Northern Ireland the IRA used RPG-7 rocket launchers against APCs with limited success – APCs are insufficiently armoured to prevent the penetration of projectiles from rocket launchers. In an urban environment, however, the close range at which terrorists are forced to engage APCs militates against a successful engagement. The limited exposure time of an armoured vehicle passing a fixed point means that the firer has very little time to recognise the target, prepare to fire, acquire the target, aim and engage. Often RPG-7 projectiles have passed behind their target, on some occasions unnoticed by the occupants of the vehicle.

An IS vehicle must be designed to allow rapid access and egress by crew and passengers. There are many examples of IS vehicles where this characteristic has been included in the design. Clearly, in a confused situation probably involving large and disorderly crowds, it is only sensible to have multiple doors in an IS vehicle. In a conventional war the enemy is normally expected from a single direction. In guerrilla warfare the enemy might attack from any quarter. The requirement is therefore to be able to leave the vehicle from the opposite side to the direction of the attack. Side doors also dictate that there should be only four wheels, an arrangement that is also sensible in the interests of simplicity and mechanical reliability.

IS armoured vehicles can be fitted with a variety of armament installations, including water cannon, tear gas launchers and machine-guns. Some can even be electrified to prevent rioters climbing on to the vehicle. In addition to armoured vehicles, a number of other types of vehicle are commonly used in IS situations: water cannon vehicles, which may or may not be armoured; conventional 'soft skin' vehicles that have been covered in a form of appliqué lightweight armour as protection against blast and low-velocity rounds; and armoured bulldozers for the removal of barricades. Appliqué armour was first developed for the British Army in an attempt to provide some protection for Land Rover crews against blast, fire and acid bombs, and low-velocity small-arms fire. GRP is a form of glassfibre used to cover the body and roof of Land Rovers, while Macralon, a form of strengthened plastic, is used to cover windscreens and windows.

Older vehicles can be adapted in many ways for IS purposes. In Northern Ireland, for example, the British Army adapted the long-serving GKN Sankey AT-104 IS vehicle, commonly known as the 'Pig', by attaching unfolding fenders to each side. Thus the vehicle, if parked in the middle of a relatively narrow road flanked by buildings, can block most of the road off and afford protection against missiles thrown by rioters. The adapted vehicle is known as the 'Flying Pig'. Other possible attachments are roof- or turret-mounted searchlights, loudspeaker systems and a strong device for removing barricades. A self-help device fitted to many jeeps and Land Rovers in the IS role is a fence piquet attached vertically to the front of the vehicle to cut steel wires stretched across roads with the intention of causing serious injury to the occupants of open vehicles.

A common threat to IS vehicles, particularly in a rural environment, is the land mine. The design of IS vehicle hulls should ideally be such that, if a mine is triggered by one of the vehicle's wheels, the upward slope of the hull deflects much of the blast and the strong

Below: A Saracen APC after being severely damaged by a landmine in Northern Ireland.

monocoque structure provides maximum protection so long as the crew are strapped in their seats. Examples of a shaped hull are the South African Hippo vehicle, the British GKN Sankey Saxon and Italy's Fiat 6614CM APC.

IS vehicles should be of simple and rugged construction. They are often used in less-developed countries with limited maintenance resources. A vehicle that closely follows such a design philosophy is the GKN Sankey Saxon. It is powered by the widely available Bedford 500 six-cylinder diesel truck engine, and the use of commercially available automotive parts means that anyone who can maintain a truck can also maintain the Saxon. Similarly, the French Berliet VXB anti-riot vehicle uses 'off-the-shelf' Berliet truck spares and is both easy and cheap to maintain. Design details are very important. For example, in the Belgian Beherman Demoen BDX, the engine air intake is located below the generous canopy over the driving position, and has a moving shutter to provide further protection against Molotov cocktails. The twin exhaust pipes run along the two sides of the roof, making it more difficult to climb on the vehicle.

A growing number of police forces and counter-terrorist organisations throughout the world recognise that discreet operational vehicles (DOVs) – standard commercial vehicles and limousines that are armoured without appearing to be so – are less provocative in low- and medium-risk IS environments than the more heavily armoured, obviously military hybrid vehicles. There will always be IS situations that warrant the attendance of highly protected military vehicles, but in many incidents the use of DOVs could be more politic and just as effective. Confrontations with lightly-armed terrorists, student demonstrations, and the carriage and escorting of government VIPs are examples. The current range of DOVs include:
● Land Rover and Range Rover-type vehicles for anti-terrorist operations, with a cross-country capability and all-round protection against handguns, submachine-guns,

grenade fragments and certain categories of rifles;
● VIP limousines with all-round protection against handguns, submachine-guns and grenade fragments;
● Saloon cars and Range Rover-type vehicles for VIP escort duties, with partial protection against handguns, submachine-guns and grenade fragments;
● Fast patrol cars for immediate response and pursuit, with frontal protection only against handguns and submachine guns.

Modern technology is narrowing the gap between what is technically feasible and operationally desirable in terms of both opaque and transparent armour. However, the design of a DOV requires thought; the answer is not necessarily to cram as much armour as possible on to a given chassis. Users often tend to ask for unrealistic and often unnecessarily high levels of armour, while insisting on minimum changes in vehicle performance and appearance. In reality the two are often irreconcilable. On the other hand, manufacturers, whose experience is usually confined to automotive engineering, tend to offer solutions that do not take sufficient account of the operating conditions and protection requirements of the user.

For instance, if a manufacturer decides that the main threat to a head of state is from the 7.62mm NATO rifle or its equivalent, the passenger section of his armoured limousine can be given complete protection against single shots from this weapon. However, to avoid significant modifications to the engine and the suspension, the driver's section would need to be left unprotected. An IS expert would advise that the death or incapacitation of a driver while travelling at speed would be likely to result in the death of the head of state anyway! Moreover, when the protected limousine is for a head of state, the need for protection to this degree can be questioned. Sensible precautions along a route should reduce the opportunities to use a high-powered rifle, and, where such use is very likely, the VIP should change his route or cancel the engagement altogether. A much more likely

Terrorist Weapons and Armour Materials Used to Resist Them

Weapon	Muzzle Velocity	Impact Energy at 50m	Aluminium		Steel		Composite		Glass		Glass Polycarbonate
	m/sec	mkg	mm	kg/m^2	mm	kg/m^2	mm	kg/m^2	mm	kg/m^2	mm
Pistols											
9mm Luger	338	47	4	11	2	14.58	6.86	13.7	25	61	-
.38 Colt	260	35	6	16.6	2	14.58	6.68	13.7	25	61	-
.38 S & W	185	16	4.5	12.5	2	14.58	6.86	13.7	25	61	-
.357 Magnum	439	101	7	19.5	2	14.58	8.66	17.1	25	61	-
Submachine-guns											
9mm Sterling	390	64	7.5	21	2	14.58	8.66	17.1	29	70	-
.45 Thomson	280	58	7.5	21	2	14.58	8.66	17.1	29	70	-
Rifles											
7.62 Ball NATO	855	380	27.5	70	5	39.38	15.23	42.3	63	150.7	35.5'
5.56mm Armalite	990	173	21	59					63	150.7	35.5'

Notes: A curved windscreen of glass/polycarbonate mix now available is capable of stopping single shots from the NATO 7.62mm rifle and the 5.56mm Armalite (both ball). The armour data is drawn from international sources. Resistance figures are derived from tests held under varying conditions. BSS 5051 Part 1 (1973) details appropriate performance requirements and test methods for security glazing. It makes provision for spall from the rear surface when attack takes place. These stringent conditions are not universally applied.

threat is from the assassin in the crowd, armed with a concealed handgun or submachine-gun. All-round protection against this threat, rather than an attempt to armour only the rear section of a limousine against the unlikely use of a 7.62mm weapon, would be the wiser course of action.

Successful DOV design should be based on the premise that no DOV will be bullet-proof. The best protection will merely buy time. The armoured Lincoln Continental limousine delivered to the US Secret Service in 1969 carried two tons of armour steel and bullet-resistant glass, and was capable of travelling at 50mph with all the tyres shot out. The Secret Service would have been the first to admit that its most attractive characteristic was its ability to maintain mobility with all its tyres deflated; the mass of armour could not have protected the occupants from sustained fire from high-power automatic rifles available on the open market. It might have resisted the first few rounds, allowing time for the agents travelling in the back-up vehicles to return fire, or for the chauffeur in the protected limousine to put his foot on the accelerator.

Some of the problems that arise in attempting to bring about a compromise of discretion, protection and performance will be apparent from the weapons and armour table. This gives the ballistic properties of a selection of weapons used by terrorists, and the necessary thickness and weight of various armoured materials currently in use. Lighter materials with similar or superior resistance qualities are under development, but they are not yet widely in use. It can be seen from the table that even all-round protection against a low-velocity 9mm SMG will impose a considerable weight penalty. Such protection would seem to be a sensible minimum for VIP limousines, with the possible addition of selected points being protected against 7.62mm high-velocity rifle attack in high-risk areas of the world. It is possible to compensate for the increased weight by restricting the number of persons in the vehicle or by modifying the chassis, suspension and engine.

If the occupants of a DOV are in a position to return terrorist fire, then there are different options.

Above: The Shorland S52 armoured patrol car provides a cost-effective aid to law enforcement, cross-country or on the streets.

A fast patrol car may need only a bullet-resistant windscreen, an armoured engine bulkhead and armour added to the inside of the front doors and the rear of the front seats. Provided only two persons used the car, it would normally require no modification to engine or chassis to achieve the same performance as the original version of the car with four persons in it. An escort vehicle, however, would normally require more extensive protection, if only because it might have to serve as a temporary refuge for a threatened VIP.

Wheels are particularly vulnerable on a DOV. Some sort of 'run-flat' capability is essential for accidental or induced blow-outs at speed, and to enable the driver to extricate the vehicle from an ambush if the tyres are shot out. There are various solutions. One involves the fitting of steel discs inside the tyres so that the weight of the vehicle is supported when the tyres are deflated. Another is the Dunlop Denovo system, which injects

a lubricant between the deflating tyre and the wheel rim. Both systems allow a vehicle to be driven out of an ambush, the Denovo system permitting it to be driven for up to 100 miles.

There is no doubt that DOVs have their place in the fight against terrorism. Assassination or kidnapping of VIPs is now a favourite terrorist tactic. Ostentatious personal protection precautions can be counterproductive in PR terms, particularly for a politician, and are likely to be exploited for propaganda purposes by political dissidents. DOVs, on the other hand, can provide an effective low-profile alternative.

There is also a category of IS vehicle that lies somewhere between the DOV and the more heavily armoured, obviously military hybrid vehicles. These are somewhat akin in appearance to a standard civilian security vehicle used to transport cash and other valuables. One such is the Glover Transac APC, which has a high 30mm ground clearance, floor protection against blast, military run-flat tyres, crew deployment via six doors, air conditioning, protection against incendiary devices, power-assisted steering, bullet-proof glass and a whole range of other special characteristics. It is simple and box-like in appearance, and not unduly antagonistic. This category of vehicle is becoming increasingly popular in many parts of the world, particularly in the Middle East and South Africa.

This chapter does not aim to cover all international IS vehicles. This would not be possible in the space available. Rather, it aims to cover a representative cross-section of IS vehicles from the international field.

BRAZIL

Engesa EE-II Urutu APC

Designed and built by Engesa of São Paulo, Brazil, this is an armoured amphibious vehicle designed to perform various roles, and which can be transformed into a family of vehicles. The engine of the Urutu is at the front on the right of the driver, which leaves the rear of the hull free for a compartment able to accommodate up to fourteen men or carry 1,800kg of cargo. A large door in the rear of the hull and a door on each side provide alternative means of entry or exit. There are four hatches in the rear compartment in addition to the driver's hatch. The vehicle is fitted with firing ports. The engine air louvres can be closed to eliminate the risk of flames from Molotov cocktails entering the engine compartment, and cooling air is then admitted into the engine from the crew compartment through a pneumatically operated hatch which is normally closed.

Variants: The design allows it to be transformed into a family of vehicles. In addition to the APC version, the Urutu can be used as an armoured ambulance, a command and

Below: Engesa EE-II Urutu APC.

communication vehicle, and an armoured cargo vehicle. The Engesa EE-9 Cascavel is an armoured car variant. The overall specification is similar, the main differences being its turret-mounted 90mm gun and the fact that it is not amphibious, although it has a fording capability of one metre.

Employment: The riot-control version is in service with the Brazilian Army and Marines, Bolivia, Chile, Colombia, Gabon, Iraq, Libya, Tunisia and United Arab Emirates.

Data: *length* 6m; *width* 2.59m; *height* 2.09m (to hull roof); *ground clearance* 0.34m; *wheel track* 2.1m; *wheelbase* 3.05m; *weight* 11,000kg (unladen), 14,000kg (laden); *engine* Detroit diesel 6v-53 developing 212hp at 2,200rpm; *crew* 14; *number of wheels* 6 x 6; *speed* 95kph; *range* 750km; *gradient* 60%; *vertical obstacle* 0.6m; *fording depth* amphibious; *turning radius* 10m; *maximum side slope* 30%; *armament* - cupola for .50cal MG *or* 20mm automatic gun and turret *or* 60mm gun mortar and turret *or* 90mm cannon with coaxial 7.62mm NATO MG and turret.

CZECH REPUBLIC

Tatra OT64 APC

The OT-64 is based on the Tatra 815 truck, development of which started in 1959. The passengers, protected by 10mm of armour, are situated at the rear of the vehicle and are provided with overhead hatches, rear exit doors and firing ports.

Variants: Model 1 (7.62mm MG in an unprotected mount); Model 2 (12.7mm or 7.62mm MG with curved shield); Model 3 (14.5mm and 7.62mm MGs in an armoured turret); Model 4 (same armament as Model 3 but with a higher turret); Model 5 (the Model 1 with two Sagger anti-tank missiles mounted over the rear of the passenger compartment); and the two command models, the R2 and R3.

Employment: Czech Republic, Egypt, Hungary, India, Libya, Morocco, Poland, Sudan, Syria and Uganda.

Data: *length* 7.47m; *width* 2.52m; *height* 2.24m; *ground clearance* 0.38m; *weight* 14,515kg (laden); *engine* Tatra T-928-14 V-8 diesel developing 300bhp at 2,000rpm; *crew* 20; *number of wheels* 8 x 8; *speed* 90kph; *range* 650km; *gradient* 60%; *vertical obstacle* 0.5m; swims.

EGYPT

Walid APC

An open-top 4 x 4 vehicle produced in Egypt and used for both military and police work.

Employment: Algeria, Burundi, Egypt, Israel, Sudan and Yemen (PDR).

Data: *engine* German Deutz air-cooled; *crew* 10; *number of wheels* 4 x 4; *armament* normally Goryunov GSM 7.62mm MG.

EIRE

Timoney BDX IS Vehicle

Design studies for this vehicle were started in January 1972 by the Irish company Technology Investments Ltd (TIL), primarily to the specifications of the Irish Department of Defence. The first prototype was completed in July 1973 and two more prototypes were built by mid-1974. These three prototypes successfully concluded an exhaustive evaluation programme. A production licence was taken out by the Belgian company Beherman Demoen of Bornem; hence the designation BDX. The vehicle is designed primarily for urban combat, but is also able to perform more conventional military duties in a rural environment. Its 12.5mm armour is thicker than that of most other vehicles of its kind, and provides protection against 7.62mm armour-piercing bullets fired at short range, yet does not add excessive weight. The driver is seated well forward to give him the widest possible field of view, and has a large windscreen of laminated glass possessing the same strength as the vehicle body, with two smaller side windows of the same material. The provision of these relatively large windows meets the need for good vision from within an armoured vehicle in urban operations. Doors in each side, as well as in the rear of the hull, meet the third requirement

for urban operations, namely the provision of multiple means of entry or exit. Production is now complete.

Variants: The BDX can be fitted with a dozer blade for clearing barricades, and there are various turret options.

Employment: Argentina, Belgium (Air Force and Gendarmerie) and Eire (Army).

Data: *length* 4.95m; *width* 2.41m; *height* 2.13m; *ground clearance* 0.38m; *wheel track* 1.9m; *wheelbase* 2.85m; *weight* c. 8,250kg (unladen), c. 9,350kg (laden); *engine* Chrysler 360 CID V-8 spark ignition, developing 200bhp at 4,000rpm; *crew* 12; *number of wheels* 4 x 4; *speed* 100kph; *range* 640-960km; *gradient* 60%; *vertical obstacle* 0.4m; swims; *turning radius* 14m; *maximum side slope* 45%; *armament* 7.62mm L37, L7 or L8 GPMG; or .50 Browning MG; or 7.62mm MG MAG; or twin 7.62mm MG; or 81mm mortar.

FRANCE

Berliet VXB 'Gendarmerie' IS Vehicle

Designed to meet the particular requirements of police armoured units, this vehicle has been in production at Berliet's Bourg factory since 1973. The characteristics that make the VXB ideal for IS missions include the large crew compartment of 11 cubic metres, the excellent visibility with no blind spots (the windows are bullet-proof glass reinforced with steel mesh), easy entry and exit (two large doors in the sides and one at the rear), effective protection against small-arms fire, mines and bombs (engine air intakes can be blocked), and good manoeuvrability. One VXB prototype was fitted with the TOP7 commander's cupola of the AMX 30 battle tank, one of the best observation cupolas available; its experimental installation illustrates the importance

Left: Belgian Army Timoney BDX IS vehicle unloading from a Transall aircraft.

given to vision in the VXB anti-riot vehicle.

Variants: The VXB 'Combat' is designed to meet the requirements of modern armoured units, and can mount a wide range of armaments. The VXB 'Gendarmerie' can be equipped with a dozer blade and/or an hydraulic winch. Production is now complete.

Employment: France (Gendarmerie), Gabon, Senegal and Tunisia.

Data: *length* 5.9m; *width* 2.44m; *height* 2.05m; *ground clearance* 0.38m; *wheel track* 2.04m; *wheelbase* 3m; *weight* 8,900kg (unladen), 12,000kg (laden); *engine* Berliet diesel developing 170bhp; *crew* 15; *number of wheels* 4 x 4; *speed* 85khp; *range* 750km; *gradient* 60%; swims; *turning radius* 15.6m; *armament* externally mounted 7.5mm or 7.52mm MG.

Below: Berliet VXB 170 'Gendarmerie' IS vehicle.

Panhard IS Vehicles
AML H60-7 Armoured Car

Development of the AML series started in 1956. The wide range of possible armaments, the good performance and low operating cost (the Panhard 4HD engine does 100km on about 26 litres) have made the AML particularly appreciated by those countries with a restricted military budget. The H600-7 version has been specially designed for IS and anti-guerrilla operations, and for use in built-up areas.

Variants: AMH 90 Reconnaissance Vehicle mounting a 90mm gun; AML 60/20 Reconnaissance Vehicle mounting a 60mm mortar and a 20mm cannon.

Employment: 4,000 AMLs of all types have been produced, including 700 for the French Army and Gendarmerie. The AML is also

used by Abu Dhabi, Algeria, Burundi, Cambodia, Chad, Congo, Ecuador, Eire, Ethiopia, Iraq, Israel, Ivory Coast, Kenya, Lebanon, Libya, Mauretania, Malaysia, Morocco, Nigeria, Portugal, Rwanda, Saudi Arabia, Senegal, South Africa, Spain, Tunisia, Upper Volta, Venezuela, Zaïre and Zimbabwe.

Data: *length* 3.79m; *width* 1.97m; *height* 1.86m (to turret roof); *ground clearance* 0.31m; *wheel track* 2.05m; *wheelbase* 2.7m; *weight* 4,800kg; *engine* Panhard 4HD 4-cylinder 1,997cc 90hp; *crew* 3; *number of wheels* 4 x 4; *speed* 90kph; *range* 600km; *gradient* 60%; *fording depth* 1.1m; *turning radius* 13.1m; *maximum side slope* 30%; *armament* one 60mm CMA1 Hotchkiss Brandt gun/mortar breech- or muzzle-loaded, and two AA-52 NF-1, or 7.62mm MAG-80 MG.

M3 VTT APC

The M3 series was designed as a troop transport complement to the AML towards the end of the 1960s. In relation to the size of its hull the vehicle has an exceptional carrying capacity of eleven men plus the driver. The M3 uses many of the components of the AML, but has the additional advantage of being amphibious without preparation. Protection for the personnel on board, who can use their individual weapons through six side ports and enter and exit through two large rear doors, is provided by 10mm armour plate, and attention has also been given to protecting all apertures against the entry of inflammable liquids.

Variants: M3 VDA AA weapon system, armed with two HS 820 SL (or M693) 20mm cannon; M3 VTS Ambulance; M3 VPC Command Vehicle, armament as for VTT; M3 VAT Recovery Vehicle. Production is now complete.

Employment: Abu Dhabi, Angola, Congo, Eire, France, Iraq, Kenya, Lebanon, Malaysia, Portugal, Saudi Arabia and Spain.

Data: *length* 5.31m; *width* 2.5m; *height* 1.75m; *ground clearance* 0.47m; *wheel track* 2.12m; *wheelbase* 2.95m; *weight* 5,800kg (laden); *engine* Panhard 4HD 4-cylinder

1,997cc 90hp; *crew* 12; *number of wheels* 4 x 4; *speed* 90kph; *range* 600km; *gradient* 60%; swims; *turning radius* 13.1m; *maximum side slope* 30%; *forward armament* one swivel-mounted weapon support for 7.5mm or 7.62mm AA-52 MG; *or* TL2 152 turret mounting two 7.62mm MG; or T20 turret mounting one 20mm cannon and coaxial 7.62mm MG; *rear armament* one weapon support revolving on semicircular rail for 7.5mm or 7.62mm AA-52 MG or a MAG-80 MG.

Buffalo

The Panhard Buffalo MO (Maintien de l'Ordre) is a 4 x 4 armoured vehicle weighing 6.6 tons, carrying six men and specifically designed for IS situations. It is equipped with an Hispano-Suiza Puma turret and is powered by a Peugeot 71 KW XD3T diesel engine. The hull, which is based on the Panhard M3 APC, has been redesigned to eliminate the sharp edges on the earlier models.

Employment: Units have been ordered by the police of an unspecified country.

VBL: The Panhard VBL is the law enforcement version of the Buffalo. Panhard estimates that the potential market for this type of light armoured vehicle in its various configurations is 5–10,000 units. Of this total, the French Army is equipped with approximately 3,000.

Saviem/Creusot-Loire VMO IS Vehicle

Saviem, in collaboration with Creusot-Loire (the two Companies formed the Société des Matériels Spéciaux Saviem-Creusot-Loire), produced the VAB, from which the VMO is derived, to meet a specification issued in 1969 by the French General Staff for a multi-role amphibious wheeled armoured vehicle to fill a forward tactical support role. The vehicle was adopted in mid-1974 by the French Army, which purchased 4,000 over a ten-year period. The VMO, an IS variant of the VAB, first appeared in 1977. Illumination on the VMO is provided by a searchlight that pivots with the gun mounting. Optional equipment comprises a periscope (magnifi-

Right: Panhard Buffalo.

cation x 1) linked to a retractable sight (magnification x 3), pivoting with the weapon mounting, plus four side observation periscopes. The weight of the turret, including weapons, ammunition and optics, is 270kg. An optional item of equipment is an hydraulically controlled dozer blade, which enables the vehicle to breach road barricades, etc.

Variants: The VAB is also produced in a 6 x 6 version and with a variety of armaments, including HOT or TOW missiles, twin 20mm AA MG and 20mm or 30mm cannon. Command and recovery variants are available.

Below: Panhard VBL.

Employment: Central African Republic, Cyprus, France (Army), Ivory Coast, Lebanon, Mauritius, Morocco, Oman, Qatar and United Arab Emirates.

Data: *length* 5.98m; *width* 2.5m; *height* 2.06m; *ground clearance* 0.4m; *wheel track* 2.07m; *wheelbase* 3m; *weight* 10,900kg (unladen), 12,900-13,900kg (laden); *engine* 235hp diesel; *crew* 12; *number of wheels* 4 x 4; *speed* 90kph; *range* 1,300km; *gradient* 50%; *swims*; *maximum side slope* 35%; *armament* in TL1G light turret manufactured by Creusot-Loire situated centrally and mounting a 7.62mm MG and a 40mm grenade launcher.

ISRAEL

Ram Light Armoured Vehicles

The Ram is manufactured by Ramta Structures and Systems, a subsidiary of Israel Aircraft Industries Ltd of Beersheba. There are five versions of the Ram: the TCM-20 20mm Twin Cannon Mount; the Close Range Tank Hunter (Destroyer) carrying a 106mm recoilless gun; the Long Range Tank Hunter (Destroyer) mounting a TOW missile system; the Infantry Fighting Vehicle; and the RAM V-11 APC. The last two are suitable for IS operations: both are basic but rugged vehicles.

Above: Saviem/Creusot-Loire VMO IS vehicle.

Above right: Ram V-11 APC.

Right: Ram Light Armoured Vehicle.

Infantry Fighting Vehicle (IFV): This configuration is equipped with three 7.62mm machine-guns, night vision equipment and a multi-channel transceiver.

Ram V-11 APC: This version carries a total of 8-10 men and all their personal equipment. Its unique system of folding armour-plate hatches, which can be fully or partly opened, provides all-round observation while affording protection against small-arms fire. Various armament combinations are possible, including 0.5in machine-guns, 0.3in machine-guns and 40mm grenade launcher. In addition it is fitted with night vision equipment and multi-channel transceiver/receiver. Both the IFV and APC versions have an exceptional power-to-weight ratio, ensuring good acceleration and a high top speed. Armour is 8mm thick and provides effective protection against close-range small-arms fire. The underside of the vehicle is 10mm steel plate, V-shaped to give maximum protection against mines.

Employment: Israel Defence Force.

Data: *length* 5.02m; *width* 2.03m; *height* 1.72m (APC 2.2m); *ground clearance* 0.38m; *wheelbase* 3.4m (long wheelbase version 5.42m); *weight* 5,400kg combat-loaded (APC 5,700kg); *engine* Deutz 6-cylinder 132bhp; *crew* 6+2 (longer wheelbase version 8+2); *speed* 96kph; *range* 800km (APC 750km); *gradient* 70% (APC 65%); *vertical obstacle* 0.8m; *fording depth* 1m; *turning radius* 7.2m; *maximum side slope* 35%.

ITALY

Fiat 6614CM APC

The 6614CM APC and its companion vehicle, the 6616BM Armoured Car, are the first armoured vehicles to be built in Italy since the end of the Second World War. With a good performance, and using the same mechanical components, these are relatively advanced vehicles without being too sophisticated. The aim is simplicity, reliability, safety and low cost. Firing ports are provided for individual weapons, and exit from the vehicles is reasonably simple through the large rear ramp and two side doors.

Below: Fiat 6614CM APC.

Above: Fiat 55-13 armoured bus.

Variants: 6616BM Armoured Car with revolving turret mounting a 20mm automatic cannon and coaxial 7.62mm MG plus a variable smoke grenade-launcher, breech-loaded from inside the turret, and six fixed-range smoke grenade dischargers. Alternatively, TOW or MILAN missiles can be fired from the turret. In 1985 Fiat announced a development of the 6614CM, the 6634G.

Employment: Italy (Carabinieri, Army), Libya, Peru, Somalia (270 ordered 1977 and delivered by 1979), South Korea and Tunisia (120 ordered in 1979). The vehicle is still in production in Italy and South Korea.

Data: *length* 5.86m; *width* 2.5m; *height* 1.78m (to hull roof); *ground clearance* 0.37m; *wheel track* 1.96m; *wheelbase* 2.9m; *weight* 7,000kg (unladen), 8,500kg (laden); *engine* Fiat 6-cylinder diesel developing 160hp at 3,200rpm; *crew* 11; *number of wheels* 4 x 4; *speed* 100kph; *range* 700km; *gradient* 60%; *vertical obstacle* 0.45m; *swims*; *turning radius* 7.96m; *maximum side*

slope 30%; *armament* 12.7mm Browning M2 Heavy MG, 7.62mm MG.

Fiat 55-13 Armoured Bus

The Fiat 55-13 armoured bus is specially designed for police use in activities such as riot control, surveillance, safe transport of personnel and the patrol of areas where the crew may be exposed to small-arms fire or to Molotov cocktails or stone-throwing. The driver has the benefit of excellent visibility, which helps to avoid collision with demonstrators when driving through dense crowds. This fast and powerful vehicle allows rapid police deployment during riots. The steel armour plating covered by the body panelling, and the windows in 27mm-thick bullet-proof glass, can stand up to pistol or submachine-gun fire. The fuel tank and radiators are also protected. The two side doors and single rear door are fitted with safety locks and a limiting device to prevent them being forced open from the outside. Firing ports can be provided to allow the crew to use weapons and to eject tear-gas bombs. There is an observation hatch in the roof. Options available are a fire-fighting system, which sprays on to the wheels, engine and fuel tank; fireproof coating for electric cables and fuel pipes; a tear-gas filtering system; and an air conditioning system.

Employment: Italy (Police).

Data: *length* 5.8m; *width* 2.1m; *height* 3m; *ground clearance* 3m; *wheelbase* 3m; *weight* 5.8 tons (gross); *engine* Fiat 8000.04 diesel, 6-cylinder developing 130hp at 3,200rpm; *crew* 1+10; *number of wheels* 4 x 2; *speed* 110kph; *gradient* over 40%; *turning radius* 5.5m.

RUSSIA

BTR-152 APC

This vehicle, based on the ZIS-151 truck chassis, first appeared in 1950. Later models used the ZIS-157 chassis. It is the most widely used of Soviet vehicles in IS situations. Although no longer in service with the Russian Army, the vehicle is still used for IS duties.

Variants: BTR-152V (with variable tyre pressure system), BTR-152K (with overhead armour), BTR-152U (command vehicle) and the BTR-152V (with twin 14.5mm guns).

Employment: Afghanistan, Albania, Algeria, Cambodia, Ceylon, China, Congo, Cuba, East Germany, Egypt, Guinea, Hungary, India, Indonesia, Iran, Iraq, Israel, Mongolia, North Korea, North Yemen, Palestine Liberation Army, Poland, Romania, Somalia, Soviet Union, Sudan, Syria, Tanzania, Uganda, Yugoslavia.

Data: *length* 6.55m; *width* 2.31m; *height* 2.01m; *ground clearance* 0.31m; *weight* 8,950kg (laden); *engine* ZIS-123 6-cylinder in-line petrol, developing 110bhp at 2,900rpm; *crew* 17; *number of wheels* 6; *range* 644km; *gradient* 55%; *vertical obstacle* 0.6m; *fording depth* 0.8m; *armament* one 7.62mm SGMB MG.

SOUTH AFRICA

Armscor AC 200 Mine Protected Armoured Support Vehicle

This vehicle is a high-mobility, mine-protected armoured support vehicle carrying up to 13 men and suitable for use on IS rural

Below: Armscor AC 200 mine-protected armoured support vehicle.

operations. The vehicle has both side and rear exits, and its windows and firing points allow the crew to engage targets from within the vehicle, while individual hatches in the roof allow riflemen to look out of the top of the vehicle. South African security forces have had to contend with mined roads, so the wedge shape of the hull of the vehicle is designed to deflect the force of an explosion upwards and outwards. The relatively high position of the crew compartment in relation to the ground gives added protection.

Variants: The vehicle is available in 4 x 4, 6 x 6 and 8 x 8 configurations. The 8 x 8 version is available as a logistics, recovery and technical support or transporter vehicle. The 6 x 6 version is available in configurations including troop carrier, ambulance, command vehicle and transporter.

Employment: South African Defence Forces.

Data: *weight* 18 tonnes; *engine* V-8 turbo-charged intercooled diesel; *crew* 3+10; *number of wheels* 4 x 4 or 6 x 6; *speed* 108kph; *range* 1,000km at 80kph; *gradient* 70%; *vertical obstacle* 0.6m; *trench crossing* 1.2m; *fording depth* 1.2m; *armament* one 7.62mm MG, two 7.62mm AA MG.

Charger

Originally developed in South Africa by Mechen, the Charger is distributed by Trojan in the UK from a Coventry base. It is suitable for a variety of roles, for which a range of equipment can be fitted with minor modifications to the structure. Both 4 x 4 and 4 x 2 versions are available. The Charger has been developed to counter attack by mines, whilst at the same time providing high levels of ballistic protection for the sides and roof. The V-body shape ensures limited damage to the capsule on contacting an anti-tank mine. In fact, the hull is designed to withstand a double TM57 landmine explosion beneath any

Left: Ingwe security vehicle.

Right: Trojan Multi Purpose IS Vehicle

wheel, and a single detonation centrally under the vehicle.

Variants: In addition to the standard eleven-man APC, there is a seven-crew APC, an anti-tank vehicle, a bomb disposal vehicle, a General Weapons Carrier, an anti-riot vehicle, a Command car, a Scout vehicle and an anti-aircraft vehicle.

Employment: It is thought that Chargers are in service in several sub-Saharan African countries.

Data

Dimensions: *length* 5.88m; *width* 2.38m; *height* 2.54m; *angle of approach* 40°; *angle of departure* 45°.

Vehicle Weights:	4x2	4x4
Unladen	4,980kg	5,076kg
Payload	1,140kg	1,140kg
GVM	6,120kg	6,216kg

Engine: direct-injection turbo-charged 4-cylinder diesel, maximum power (DN) 85kW at 2,800rpm, maximum torque (DN) 378Nm at 1,500rpm; *transmission* Gearbox-type 5-speed synchromesh manual; *suspension* semi-elliptic leaf spring front and rear; *shock absorbers* double-action telescopic hydraulic.

Performance: *maximum speed* 105km/h; *range* paved roads, 800km, cross-country 600km; *gradability* forward (4 x 2) 40%, forward (4 x 4) 60%; *turning circle* ±15.150m.

Sandock-Austral Ingwe Security Vehicle

The Sandock-Austral Ingwe is a high-mobility four-wheel drive IS vehicle suitable for

use by civilian security companies, police or military. Its hull design offers excellent protection to crew and passengers against land mines, and its hull provides protection against small-arms fire up to 7.62mm ball ammunition. In its standard form the interior layout will accommodate fourteen persons, but different seating layouts may be specified and a range of optional extras are available, including various radio fits, searchlights, weapons mounting points and turrets and heavier armour protection. Ingwe uses proven, commercially available equipment with ease of maintenance in mind. The vehicle is a simple and highly practical IS vehicle.

Employment: Thought to be about to enter service with the South African Defence forces.

Data: *weight* 10,000kg; *engine* 6-cylinder diesel developing 124kw at 1,700rpm; *crew* 2+12; *number of wheels* 4 x 4; *speed* 100kph; *range* 500km; *gradient* 60%; *vertical obsta-cle* 0.6m; *trench crossing* 1.04m; *fording depth* 1.2m.

Trojan Multi Purpose IS Vehicle

The Trojan Multi Purpose IS vehicle is marketed by Integrated Trade Services (ITS) of Hamburg and manufactured in South Africa. It is ideally suited to the urban riot situation. The monocoque hull design is manufactured from armoured plate. Ballistic resistance up to 7.62mm NATO ball ammunition is provided by the body and bullet-resistant glass. All windows, lights and externally mounted auxiliary equipment are protected from hand-thrown missiles by heavy-duty welded mesh screens. The pneumatically operated bull bar can be operated from within the vehicle to bulldoze obstacles from its path. Also, the Trojan's unique pneumatic 'plug' doors allow for crew deployment via both doors in a restricted space as little as 2.8m wide, such as an alleyway or between buildings. A water cannon can be fitted to the top of the vehicle, though obviously the 25-litre water tank reduces crew space inside the vehicle. The six-cylinder, six-litre diesel engine gives a top speed of approximately 100kph (60mph), and the 4 x 4 configuration gives an impressive off-road capability.

Variants: In addition to the APC version, water cannon and ambulance versions are available. The casualty compartment in the ambulance version can be fitted for 5+2 stretchers or 2+3 stretchers.

Employment: It is thought that APC versions are being supplied to several Middle Eastern customers.

Data

Dimensions: *height* 2.64m; *width* 2.50m; *length* 5.20m; *wheelbase* 3.0m.

Weights (4 x 4): *tare* 7,420kg; *payload* 1,780kg; *gross* 9,200kg. **(4 x 2):** Tare 7,050kg; *payload* 1,750kg; *gross* 9,200kg.

Performance:	**4 x 2**	**4 x 4**
Maximum speed	104kmh	100kmh
Gradability	30% 14°	60% 33°
Turning circle	13.5m	13.5m

Engine: 6-cylinder in-line, 5,958cc compensated/turbo diesel.

SWITZERLAND
Mowag IS Vehicles

Mowag of Kreuzlingen has produced a family of wheeled vehicles, most of which are either specifically designed for, or are suitable for, IS work. The principal vehicles are detailed below.

Mowag Piranha IS Vehicle

The Piranha family of 4 x 4, 6 x 6 and 8 x 8 armoured vehicles are fairly recent Mowag developments. There are three different hull lengths, with two, three and four axles, accommodating eight, ten and eleven men respectively. The vehicle is available in an amphibious 4 x 4 version, and this is the most suitable for IS operations. The front, side and rear armour is capable of withstand-

Below: Mowag Piranha IS vehicle.

ing horizontal fire from NATO 7.62mm ammunition, the floor is proof against anti-personnel mines and the roof against splinters.

Employment: Details not available.

Data: (non-amphibious 4 x 4 version): *length* 5.39m; *width* 2.5m; *height* 1.85m (hull); *ground clearance* 0.5m; *wheel track* 2.18m (front); *wheelbase* 2.5m; *weight* 7,750kg (laden); *engine* Detroit diesel 8.2-litre V-8; *crew* 8; *number of wheels* 4 x 4; *speed* 100kph; *range* 700km; *gradient* 70%; *turning radius* 12.6m; *maximum side slope* 35%; *armament* turret for .50 M2 MG (4 x 4D) or remote-control 7.62mm MG (4 x 4P).

Mowag Roland IS Vehicle

A smaller, lighter and faster 4 x 4 APC, in all other respects similar to Piranha.

Employment: In service with a number of unspecified countries, including several in South America.

Data: *length* 4.73m; *width* 2.05m; *height* 2.1m (to top of turret); *ground clearance* 0.42m; *wheel track* 1.67m (front); *wheelbase* 2.65m; *weight* 4,900kg (laden); *engine* Chrysler 8-cylinder V90; crew 5-6; *number of wheels* 4 x 4; *speed* 110kph; *range* 570km; *gradient* 60%; *fording depth* 1m; *turning radius* 13.7m; *maximum side slope* 30%; *armament* turret for .50 M2 MG or remote-control 7.62mm MG; optional equipment includes obstacle-removing equipment and searchlight on turret.

Mowag Spy

The Spy is the latest in the range. It has been specifically designed as a reconnaissance vehicle for all types of terrain and climate; so were the British Ferret and the French Panhard AML H60-7, but both were more widely used on IS duties than any other Western vehicles during the 1950s and '60s and into the '70s. The excellent power-to-weight ratio of 27hp/ton gives the Spy exceptionally good

Below: Mowag Spy.

Above: Mowag Wotan IS vehicle.

acceleration and mobility. Its crew of three makes it more suitable for rural IS operations, providing escorts for convoys or VIPs. **Data:** *length* 4.5m; *width* 2.5m; *height* 1.67m (hull); *ground clearance* 0.5m; *wheel track* 2.18m (front); *wheelbase* 2.5m; *weight* 7,500kg (laden); *engine* Detroit diesel 8.2-litre V-8; *crew* 3; *number of wheels* 4 x 4; *speed* 110kph; *range* 700km; *gradient* 60%; *fording depth* 1.3m; *turning radius* 12.6m; *maximum side slope* 35%; *armament* as Roland, plus option for twin .30 and .50 MGs.

Mowag Wotan

This was first produced in 1957/8, and in 1959 23 were supplied to the German Frontier Police, who subsequently decided to equip all of their mobile units with it. In 1962 Henschel (now Thyssen-Henschel) produced 260 under licence, most of them without armament and fitted only with an observation cupola for the vehicle commander; this version was designated SW-1 Kfz-91. A number were fitted with a turret mounting a 20mm Mk 20-1 (HS 820) cannon, and this version was designated SW-11 Kfz-91.

Employment: Wotans are still in service in limited numbers in Germany as well as in Chile.

Data: *length* 5.31m; *width* 2.2m; *height* 2.2m (to top of turret); *ground clearance* 5m; *wheel track* 1.95m; *wheelbase* 2.6m; *weight* 8,600kg; *engine* Chrysler R-319 six-cylinder petrol, developing 161bhp; *crew* 7; *number of wheels* 4 x 4, steering on all; *speed* 85kph; *range* 400km; *gradient* 60%; *armament* manually operated 7.62mm MG mounted externally.

Mowag Grenadier

Like the Wotan, this is an older member of the family, but is still in service in many parts of the world. It was developed to fulfil several roles, including that of an IS vehicle. A variant lacks the propeller drive.

Data: *length* 4.9m; *width* 2.43m; *height* 1.75m (to hull roof); *ground clearance* 4m; *wheel track* 1.99m (front), 2m (rear); *wheelbase* 2.5m; *weight* 5,000kg (unladen), 6,000kg (laden); *engine* as Roland; *crew* 8; *number of wheels* 4 x 4; *speed* 100kph; *range* 750km; *gradient* 70%; swims; *turning radius* 12.9m; *maximum side slope* 30%; *armament* as Roland, but can also mount 25mm Oerlikon cannon.

UNITED KINGDOM

Avon Inflatables
Avon Special Forces Searider

Searider craft are produced by Avon Inflatables of Llanelli, Wales. The R6M Searider was originally designed as a safety boat for the North Sea oilfields. However, specially equipped craft are produced for law enforce-ment, firefighting, fishery protection and special forces use. These craft have self-righting equipment and immersion-proofed engines and electrical systems. Their inflatable buoyancy and deep V seagoing hulls enable Seariders to operate in the most difficult of conditions. They are suitable for off-shore counter-terrorist use, such as in the protection of oil rigs, and also on sea borders to intercept infiltrators or gun runners.

Employment: Royal Navy, UK Coastguard, and other navies.

Data: *length* 6.05m; *beam* 2.34m; *weight* 681kg; *capacity* 1,125kg, 15 persons; *power* 2 x 90hp; *speed* 40kt.

GKN Sankey IS Vehicles
AT-104

This vehicle was developed from the 1-tonne 4 x 4 Humber 'Pig' (FV1611) armoured truck, which was the Humber FV1601 truck chassis powered by a 120hp six-cylinder Rolls-Royce B-60 Mk 5A petrol engine, on

elow: Avon Special orces Searider.

which was mounted an armoured shell produced by GKN Sankey of Telford, Shropshire, and the Royal Ordnance Factories. The AT-100 (4 x 2) and the AT-104 (4 x 4) were produced in 1972 by GKN Sankey to meet the specific requirements of urban anti-guerrilla operations. Utilising Bedford civilian truck parts already in production, to keep down costs, these vehicles are among the first to have been specially designed for this type of work.

Variants: The AT-104 has a number of optional items that can be fitted on request, including spotlights, an hydraulic winch, a loudspeaker system, a barricade remover, flashing beacons and/or sirens. The basic vehicle has been adapted variously, and provides a classic example of how a single machine can be modified to meet a multiplicity of different roles.

Employment: Brunei, Netherlands (Police); some 500 uparmoured Humber 'Pigs' are available for service with the British Army in Northern Ireland.

Data: *length* 5.49m; *width* 2.44m; *height* 2.49m (to standard cupola roof); *ground*

Left: AT-104.

Below: Saxon with wings to guard against hand-thrown objects.

clearance 0.51m; *wheel track* 1.72m; *wheelbase* 3.33m; *weight* 8,074kg (unladen); *engine* varies according to petrol or diesel power unit fittings, to provide power in the range of 100-150bhp, using standard units from General Motors; *crew* 11; *number of wheels* 4 x 4; *speed* 80kph; *range* 500km; *gradient* 50%; *fording depth* 1m; *maximum side slope* 30%; *armament* in standard form is not fitted, but the cupola can be replaced in manufacture by a specially designed turret to mount single or twin MGs of 7.62mm or 5.56mm calibre; alternatively a MG can be externally mounted, and grenade launchers can also be fitted.

Saxon (IS version)

Designed for anti-riot requirements in urban areas, and for counterinsurgency and guerrilla warfare, the IS version of the Saxon has a turret that can mount a wide variety of specialist weapons including smoke, CS gas, submachine-guns and rifles. The hull is resistant to 5.56mm and 7.62mm AP or ball at point-blank range. The specially shaped hull avoids mine blast pockets and affords maximum protection to the crew, engine, gearbox and radiator. Runflat tyres are fitted as standard. Accessibility is excellent via two large doors in the rear, which are controlled by the driver, and two side doors.

Above: Saxon.

There are six observation/firing ports, and the driver has four small windows fitted with bullet-proof glass giving the same degree of protection as the armour plate. The combination of good vision for crew and driver, power steering and small turning circle gives high manoeuvrability in built-up areas.

Variants: The IS version of Saxon has three additional operation fits:

Armoured Ambulance

The protection of injured police, security forces and VIPs is of prime importance, and speed in evacuation is crucial to the survival of the severely injured. The internal arrangement allows for up to four stretcher cases, or two stretcher cases and six sitting wounded, or ten sitting wounded.

Employment: Bahrain, Kuwait, Malaysia

range 480km; *gradient* 66%; *vertical obstacle* 4.0m; *folding depth* 1.12m; *turning radius* 8.75m; *maximum side slope* 36%.

Armament: not fitted as standard, but a pintle-mounted MG can be fitted in the command cupola; alternatively, a 7.62mm GGMPG turret can be mounted.

Border Patrol/Airport Security

Security Forces face a multitude of threats, such as international terrorism and arms and contraband smuggling across national boundaries; they also have to maintain constant vigil at key points such as airports, border crossing points and seats of government

Incident Control Vehicle

Of similar silhouette to the standard vehicle, this variant accommodates a wide variety of sophisticated electronic, communication and surveillance equipment. The vehicle enables commanders rapidly to achieve control at an incident in a secure, protected environment..

Simba FS100 APC

Simba is a fast, highly mobile APC. It has two side exits and double rear doors, and comes in two armour options.

Option 1 (High Mobility): a lightweight hull design of high-hardness ballistic steel gives immunity against 7.62mm ball rounds at any angle and any range. The shaped hull ensures survival against close-quarter attacks by 7.62mm AP rounds.

Option 2 (High Protection): an increased-thickness hull provides complete immunity against 7.62mm AP or ball rounds fired from any distance or from any angle between +40° and -10°. this option gives enhanced protection against fragments resulting from mortar and artillery attacks.

Variants: FS 100/APC armoured vehicle, FS 100/AA vehicle, FS 100 20mm armoured fighting vehicle, FS 100 ATGW vehicle, FS 100/90mm armoured fighting vehicle.

Employment: The vehicle is particularly suited to IS operations. The Philippines government has confirmed that it is to buy 150 Simba 4 x 4-wheel armoured vehicles from the UK company Defence in a deal worth £30 million (US$57 million), including

(40 in service with the Army), Nigeria, Oman and United Kingdom.

Data: *length* 5.34m; *width* 2.5m; *height* 2.86m (to top of turret); *ground clearance* 3.3m; *wheel track* 2.06m; *wheelbase* 3.12m; *weight* 9,600kg (unladen); *engine* General Motors Bedford-type 500 6-cylinder diesel, developing 167bhp at 2,800rpm; *crew* 2+8-10; *number of wheels* 4 x 4; *speed* 96kph;

Left: Simba FS100 APC.

Right: Glover Transac 4x4 APC Mark I.

Below right: Glover Transac 4x4 APC Mark II.

spares and training. Simba, derived from the Saxon armoured personnel carrier which is widely in service, will be built in the Philippines by Asian Armoured Vehicle Technologies Corporation (AAVTC), a joint-venture company formed by GKN, the Philippine Veterans Development Corporation and others.

Data: *length* 5.26mm; *width* 2.54m; *height* 2.1m; *ground clearance* 0.33m; *wheel track* 2.07m (front), 2.12 (rear); *wheelbase* 2.97m; *weight* 8.2 tonnes; *engine* Perkins TV8 540 diesel, developing 210bhp at 2,500rpm; *crew* 12; *number of wheels* 4 x 4; *speed* 110kph; *range* 640km; *gradient* 52%; *turning radius* 8.25m; *maximum side slope* 35%.

Glover
Glover Transac 4 x 4 APC

The Glover Transac 4 x 4 APC is one of the most impressive IS vehicles currently on the market. Its six full-size doors allow a trained fourteen-man crew to debus in four seconds. It has a total of ten gun firing ports; four per side and two in each rear door. Its relatively narrow 2.2m width is ideal for an urban environment. It has a high 0.3m ground clearance to traverse debris.

Variants: 7.62mm protected water cannon, command and communications unit, ambulance, airport security vehicle.

Employment: Transac GS 4 x 4 Mk II are operating in Pakistan, SE Asia and the Middle East including Kuwait.

Data: *crew* 2+12; *payload* 2,000kg; *unladen weight* 6,300kg; *front axle* 4,400kg; *rear axle* 4,400kg; *power : weight ratio* 17.22bhp/tonne; *gross vehicle weight* 8,300kg; *length* 5.6m; *width* 2.2m; *height* 2.35m; *ground clearance* 0.28m; *track* front/rear (approx) 1.95m; *wheelbase* 3.3m; *angle of approach* 35°+; *angle of departure* 35°+; *side angle* 35°+; *turning radius* 8m; *maximum speed* on road 105kmh; *fuel capacity* 170 litres; *maximum range* (standard tank) 650+km; *standard engine* Perkins 'Phaser' diesel 145T, 143bhp; *engine option* Renault Midliner diesel MIDS 06 02 12B, 147bhp.

Hotspur Armoured Vehicles
The Commander

The Hotspur Commander, with its fully armoured monocoque hull, is based on the Reynolds Boughton RB-44 vehicle recently selected by the British Army to meet their

2-tonne-vehicle requirement. The vehicle is powered by a Perkins Turbocharged four-cylinder diesel engine developing up to 120bhp at 2,600rpm. The permanent four-wheel drive system offers good rough terrain capability, and complete protection for the twelve-man crew is provided by the fully welded armoured body. The steel armour is designed to provide ballistic immunity from 7.62mm NATO ball ammunition at 25m and at 90° attack angle.

Data: *length* 5.7m; *width* 2.25m; *height* 2.33m; *combat weight* 6,600kg; *engine* (standard) diesel 110T (military); *power : weight ratio* 16.51bhp/tonne; *ground clearance* 0.236m (9.00 x 16 tyres); *wheelbase* 3.226m; *angle of approach* 40°; *angle of departure* 24°; *turning radius* 7.7m; *maximum speed* (on road) 105kph; *fuel capacity* (standard tank) 128 litres; *maximum range* (standard tank) 550km; *gradability* 50%.

Armoured Saloon Cars

Hotspur Armoured Products, a division of Penman Engineering Ltd, can supply customised armouring for a range of saloon cars. In many cases the armouring system has been developed in conjunction with the vehicle manufacturer, so that the general per-formance of the vehicle can be retained as far as possible. The vehicle is detrimmed and, depending on the desired level of protection, high-hardness steel, ceramic, or ballistic nylon armour is fitted to the internal skin of the passenger compartment. For most applications an extremely hard steel of low alloy content is used, which will withstand multiple impact and continue to give protection against further attack. Ballistic protection can be offered up to high-velocity rifle standard, and at the highest level this forms a ballistic cell encompassing floor, roof, and all vertical surfaces, with overlaps and slave plates protecting virtually all possible points of ballistic penetration including door and window apertures, locks, cable ways, etc. The original glazing is replaced with transparent armour offering protection to a level consistent with that of the opaque armour, and at the higher protection levels utilises glass/polycarbonate composites. The vehicle is retrimmed to be virtually indistinguishable from the original trim. The same attention is devoted to the external appearance of the vehicle, to ensure that it displays no obvious outward signs of having been protected. The protection levels offered range from anti-kidnap through handguns (.38, .45 ACP,

Above: Hotspur Commander.

46

.357 Magnum, .44 Magnum using metal-piercing ammunition), 9mm submachine-gun, shotguns and .30 M1 carbine, to 7.62 and 5.56mm high-velocity weapons such as Enfield, Heckler & Koch, Kalashnikov and Colt M16. The range of vehicles which have been protected embraces Rolls-Royce, Range Rover, Land Rover and even heavy commercial vehicles.

Employment: Hotspur conversions have been supplied to heads of state, government ministers and officials, the diplomat corps and police and military forces in many countries around the world.

Data: As well as the armouring of the vehicle and glazing, special fittings can be added, including air conditioning, explosion-proof/self-sealing petrol tanks, run-flat wheel inserts, passenger-controlled centralised door locking with anti-hijack bolts on each door, engine immobilising devices, a rein-

forced suspension system, discreet identification lights alongside or behind the radiator grille, emergency spotlights for use if normal lighting is destroyed, a distress siren or two/three-tone driving horns, automatic fire-extinguishing systems for engine compartment and boot, a concealed microphone and loudspeaker system allowing communications between occupants and persons outside the vehicle without loss of ballistic protection, a radio telephone or two-way radio system, smoke or gas dischargers, public address systems, and hostile fire indicating systems, which through radar sensors detect and display the direction or directions from which shots are being fired at the vehicle.

Hotspur Pinzgauer Ecosse APC

One of Hotspur's latest products, the Pinzgauer Ecosse is a rugged and simple APC designed for a driver, front passenger and

Below: Hotspur Pinzgauer Ecosse APC.

eight passengers in rear. It is armoured to provide immunity from 7.62mm NATO ball ammunition at 25m at 90° attack angle. Rapid deployment through wide access doors is a particular feature of this APC. It has six gun firing ports and vision blocks.

Data: *gross vehicle weight* 4,500kg; *tailer weight* (on road) 5,000kg, (off road) 1,800kg; *payload* 800kg; *maximum speed* 112k/h; *gradability* (fully laden) 84%; *turning circle* 13m; *ground clearance* 0.335m; *fording depth* (approx.) 0.7m.

Hussar APC

This is a light armoured car for IS situations. It has single access doors on either side and a double door at the rear. Three gun slots and vision blocks are provided on each side of the vehicle, and one in each of the rear doors. The front and side windows are glazed in transparent armour and offer the same degree of protection as the hull, which is proof against 7.6mm high-velocity ball rounds at 25m. The vehicle has an armoured monocoque hull encompassing both crew and engine compartments. A light armoured turret or rotating MG hatch are mounted on top of the vehicle. Optional equipment includes a run-flat tyre system, multiple grenade launchers, a night vision facility for the driver, a self-sealing petrol tank, spot lamps, an intercom and siren and a PA system.

Above: Hotspur Hussar.

Above: Hotspur Polisec 8/12-man police vehicle

The Hussar fourteen-man Internal Security Vehicle (ISV) Police/Paramilitary is the same vehicle as the Hussar APC, except that it lacks a turret and is designed to look more like a police vehicle than a military APC. To that end it is painted white and is equipped with spot lamps, a PA system and blue flashing lights.

The Hussar Polisec eight/twelve-man Police vehicle again uses the same chassis as the APC and ISV, but is designed purely for police use. Although the vehicle looks like a modified Land Rover, additional armour fitted on the inside of the vehicle's body provides protection against small-arms fire. The armour is thought to be based on that employed in the earlier Hotspur Armoured Land Rover. This was fabricated from 4.76mm Hotspur steel, with windscreen and side and rear windows of laminated armoured glass.

Employment: Hussar is now in service with at least five overseas countries. The Hussar is also built under licence in Spain by IMAHO for the Spanish Army.

Data: *length* 5.74m; *width* 1.85m; *height* 2.28m (with hatch) 2.62m (with turret); *wheel track* 1.48m; *wheelbase* 3.81m; *weight* 5,350kg; *engine* Rover 3.5 litre V-8 petrol, developing 114bhp at 4,000rpm; *crew* 14; *number of wheels* 6 x 6 or 6 x 4.

The Skirmisher

The Skirmisher is a versatile 4 x 4-wheel drive armoured personnel carrier, based on the Land Rover 110in coil sprung chassis. It has a well proven record, being deployed in many countries in civil unrest situations. The Skirmisher monocoque armoured steel hull is designed to give complete crew protection against 7.62mm NATO ball ammunition. The V-shape hull gives enhanced ballistic protection, since few surfaces are at normal angle to attack. The floor is protected against mine and grenade fragmentation. The Skirmisher is capable of transporting up to eight crew, including driver, over difficult terrain, and is fitted with six gun firing ports designed for rapid deployment of weapons. The hull is a fully welded body unit complete with seats for up to eight people including the driver. It is fabricated from lightweight high-hardness steel armour, and is bolted in the chassis. Windscreen and front side windows are of laminated armoured glass with anti-splinter screens of polycarbonate. The

Above: Hotspur Skirmisher.

vehicle shell also affords protection to the engine compartment. The driver and co-driver's doors and the rear crew doors are provided with internal operated shoot bolts. Special attention has been given to the design of the door apertures to ensure complete spall protection. The armoured door overlap strips fitted incorporate a double seal unit and spall return strip, giving proof against petrol ingress and spall fragments.

Variants: armoured personnel carrier (APC), command/communications, ambulance, EOD transport and command, cash and valuables transport, narcotics unit, prisoner transfer, escort vehicle.

Data: *length* 4.865m; *width* 1.85m; *height* 2.21m; *wheelbase* 2.794m; *height with turret* 2.62m; *fuel capacity* 98 litres; *minimum ground clearance* 0.215m; *approach angle* 49.5° (laden); *departure angle* 30° (laden); *weight* 3,800kg; *engine* standard V8 petrol; option turbo-charged diesel; *transmission* 5 speed with dual range transfer gearbox, 4 x 4 drive.

Land Rover

Land Rover vehicles have been in service with military forces throughout the world for over 40 years, and are currently used by more than 100 military and paramilitary authorities worldwide. The latest coil-sprung versions of the Land Rover were introduced in 1983. The current Land Rover range consists of the 90, 110 and 127, and there is a high degree of commonality of components between the three models, enabling users to exploit the flexibility offered without complex logistics. Land Rover 90, 110 and 127 vehicles are in service with military forces around the world, and are used by the British Army as the standard truck utility light and truck utility medium. Land Rover 127 vehicles are in service with the Royal Air Force as ambulances, and also as the primary support vehicles for the British Aerospace Rapier anti-aircraft missile system. A wide range of power units is available; four-cylinder, 2.5 litre petrol, diesel or diesel turbo engines, or a V8 3.5 litre all-aluminium petrol engine.

Left: Land Rover 110 Station Wagon.

These power units are particularly suited to the demanding requirements of off-road vehicles.

Data	90	110	127	6 x 6
Dimensions/weights				
Wheelbase (m)	2.36	2.794	3.226	3.94
Overall width (m)	1.79	1.79	1.79	2.062
Overall length (m)	3.883	4.438	5.132	6.001
Cab height (m)	2.035	2.035	2.035	2.08
Cargo bed length (m)	1.14	2.01	2.58	3.147
Cargo bed width (m)	1.43	1.67	1.865	2.0
GVW (kg)	2,550	3,050	3,500	5,600
Capacities				
Fuel capacity standard (litres)	54	80	80	130
Seating				
Maximum	7	12	14	17
Performance				
Turning circle, kerb to kerb (m)	11.7	12.8	15.0	16.8
Approach angle	48°	50°	50°	45°
Departure angle	49°	35°	35°	33°
Ramp break over angle	150°	152°	155°	148°
Maximum gradient (EEC kerb weight)	45°	45°	45°	45°
Minimum ground clearance (m)	0.191	0.215	0.215	0.215
Wading (without preparation)	0.6m	0.6m	0.6m	0.6m

Lower left: Land Rover 127 Shelter.

Below: The Land Rover 6x6 long-range patrol vehicle.

Variants: It is not possible to cover all of the Land Rover variants in this volume. Some of the notable variants are:

The Land Rover Armoured Patrol Vehicle

This is based on the Land Rover 110 chassis. The concept was to create a powerful, highly mobile, low-profile vehicle with outstanding ballistic protection. The vehicle has a fully-armoured monocoque hull manufactured from special armoured steel. The front wind-screen and cab windows are constructed of bullet-proof multilaminates of glass with a polycarbonate anti-space liner. Both armour

and glass give protection against 7.6mm at point-blank range. Machine-pressed GRP plates are fitted to the floor area, plus an additional belly plate under the front crew area to give protection against grenade fragmentation and nail-bomb attack.

Land Rover Defender SOV

The Defender Special Operations Vehicle (SOV) is being offered by Land Rover to meet the needs of special forces and rapid reaction forces. Carrying up to six crew, it has a greater range and load capacity than the light strike vehicles used by US and UK special forces during the Gulf conflict, enabling it to undertake long-range surveillance and strike missions. The SOV was developed to meet a customer's requirement, involving an order for 45 vehicles. It is based on the four-

wheel-drive Defender 110, powered either by Land Rover's 200 Tdi 2.5 litre turbocharged direct injection diesel or by a petrol 3.5 litre V8 engine. The Defender SOV can be tailored to meet specific operational and logistics requirements. The main weapons ring mount attached to the roll bars can accept a variety of weapons, including the ASP 30mm cannon, the Mk 19 40mm grenade launcher or a 12.7mm machine-gun. Lighter weapons can be pintle-mounted at the front crewman's station and in the rear compartment. Anti-tank missiles, mortars and other support weapons can be stowed. Space has been provided between the driver and the front crewman's seat for communications equipment and for the installation of a global positioning system or navigation aids. An electric winch, infra-red lighting

Below: Land Rover Desert Patrol Vehicle.

Above: Glover Webb Desert Land Rover equipped with a .5in Gatling gun (see overleaf).

and extra fuel tanks are among the optional equipment that can be fitted. The Defender can be underslung from medium- and heavy-lift helicopters, carried internally by helicopters such as the CH-47 and C-130-size aircraft, or it can be air-dropped.

Land Rover Desert Patrol Vehicle
The Land Rover Desert Patrol Vehicle is another variation of the standard short-wheelbase Land Rover. A GPMG is mounted on the bonnet for forward firing, while four GPMGs are mounted in the rear for anti-aircraft purposes. This vehicle is thought to be in service with several Middle Eastern armies.

Northern Ireland Patrol Vehicle
The standard Northern Ireland patrol vehicle is still in use with the British Army and Royal Ulster Constabulary in Northern Ire-

land. A standard Land Rover is used with GRP and Macralon armour added. The former is glassfibre based and gives some protection against low-velocity small-arms fire and grenade fragments. Macralon, a form of strengthened plastic, is used to strengthen windscreen and windows.

Glover Hornet
Hornet is the result of an in-depth study undertaken by Glover Webb Ltd to create the new generation of turreted scout car based on the now established and highly successful heavy-duty military 110 Land Rover chassis. The armoured bodywork is built to an already accepted military standard, with full ballistic overlaps and splash returns fitted to all apertures. Glass and vision blocks have been tested to withstand the same level of attack as armoured steel areas, and full certification is provided for all armoured materi-

als used on the vehicle. Floor areas are protected against grenade attack by high-yield steel plate. In keeping with the body and chassis, a new low-profile turret has been designed and developed for Hornet, providing a smoke-free firing position, good all-round vision and the same level of protection as the armoured body. The periscope is co-axial, operating with the weapon from -10° to +50°.

Employment: Land Rovers of various types are in service all over the world. It is of some note, however, that the unusual Land Rover 6 x 6 was originally developed to meet the requirements of the Australian Army. The vehicle is now manufactured in Australia by Land Rover Australia. Land Rover 4 x 4 vehi-

cles are also used by the Australian Army.
Data: *length* 4.429m; *width* 1.84m; *height* (with turret) 2.1m; *wheelbase* 2.794m; *gross vehicle weight* 3,600kg; *engine* 3.5 litre V8 petrol.

Glover Webb Desert Land Rover
This long-wheelbase Land Rover has been converted to a desert patrol vehicle by Glover Webb Ltd. It has an Astra Gecal 50 .5in Gatling gun mounted in rear.

Pilkington Triplex Bullet Resistant Composites for Vehicles
For more than ten years, Triplex has been providing discreet protection for the world's most important people. The lifestyle of many

of these VIPs places them constantly in the public eye, but those who are the most visible are also the most vulnerable to the escalating attacks by armed terrorists and criminals. The personal protection for VIPs has to be totally effective but discreet. A leading force in the application of glass and polymer technology, Triplex has directed its extensive R and D programme towards keeping VIPs visible but protected. As a result, the company is now firmly established as one of the world's major suppliers of bullet-resistant transparencies affording the highest levels of protection to the international armoured limousine industry. Weight is a crucial factor to all of those involved in this industry. Any significant weight saving cuts the loading on the vehicle chassis, reducing, in most instances, the need for complex re-engineering of the limousine's basic structure. Many major advances have already been made, and research continues to focus on the need to minimise the weight and thickness of transparent armour whilst at the same time increasing levels of protection and maintaining visibility. The development of glass/polycarbonate composites is just one such advance. Because of the ductile nature of the material, the addition of a polycarbonate ply to the protected side of the transparency significantly increases the bullet resistance of the laminate. Since this allows a reduction in the number and thickness of the glass plies, important weight savings are

Left: Glover Hornet.

Right: The 'Popemobile' is protected by Triplex bullet-resistant glass.

also achieved. To capitalise on the benefits of weight and thickness reduction made possible by the development of Triplex glass polycarbonate composites, the Division's research programme has also concentrated on improving the techniques of discreet armouring by developing design features and manufacturing technology which allows for the close reproduction of a vehicle's original glazing lines. Each Triplex composite is designed by the Division's team of specialists to match the curvatures of the original equipment glass. Triplex has also developed special glass-curving furnaces to allow for

manufacture to minimal tolerances on the most severe radii, cambers and cross-curvatures.

Saker Light Strike Vehicle (LSV)

The Saker LSV is based on a space-frame chassis allowing a wide variety of role options. Tow, Milan and Hellfire anti-tank missile systems can be fitted, as can M19, GPMG, Twin Browning and 0.50 machine-guns, 30mm ASP cannon, the Gecal 0.50 Gatling gun and almost any other weapon fit. Saker's low profile, exceptional mobility and thermal low signature make it extremely

Right: Saker Light Strike Vehicle with .5in Browning and 7.62mm machine-guns.

Below: Saker Light Strike Vehicle.

evasive and difficult to track. It has exceptional ground clearance, coupled with a light footprint, and is designed to carry its crew over ranges extending up to 1,500 miles. Because it has a space frame its inherent strength is immense, yet it is designed to be repairable in the field, using basic tools. Wessex Defence of Plymouth market the vehicle, which was designed by Longline Ltd of West Sussex.

Employment: UK Ministry of Defence, almost certainly Special Forces (SAS).

Data: *length* 4.015m; *width* 1.830m; *height* 1.625m; *engine* rear-mounted petrol, VW Flat 4 1,600 tuned, normally aspirated, producing 64bhp at 4,800rpm; *torque* 90; *engine* rear-mounted diesel, Perkins Turbo-charged

2-litre direct injection, state-of-the-art technology, developing 80bhp at 4,500rpm and 116lb/ft torque at 2,400rpm; *gearbox* four-speed manual; *suspension* independent front and rear with adjustable torsion bar rear, extra-long-travel double-acting shock absorbers mounted in pairs; *brakes* hydraulically operated discs all round; *steering* rack and pinion; *tyres* 6.50 x 15.

Shorland Armoured Vehicles
Shorland S55 Armoured Personnel Vehicle and S52 Armoured Patrol Car

The Shorts Shorland Series 5 vehicles are based on a specially strengthened 110in Land Rover chassis and are powered by a 2.5 litre V8 engine coupled to a permanent

four-wheel drive. The armour has been proven as effective against both 7.62mm rifle and machine-gun fire, even at very close range. The floors of the vehicles are constructed of tough, glass-reinforced plastic which affords excellent protection against blast, nail and pipe bombs. The Shorland Series 5 consists of four variants – the S52 armoured patrol car, S53 air defence vehicle, S54 anti-hijack vehicle and S55 armoured personnel carrier. All Shorland Series 5 vehicles share over 80% commonality of spares with the standard Land Rover.

Employment: Shorland vehicles are in service with the British Army and Royal Ulster Constabulary and with more than 40 overseas countries.

Data	D52/S54	S53	S55
Seats	3	2/3	8
Maximum speed,			
road	120kmh	120kmh	120kmh
Maximum speed,			
cross-country	48kmh	48kmh	40kmh
Range	700km	700km	625km

Maximum operational weight 3,600kg
Engine Land Rover V8 Petrol
Power : weight ratio 31.6bhp/tonne
Suspension Heavy-duty-travel coil springs all round. Anti-roll bars front and rear.
Steering Power-assisted worm and roller
Turning circle 6.6m
Maximum gradient Greater than 1 in 1

Submarine Products Ltd
Sub Tug

Sub Tug is a rugged, heavy-duty, divers' tug which enormously increases a diver's underwater range and capabilities. For several years the company was aware of the lack of a purpose-built military divers' tug. Those available on the sporting market failed to meet the demands of naval or special forces divers in terms of speed, endurance or

Above left: Shorland S52.

Above: Shorland S55.

strength. Sub Tug has therefore been developed with the assistance of former Royal Marine divers to the best possible specification for military use. It comprises a torpedo-shaped body, a rear-mounted propeller and a tubular steel frame. The propulsion system is a development of the well-proven Subskimmer thruster unit. The frame gives protection from accidental damage and enables two people to carry Sub Tug easily between them. It also provides extra handholds and equipment attachment points so that divers may remain unencumbered during their mission. Also incorporated into the

unit are permanent buoyancy pads and ballast attachment points, so that neutral buoyancy may be achieved in any water conditions. The main body of the vehicle houses the batteries, which may be recharged very easily, or a spare set can be permanently maintained fully charged and exchanged swiftly and simply for the depleted set, keeping downtime to a minimum. The whole vehicle is streamlined and faired to reduce drag. The first diver holds the rear end of the vehicle frame and operates a simple on/off switch with his right hand. If he should accidentally let go, the vehicle automatically

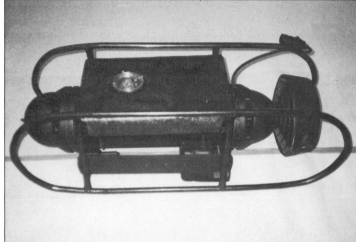

stops, preventing a potentially dangerous situation. His companion either holds a removable trapeze, which tows him behind the first diver, or he may hold on to the steel frame, so that the two divers travel side-by-side and may communicate.

Data: *length* 1.400m; *width* 0.600m; *weight* 90Mg with batteries; *max operating depth* 60m; *max speed* with two divers 2.5kt; *batteries,* lead/acid rechargeable motor, 24V; 1.3Kwh; *power* 24V, 1.5 Kw; *motor speed* 3,000rpm; *gearbox* 5:1; *propeller speed* 600rpm; *endurance* 1 hour.

UK/BELGIUM

Vickers Valkyr IS Vehicle

The Valkyr is a versatile wheeled armoured vehicle developed and produced by Vickers Defence Systems in association with Beherman Demoen. Amphibious without preparation and easily air portable, it is designed to meet the needs of military or police forces anywhere in the world requiring fast, dependable, comfortable and well-protected transport over all kinds of terrain. It is available as a purpose-built personnel carrier or fire-support vehicle, or for a variety of other roles, such as ambulance, mobile command post, or IS vehicle. Valkyr's high-hardness-steel monocoque hull provides protection against 7.62mm armour-piercing ammunition fired at point-blank range against the frontal arc (including windscreen), and all-round protection against 7.62mm ball fired at point-blank range and 155mm shell splinters. If required, appliqué armour can be added to give increased protection against 7.62mm armour-piercing ammunition. The engine and transmission are fully enclosed within the hull armour, providing the highest degree of protection for the automotive system, transmission and brakes. The General Motors 453T diesel engine combines high power-to-weight ratio with speed and fuel economy. The option of two- or four-wheel drive greatly increases the range available from the 100 litre fuel tank, while the locking differentials and fully independent suspension, coupled with power-assisted steering, give the vehicle an excellent cross-country performance. For the IS role, Valkyr allows a ten-man force with all its equipment to deploy quickly and safely. A wide range of specialist equipment is avail-

Far left and left: Sub Tug.

able, including searchlights, water cannon, grenade launchers and a bulldozer blade. The excellent visibility for the driver provided by three armoured glass screens greatly simplifies manoeuvring in confined spaces.
Data: *length* 5.6m; *width* 2.5m.

UK/GERMANY

Transac International
Transaif Multi-Role Armoured Vehicle
Designed and marketed worldwide by Transac International Ltd of the United Kingdom, this vehicle is constructed on a standard Mercedes truck chassis. The hull is constructed of steel armour capable of with-

Below: Valkyr IS Vehicle, police version.

standing high-velocity rifles at point-blank range. The strength of the windows is 'compatible to hull protection'. The vehicle has three exits, and is equipped with bullet-proof run-flat tyres and a fire extinguisher system.
Variants: The vehicle is available in three versions.

Law Enforcement Vehicle: This version is intended for riot-control, civil unrest and anti-terrorist activities. It is capable of transporting fourteen fully-equipped men and provides protection against small-arms fire, petrol bombs and blast or fragmentation attack. The styling of the Transaif can be refined to provide a deterrent or passive appearance, and it is capable of continuous high speed on motor-

ways – useful for fast deployment or when carrying out VIP escort duties.

Police Command Vehicle or Communications Centre: This version provides a protected environment for police officers commanding an operation.

Airport Security: This is equipped with short-wave radio systems, radar and laser scanners, CCTV systems and noise/movement detectors. It can be used as a command vehicle, for the transportation of VIPs within airport boundaries, or can deliver a reaction force to the scene of an incident.

Data: *length* 7.3m; *width* 2.5m; *height* 3.1m; *weight* 10,000kg (unladen) 14,800kg (laden); *engine* Mercedes Type OM352A 6-cylinder diesel, 168hp; *crew* 14; *number of wheels* 4 x 4; *speed* 105kph; *range* 680km.

Transac Bomb Disposal Vehicle

This is a standard Mercedes van fitted with the complete range of bomb disposal equipment. All of the items shown in the photograph (including the robot) are carried in one vehicle. The interior is specially designed to

allow an EOD team to operate efficiently and quickly.

UK/SWEDEN

Transac ACEe

The Armoured Combat Engineer Equipment (ACEe) is a heavily protected Volvo loader with proven appliqué armour. It can be used for barricade removal in riot control situations.

Data: *height* 2.27m; *ground clearance* 0.4m (laden); wheelbase 3.1m; *weight* 11,500kg (laden); *engine* General Motors 453T diesel, developing 780hp at 2,800rpm; *number of wheels* 4 x 2 or 4 x 4; *speed* 100kph; *range* 700km; *gradient* 60%; *turning radius* 8m; swims.

UNITED STATES OF AMERICA

Cadillac Gage Armoured Vehicles
Commando V-150 APC: A prototype of the Commando was produced in March 1963, and it went into production in 1964. The

Above: Transaif Multi-Role Armoured Vehicle.

Opposite page, top: Transac Bomb Disposal Vehicle.

Opposite page, bottom: Transac ACEe.

Above: Commando V series.

Commando uses many components already in use in other vehicles, such as the Rockwell Standard axles used in the M-34 series of trucks and the 210hp Chrysler V-8 engine used in the M-113 APC. The Commando, which proved itself in Vietnam, has excellent mobility with a high top speed and a good range, and can carry twelve men. It offers good protection against inflammable liquids and close-range small-arms fire, and individual weapons can be fired through ports.

Variants: There are four different models of hull: V-100, V-150, V-200 and V-300. The V-100 is the basic version, while the V-150 has stronger suspension and axles and can be fitted with a different engine and transmission. The V-200 is powered by a 275hp diesel. All versions are available in a wide range of configurations, of which three are suitable for IS duties: the simple turretless APC, the turreted version and the fixed superstructure version, which can be used as a mortar or command vehicle.

Employment: Bolivia, Botswana, Cameroon, Dominican Republic, Ethiopia, Gabon, Guatemala, Haiti, Indonesia, Jamaica, Kuwait, Laos, Lebanon, Malaysia, Mexico, Muscat and Oman, Panama, Peru, Philippines, Portugal, Saudi Arabia, Singapore, Somalia, Sudan, Turkey (police), USA (Air Force, Army and various state police forces). To date, more than 4,000 of these vehicles have been sold.

Above: Commando Scout.

Data: *length* 5.69m; *width* 2.26m; *height* 1.96m (to hull roof); *ground clearance* 0.38m; *wheel track* 2.1m; *wheelbase* 2.85m; *weight* 6,804kg (unladen), 8,185kg (laden); *engine* Chrysler 361 210hp petrol or Cummins V-6 155hp diesel; *crew* 12; *number of wheels* 4 x 4; *speed* 90kph; *range* 750km; *gradient* 60%; *vertical obstacle* 0.61m; swims; *turning radius* 16.7m; *maximum side slope* 30%; *armament* externally mounted MG or manual turret mounting twin .30 7.62mm/.30/.50 combination MGs.

Commando Scout

Designed as a reconnaissance vehicle. Scout is suitable for both conventional and IS situations. It is a highly agile, low-silhouette vehicle suitable for operations in open terrain or, with its small size and turning radius, it is equally at home in an urban environment.

Variants: command vehicle with 7.62mm MG mount; turreted version mounting twin .50 or 7.62mm MG; turreted version with 40mm/.50 MG; scout with TOW missile system; and 20mm turret.

Employment: Negotiations are in hand with several customers.

Data: *length* 2.5m; *width* 2.06m; *height* 2.16m; *wheelbase* 2.67m; *weight* 6,800kg; *engine* V-6 diesel, 149bhp at 3,300rpm; *crew* 2-3; *number of wheels* 4 x 4; *speed* 55mph; *range* 500 miles; *gradient* 60%; *vertical*

Left: Commando Ranger.

obstacle 0.61m; *fording depth* 1.17m; *turning radius* 7.8m; *maximum side slope* 30%; *armament* twin 7.62mm MG, combination 7.62mm/.50 MG or 7.62mm/40mm grenade launcher.

Commando Ranger

Designed to provide good ballistic protection and high mobility at low cost, this simple, rugged and effective vehicle offers crew protection against small-arms fire and grenade fragments by using Cadillac Gage lightweight Cadloy armour, which holds the vehicle weight to 4,536kg.

Variants: APC, command vehicle, ambulance and Ranger with MG turret.

Employment: US Air Force, US Navy, Indonesia and Luxembourg.

Data: *ground clearance* 20cm; *weight* 4,536kg; *engine* petrol V-8, 180hp; *crew* 8 (APC configuration), 3 (turret configuration); *number of wheels* 4 x 4; *speed* 113kph; *range* 490km at 72kph; *gradient* 60%; *vertical obstacle* 25cm; *maximum side slope* 30%; *armament* 7.62mm MG, twin 7.62mm or one 7.62mm with .50 cal turret.

Harley Davidson Military Motorcycles

Motorcycles are a useful tool in the anti-terrorist war. Terrorists themselves have been known to use them as getaway vehicles after bomb attacks. The best vehicle for chasing a motorcycle in heavy traffic is clearly another motorcycle. They are also useful for the provision of outriders to escort VIPs. It is not possible to include more than one in this volume, but the Harley-Davidson provides an excellent example.

Data: *unladen weight* 152kg; *max width across handlebar* 0.790m; *max length* 2.168m; *wheelbase* 1.45m; *ground clearance* unladen 0.22m; *engine* aircooled single-cylinder four-stroke 'Electric Start', 349cc, 29bhp; *acceleration* 0-106kph - 10sec; *maximum speed* 128kph.

Below: Harley Davidson Military Motorcycle.

2

Counter-Terrorist Air Operations

Helicopters are particularly suited to IS operations. None have been specifically designed for IS work, but virtually all military and some civilian helicopter types are suitable for IS operations. In a rural environment they are used for placing quick-reaction forces in cut-off or ambush positions. They are highly suitable for mounting what the British Army in Northern Ireland call 'Eagle' patrols – swooping down on a country lane, dropping a small party of soldiers and mounting an instant road block for a limited period. The helicopter loiters nearby until the road block party recalls it. In a rural environment, helicopters are very useful for surveillance duties, liaison and logistic support. In many IS situations, security force bases are dangerous and difficult to reach by road. If a large convoy is used for resupply purposes, its route has to be cleared and picqueted, a time-consuming and manpower-intensive pastime. Clearly the simplest and most efficient method of routine supply and liaison for such outposts is by helicopter, and this was the method normally used by the British Army to resupply was bases in South Armagh in Northern Ireland.

In an urban environment, helicopters are of more limited use, but can be used in the crowd surveillance and control roles with searchlights, cameras or loudspeakers. They can also be used as mobile command posts. Indeed, there are occasions, particularly in a confused urban situation, when the only way a commander can get an overall impression of a situation is from the air. Finally, and perhaps most importantly, helicopters are used in IS situations for casualty evacuation. Many lives have been saved in Northern Ireland and elsewhere by flying grievously wounded soldiers direct to a hospital helipad. Certainly in Northern Ireland all of the main casualty hospitals have helipads.

Helicopters have remained remarkably immune to small-arms fire – their tolerance to several hits is considerable. While some have been forced to land at the first opportunity owing to damage caused by small-arms fire, few have been 'shot down'. Where, however, terrorists or guerrillas have managed to obtain hand-held surface-to-air missile systems, such as the Soviet designed SAM-7, helicopters have been successfully engaged. There is photographic evidence of successful engagements of Soviet helicopters in Afghanistan by the Mujahadin using US manufactured 'Stinger' missiles. The counter to the hand-held surface-to-air missile is to fly at 50ft or less, so that the operator does not have sufficient time to acquire his target, fire the missile and achieve lock-on with the infra-red heat-seeking system during the brief exposure time of the target.

It is not the aim of this short chapter to catalogue all of the world's military helicopters. However, some helicopter types used in IS operations will be included to illustrate various missions. In addition, some examples of attachments to helicopters, illustrating how helicopters have been adapted to IS situations, are given. Helicopters can be used to land assault teams on top of high-rise buildings or other inaccessible spots. Most counter-terrorist organisations retain quick-reaction teams able to operate from helicopters. Methods of exit vary from free-falling to abseiling or jumping.

Fixed-wing aircraft can also prove useful in counter-terrorist operations; they provide

a much more stable platform for air-to-ground surveillance operations or for insertion by parachute. Surveillance of oil rigs is carried out by conventional maritime surveillance aircraft such as the Nimrod. Such installations are always vulnerable to terrorist attack.

Training in air-to-ground co-operation and helicopter support operations is vital for effective counter-terrorist air operations. There are a few organisations which specialise in the business. One such is E2-G, a UK based company which can train fixed-wing and helicopter pilots from *ab initio* up to and including the specialist techniques used in support operations, such as training in short take-off and landing (STOL) methods including the selection, marking and layout of improvised landing sites. E2-G can also locate and procure suitable aircraft for special operations, as well as advise on an equipment and sensor fit, including avionics and air-to-ground operation devices. E2-G can also provide expertise and advice in the construction of helicopter pads and forward operating bases; in other words, it can offer valuable expertise on anything connected with counter-terrorist air operations, an unusual service which could prove useful in parts of Asia, the Middle East, Africa and South America.

AUSTRIA

HB-23 Scanliner

The HB-23 Scanliner is built by HB Aircraft Industries of Hofkinchen, Austria. It it is an increasingly versatile aircraft suitable for oil and powerline inspection, border patrol, coastal patrol, police duties, traffic observation, farm and forest survey, pollution control and any other surveillance and observation duty. In this respect is suitable for counter-terrorist operations in the surveillance mode. It is an extremely efficient machine owing to its outstanding aerodynamics and low weight and, with a precise manoeuvring capability down to zero altitude and a stalling speed of only 41kt, it offers virtually all the advantages of a helicopter at 10 per cent of the purchase and operating costs. Aircraft retail at about £100,000.

Data: *power plant* VW-HB/2400 G/2; *take-off run* 160m; *rate of climb* 360m/sec; *cruising speed* 172kph (75% output); *radius of turn* 106m; *stalling speed* 76kph; *range/option* 821km/1,610km.

Right: HB-23 Scanliner.

FRANCE

Aérospatiale SA 330 Puma

The various versions of the Puma and the Super Puma are used in a range of countries (see below). It is illustrated here as an example of the category of helicopter which is so useful in counter-terrorist operations for lifting up to 21 troops into an operational area. Many other troop lift helicopters meet the same requirements.

Employment: Algeria (Puma), Argentina (air force, Super Puma; army, Puma and Super Puma), Brazil (air force, L Puma and M Super Puma for SAR and transport; navy, F Super Puma for SAR and transport), Cameroun (L Super Puma), Chad (Puma), Chile (air force, B Super Puma; navy, F1 Super Puma for ASV), China (B Super Puma), Cote d'Ivoire (Puma), Ecuador (air force, F Puma and B Super Puma; army, Puma and B Super Puma), Ethiopia (IAR-33OL Puma), France (air force, B and H Puma and Super Puma for SAR training and transport; army, B Puma and MI Super Puma), Gabon (C and H Puma), Republic of Guinea (IAR-33OL Puma), Indonesia (air force, IPTN J/L Puma, and IPTN HAS-332 Super Puma; navy, IPTN HAS 332 Super Puma for armed assault, SAR and other roles including two helicopters for ASV with Exocet), Iraq (Puma), Japan (army, L Super Puma), Kenya (Puma and IAR-330L Puma), Kuwait (armed H Puma and F Super Puma for SAR and ASV with Exocet), Lebanon (L Puma), Malawi (Puma), Malaysia (IPIN Super Puma), Mexico (Puma for SAR and transport, and L Super Puma), Morocco (C Puma), Nepal (C Puma and L Super Puma), Nigeria (Puma and M Super Puma), Oman (Super Puma for Royal Flight), Pakistan (air force, J Puma: army, F and J Puma), Panama (L super Puma), Portugal (C Puma for SAR), Qatar (F Super Puma), Romania (IAR-330L Puma), Saudi Arabia (Super Puma, some for ASV with Exocet), Senegambia (F Puma), Singapore (M Super Puma for SAR, etc.), South Africa (F, J, L Puma for armed SAR, evacuation and transport), Spain (air force, C, H, J Puma and B Super Puma for SAR

Right: Aérospatiale AS 350.

Left: Puma landing at a fortified base in Northern Ireland.

and transport; army, B Super Puma), Sudan (IAR-330L Puma), Sweden (MI Super Puma for SAR), Togo (Puma), Switzerland (MI Super Puma), Tunisia (Puma), United Arab Emirates (Puma and B, F, L Super Puma), UK (E/HC.1 Puma), and Zaire (Puma and L super Puma).

Data: *rotor diameter* 15.60m; *length of fuselage* 15.53m; *height* 4.92m; *rotor disc area* 191.1m^2); *number of crew* 2 or 3. Provision for 21 troops, 9 stretchers plus 3 seated casualties, or cargo; *take-off weight* 9,000–9,350kg; *weapon load* see armament; *cruising speed* 240kph; *range* 870km without auxiliary tanks; *ceiling* 4,100m; *rate of climb at sea level* 6.2m/sec; *radar* Thomson CSF Varan radar in nose for ASW/ASV, RCA Primus 500 or Bendix RDR 1400 search radar for SAR; *power plant* two Turbomeca Makila 1A1 turboshaft engines, each maximum continuous rated at 1,162kW; *arma-*

ment two Exocet anti-ship missiles or two torpedoes. Other weapon options for Super Pumas (usually non-naval versions) include two 7.62mm machine-guns, one 20mm cannon or two pods for 68mm or 2.75in rockets.

Aérospatiale AS 350

The Aérospatiale AS 350 series is used by various British police forces, and can be adapted for counter-terrorist purposes.

Employment: Different versions are used by 18 countries including Argentina, Australia, France, Brazil, Denmark, Malawi, Sierre Leone, Tunisia and the UAE.

Data: *rotor diameter* 10.69m; *length of fuselage* 10.93m; *height* 3.34m; *rotor disc area* 89.75m^2; *number of crew* 2 plus 4 other persons when required; *take-off weight* 2,200-2,450kg; *armament* see versions; *cruising speed* 230kph; *range* 655km; *ceiling* 4,500m; *rate of climb at sea level*

| Nightsun | High Skids | High viz. windows | Skyshout | Extended steps | Sliding doors |

7.5m/sec; *radar* none; *power plant* one Turbomeca Arriel 1D turboshaft, rated at 510kW.

McAlpine of Hayes, Middlesex, UK, specialises in the fitting out of Aérospatiale AS 355F Twin Squirrel helicopters for UK police forces. Helicopters can have a range of facilities, but these usually include:

● A purpose-built six-place intercom and audio system with the dedicated operator station boxes essential for good internal and external communications;

● Three police tactical Comms systems covering the UHF.FM, VHF AM/FM and VHF.FM frequency bands;

● Hands-free operation of all transmitters;

● A 30-million candlepower searchlight, 'Nightsun', with vertical and azimuth control with wide and narrow beam focusing;

● Infra-red filter option for covert surveillance is available;

● A 700W high-powered eight-horn PA system, 'Skyshout', operable from heights up to and in excess of 1,500ft with speech, siren and trill options;

● A complete role equipment package protected by an Automatic Electrical Shedding system in the event of an engine or generator failure. This enhances flight safety and relieves pilot workload;

● Flight station ergonomics carefully designed for a safe and user-friendly environment;

● A chin-mounted FLIR turret with Telemetry Downlink for live picture monitoring. Compatibility with video camera is also available.

The helicopter also carries a full airways, IMC-capable avionics package complete

Above: An Aérospatiale AS 350 adapted for IS duties.

with three-axis autopilot stabilisation and upper mode coupling facilities.

ITALY

Agusta A109 Mk II 'Law Enforcement'

Designed for high performance in all weather conditions, and for operations from unprepared areas, the A109 Mk II has proven to be highly effective for law enforcement operations. Experience with various Italian police forces, including the Carabinieri, which presently operate more than 50 A109s, has permitted Augusta to develop a number of configurations that meet most law enforcement requirements. With a cruising speed of over 280kph, a range of over 800km, an endurance of over 4hr and the ability to accommodate up to seven passengers, the A109 is an ideal helicopter for IS operations.

Data: *overall length* (rotor turning) 13.05m, (rotor stopped) 11.114m; *maximum height* 3.3m; *cabin width* 1.44m; *main rotor diameter* 11m; *tail rotor diameter* 2.03m; *maximum gross weight* 2,600kg, *empty weight* 1,418kg; *useful load* 1,182kg; *engine ratings* twin-engine take-off 672kW, maximum continuous 672kW; *maximum cruising speed* 282kph; *rate of climb* (twin-engine) 8.9m/sec, (single-engine) 2.3m/sec; *service ceiling* (twin engine) 4,572m, (single engine) 2,530m, *maximum range* 815km; *maximum endurance* 4.35hr; *operating conditions* -40°C to +50°C.

UNITED KINGDOM

British Aerospace Steadyscope Monocular GS 907

A hand-held gyrostabilised viewing device intended to avoid the blurring of images

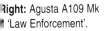

Right: Agusta A109 Mk II 'Law Enforcement'.

while moving at speed in boats, vehicles and aircraft. Offering magnifications of x10 and x7, it features an internal steering device. The x7 magnification unit can be augmented with a night vision image intensifier. Weights are 2kg (day unit) or 2.4kg (night unit). Dimensions are 251mm x 225mm x 96mm (day) and 270mm x 225mm x 96mm (night).

Variant: Steadyscope Binocular GS 982 incorporates a similar mechanism and weighs 2.3kg.

British Aerospace Nimrod

With its immensely long endurance, impressive range and comprehensive sensor fit, the Nimrod maritime patrol aircraft is just one example of several such aircraft worldwide (the US P-3 Orion and French Atlantique are others) that can be utilised for surveillance of offshore facilities such as oil rigs. They can also be used to watch ships suspected of carrying supplies of weapons and explosives for terrorist organisations. An example of such an operation was the successful interception of the trawler *Eskund* off the French coast in 1989, which was transporting an illegal shipment of arms from Libya to Ireland for the IRA.

Employment; Royal Air Force.

Data: Nimrod MR.Mk 2P; *wing span* 35m; *length* 39.35m; *height* 9.08m; *wing area* 197m^2; *number of crew* 12, comprising two pilots, flight engineer, two navigators, radar operator, two sonics operators, MAD and ESM operator, and two observers; *take-off weight* about 87.090kg; *stores load* 6,123kg; *maximum speed* about 926kph; *endurance* 12hr; *ceiling* 12,800m; *power plant* four Rolls-Royce RB.168-20 Spey Mk 250 turbofans, each rated at 5,507kg thrust; *armament* typically nine torpedoes plus bombs in bay. Two underwing stations for Harpoon anti-ship missiles, four Sidewinder self-defence AAMs, mines, rocket launchers or cannon pods.

Marconi Elliott Heli-Tele

The Electro-Optical Systems Division of Marconi Elliott Avionics Systems has devel-

Above: Steadyscope Monocular GS 907.

oped the remarkable air-to-ground television surveillance and reconnaissance system known as Heli-Tele. It consists of a colour television camera mounted on a helicopter, a microwave link with multi-range aerials, and a number of display units both in the helicopter and at base headquarters. Of cardinal importance in the operation of the system is the stablilised platform on which the camera is mounted. The platform stabilises the camera along its line of aim to better than 1/1600th of a degree, and isolates the camera from the vibrations and positional changes of the helicopter. The camera attitude and its zoom lens are controlled from a joystick with a two-axis movement. The camera's field of view extends down to about 1°, which enables the pinpointing of subjects from very considerable distances. Although a monochrome camera may be employed, the use of a colour system enhances not only the

Right: Nimrod MR Mk II flying over an oil rig in the Moray Firth.

general monitoring of subjects, but also the differentiation between subjects of a similar type. If a low-light camera tube is fitted, surveillance under starlight conditions is possible. The advantages of Heli-Tele are immense for reconnaissance and surveillance in urban, rural and offshore areas. Unit commanders can rapidly survey and search large areas by operating a number of helicopters simultaneously, relaying pictures back to centralised monitors and videotape recorders. They can develop their strategy based on what they can see, rather than on what they are told, and can deploy their men and equipment immediately to counter a rapidly changing situation. The short-range ground station is transportable and can be unloaded and set up by two men in less than ten minutes in any convenient building or in the open air. It can also be fully mobile in a vehicle such as a Land Rover, either stationary with the antenna erected or on the move with the aerial down. The short-range ground station is complementary to the command post installations, and allows multiple simultaneous reception of the aircraft television transmissions by a number of mobile or stationary ground receivers.

Employment: Belgium (Gendarmerie), United Kingdom.

Data: *weight* 150kg; *field of view* 1°-20°; *elevation* 4.25°-60°; *transmission link range* 4-6km (short-range station), 40-60km (long-range station).

Night Vision and Navigation Aids

Night landing aids: To effect a rendezvous between security forces and a helicopter, a relatively compact and simple system of homing-in is needed. The 'Pal' range of night landing aids developed by Security Research provides an example. It consists of an angle-of-approach indicator and tactical approach lights: the standard system is one indicator and five lights. It comes in a carrying case complete with a charger unit.

Thermal imaging: The helicopter pilot will need equipment for enhancement of night vision, such as the LT1069 Helicopter Thermal Imaging System developed by Lasergage and Barr & Stroud. Compact and lightweight, this has been specially developed for helicopter use; it is completely passive, operates independently of ambient light levels and sees through mist, smoke and glare from the sun, flares or searchlights. The thermal imager is mounted via a gimbal and yoke mechanism, the controls and display being mounted within the helicopter.

Flares: Unlikely in a conventional war situation is the need to provide illumination of an area of ground. However, in IS operations illumination of terrorists may be required. This can be achieved by use of flares, such as the Schermuly Mk 5 emergency flares, twin-mounted on a helicopter airframe.

Searchlights: More durable high-intensity illumination requires a searchlight. One such is Spectrolab's SX-16 Nightsun. Developed by Spectrolab of California, this is a lightweight high-power searchlight. The Nightsun's brilliant but accurate beam is an ideal aid in an IS situation – it can be directed by the operator to illuminate those areas

Above: Marconi Elliott Heli-Tele.

he wants lighted, without creating secondary disturbances in surrounding areas. The high power of the searchlight allows helicopters to fly at higher altitudes, thus avoiding small-arms fire. When equipped with a special IR filter, Nightsun may be used to observe activities at night without a terrorist knowing that the beam is directed at him.

Employment: Various US police forces (fitted to Bell JetRanger), British Army Air Corps (fitted to Scout helicopter and used in Northern Ireland), and other police forces.

Data: *dimensions* 27.9cm x 45.7cm (remote-control unit 15.2cm x 10.1cm x 7.2cm); *weight* 11.34kg (remote-control unit 0.85kg); *beam spread* 4° in search mode, adjustable to 20° in flood mode; *beam intensity/size* 50 x bright moonlight at 1,000m for 100m diameter beam; *average beam power* 25,000 Lumens.

Pilot Protection

Helicopters can survive a remarkable number of bullet strikes to the airframe, but clearly the same cannot be said of the pilot. Armoured helicopter seats are made by most aircraft-manufacturing nations, mainly for military purposes. However, their use is particularly relevant to the IS helicopter. An example is the range of ceramic/fibre composite armour made by Bristol Composites. The armour, which can be designed to fit inside an existing crew seat or can be bolted on to the seat exterior, is available in a number of different grades. The heaviest is capable of stopping multi-hits of 7.62mm AP ammunition from an FN FAL rifle at 90m range. Crew members can also be provided with breastplates of similar material – the pilot is vulnerable to a round entering the front of the aircraft.

Shorts 3M Skyvan

The Shorts 3m Skyvan STOL aircraft is typical of a range of aircraft produced by various manufacturers around the world, but the Skyvan is one of the most impressive of its type. It can operate in demanding terrain, achieve very short take-off runs, and carry impressive loads. It is ideal for providing

Above: Lynx protective pilot seat.

Right: Skyvan of the Sultan of Oman's armed forces.

troop transport and logistic support in counterinsurgency situations. Although Shorts now produces more modern equivalents, such as the Shorts 330 and the Sherpa, the Skyvan is a good example of the type of basic, rugged aircraft that is suitable for counterinsurgency operations in the Third World.

Employment: Sultan of Oman's Armed Forces (15 aircraft), Argentina, Austria, Botswana, Ecuador, Ghana, Indonesia, Lesotho, Mauritania, Nepal, Panama, Singapore, Thailand and Yemen.

Data: *wing span* 19.79m; *length* 12.6m; *height* 4.6m; *maximum speed* 155kph, range 416km.

Skylink Surveillance System

This ingenious system uses ultra-low-cost aircraft to mount a Minerva Gyro-stabilised camera platform to take long-range oblique photographs of targets up to many thousands of metres away. Car registration numbers can be read at 100m range, and a specific human

face recognised at 200m range. Human movement can be recognised up to ranges of 1,000m, truck movement up to 4,800m. Human movement can be detected up to ranges of 3,800m, truck movement up to 18,000m. The Skylink Surveillance System is best used with several aircraft transmitting full-colour, free-motion video directly to a ground station. An airborne command post can be used to co-ordinate large numbers of Skylink aircraft and to monitor the pictures taken by the cameras or infra-red sensors on the Skylink aircraft. The system is effective for the surveillance of borders or to reach large areas for small targets.

Westland Lynx

The Lynx helicopter has been produced in many versions. The versions most used in the military (and specifically counter-terrorist) context are the Mks 1, 7 and 9. They are used for troop transport in Northern Ireland. Of course other similar helicopters could be used in the same role. The Lynx is illustrated

Above: Bell 206L-3 LongRanger III.

Left: Soldiers from 6 UDR emplaning on a Lynx.

because it is in daily use in Northern Ireland for counter-terrorist operations.

Employment: Currently used by Brazil (navy, Mk 21 for ASW), Denmark (navy, Mks 23, 80 and 90 for ASW and fishery protection), France (navy, HAS Mk 2(FN) and Mk 4 for ASW and SAR), Germany (navy, Mk 99 for ASW), Netherlands (navy, Mks 25, 27 and 81 for ASW, SAR and utility), Nigeria (navy, Mk 89 for ASW and SAR), Norway (coast guard/air force, Mk 85 for maritime patrol), Qatar (police, Mk 28), and UK (navy, HAS.Mk 2 and 3 for ASW, ASV, etc.; army AH.Mk 1, 7 and 9 for anti-armour, liaison, utility). In addition, South Korea has selected Lynx for its navy, carrying Ferranti Seaspray Mk 3 radar and armed with Sea Skua for ASV role.

Data: *rotor diameter* 12.8m; *length, including rotors* 15.16m; *height* 3.20m; *rotor disc area* 128.71m^2, *take-off weight* 4,763kg; *cruising speed* 232kph, *range* 593km, *rate of climb at sea level* 11m/sec; *radar* see versions; *power plant* army versions i.e. Mks 1, 7 and 9, are powered by Rolls-Royce 671kW Gem 42 or 835kW Gem 41-1 turboshaft engines.

USA/UK

Bell 206L-3 LongRanger III

The Bell LongRanger is specifically designed for law enforcement missions. It is equipped with forward-looking infra-red

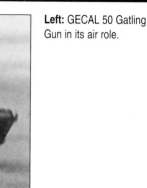

Left: GECAL 50 Gatling Gun in its air role.

(FLIR) to search through foliage or undertake night-time surveillance. It has specialised communications equipment that allows it to communicate with a number of ground stations and other airborne units, and specialised radar to permit long-range tracking surveillance, cameras and the Nightsun Searchlight System.

Data: *maximum gross weight* 1,882kg; *empty weight* standard configuration 998kg; *useful load* 884kg; *maximum continuous cruise at sea level* 203kph; *range at sea level* 593km; *hovering in ground effect* 5,030m, *hovering out of ground effect* 1,650m; *service ceiling* 6,090m.

Note: Performance shown is at maximum gross weight.

GECAL 50 Gatling Gun

GECAL 50 is being developed, manufactured and marketed jointly by Astra of Grantham, Lincolnshire, UK, and General Electric Company of the USA. It is available in a three- or six-barrel configuration, with maximum firing rates of 2,000 rounds per minute and 4,000 rounds per minute respectively. As with all Gatling guns, reliability is extremely high, with a mean rounds between failures of 50,000 rounds. Other features are accuracy and light weight, and the gun will fire all types of 12.7mm ammunition currently in production or development. When installed in the Black Hawk helicopter, the GECAL 50 pintle-mounted gun system gives the Black Hawk an impressive self-protection capability at greater stand-off ranges.

Data: *gun type* 50 calibre (12.7mm Gatling); *weight* - gun (3-barrel) 30kg, (6-barrel) 43.6kg - recoil assembly and ancillary equipment 48kg - ammunition handling equipment (empty) 38kg (100rds) 184kg - ammunition (100 rds) 146kg; *rate of fire* 3-barrel up to 2,000 rounds/min, 6-barrel up to 4,000 rounds/min; *ammunition type* TP, M-8 API, APHC(1) nm 140, M-17 Tracer, SLAP, WALAP; *muzzle velocity* 884m/sec; *average recoil force* 3-barrel 3.5kN at 2,000 rounds/min, 6-barrel 5.3kN at 4,000 rounds/min; *dispersion* (80% of rounds fired) 3 mils; *feed system* linked.

3

Bomb Disposal and Detection Equipment

One of the most widely used terrorist weapons is the bomb. Bombings are aimed at military targets (vehicles or soldiers or military installations) or economic targets; or they can be indiscriminate. The rationale behind an attack on a military target is clear enough. That against an economic target incorporates a longer-term strategy, and is designed to undermine the ability and determination of the state to carry on the war against terrorism. Clearly, the more expensive a campaign becomes, the more difficult it is to justify to the taxpayer in a democratic state. The IRA in Northern Ireland quite regularly bombed factories and other economic targets. Their attacks on the City of London in 1992 and 1993 had a clear economic motive. Indiscriminate bombing is, perhaps, terrorism in its purest form. By creating an atmosphere of terror indiscriminately it is hoped to so terrify and intimidate the population that they will be cowed into submis-

Below: Preparing the operator.

sion. Aircraft, shopping precincts, hotel lobbies and airport check-in facilities are but a few of the many public targets that have been bombed by the Red Army Faction, the Bader-Meinhof group, Palestinian terrorists, Sikh extremists, the IRA and other terrorist groups in recent years.

The form of terrorist explosive devices varies according to the nature of the planned target and the skill of the bomber, and may therefore incorporate commercial or home-made explosive materials and be initiated by command detonation, a timing device, or target influence. Perhaps the most common method of transporting and placing a bomb is by using a car. The so-called 'car bomb' has become almost commonplace as a method of terrorist attack throughout the world. In the Lebanon in 1983-4 even larger amounts of explosive were packed into lorries and driven by suicidal Palestinians straight at buildings occupied by US and French troops of the four-power peacekeeping force. The method proved horrifically effective when 241 US marines were crushed to death in their collapsed barrack block. A variation of the car bomb is the so-called 'proxy' bomb, a technique developed by the IRA in Northern Ireland, whereby terrorists intimidate an individual (usually by holding the victim's family hostage under threat of death) to drive a car bomb up to a target and leave it there. 'Proxy' bombs are normally activated by means of a timing mechanism. This is sometimes associated with a telephoned warning, which allows the security forces to evacuate innocent civilians. This technique causes maximum disruption and damage while at the same time giving the impression that it is not the terrorists' wish to harm anyone.

The Command Wire Improvised Explosive Device (CWIED) and Radio Controlled Improvised Explosive Device (RCIED) are the most difficult to guard against. The first requires the individual initiating the bomb to be at the end of the wire and to be able to see the target. The second provides the bomber with great flexibility, but it also requires more sophisticated initiation equipment.

Much research is going into ways of countering the RCIED. The third main category of initiation of an explosive device is target influence, in which the presence of the target initiates a trembler or similar device. Vigilance, good tactics and timely intelligence remain the best defence against such a threat.

One of the most horrific examples on the British mainland of command detonation occurred on 20 July 1982, when, shortly before one o'clock, a bomb exploded underneath the bandstand in Regent's Park, London, upon which a military band was playing. Six members of the band were killed instantly, and one died later of his wounds. A few hours before, men of the Household Cavalry mounted squadron had been cut down by a car bomb as they rode through Hyde Park on their way to ceremonial duties in Whitehall. Nobody will ever forget the horrific photographs of men and horses lying stricken in the road.

The twin atrocities of the assassination of Earl Mountbatten on his boat *Mullaghmore* in the Republic of Ireland and the Warrenpoint explosion, which killed 12 paratroopers, occurred on 27 August 1979. The first of these bombs was probably detonated remotely from a vantage point on the shore, the bomb comprising 50lb of explosives hidden beneath the boat's decking. The second, 500lb of explosives in milk churns hidden in hay bales, was detonated by men just across the border as the paratroopers' truck was passing.

Another method of delivering high explosive to a target, much favoured by the IRA in Northern Ireland, is the home-made mortar. Guerrilla movements all over the world have used mortars to attack targets remotely, but have usually been able to acquire properly manufactured mortar systems, either on the international arms market or by capturing them in actions against government troops. In Northern Ireland it proved too difficult for the IRA to smuggle such bulky weapons into the country. Moreover, their sophisticated sighting systems made them unnecessarily complicated for the IRA's simple requirement – to lob high-explosive a short distance

Below: Briefing the team.

into a security force base. Ingeniously, the IRA developed a series of home-made mortars, which, although unreliable and unpredictable, sometimes managed to inflict casualties inside security force bases. The most spectacular use of this method was in February 1991, when the IRA fired a number of mortar bombs at No 10 Downing Street from the back of a truck in Whitehall. One bomb landed in the garden during a Cabinet meeting.

A distinction should be made between bombs designed to cause maximum damage to buildings or military vehicles, and those targeted against individuals. The former

often consist of hundreds of pounds of explosives, and can be secreted in a vehicle or large container (a beer keg or milk churn) and placed behind a wall or under a culvert. They can be detonated either remotely or by means of a timing mechanism. Bombs of the second kind are altogether smaller and often more sophisticated, and can be attached to the underside of a car or to a door, or can even be delivered by post. It is a common terrorist tactic to place bombs underneath cars or in the engine compartments of cars belonging to members of the security force during the night, so that when the victims drive away next morning a trembler device

detonates the explosive. This method was used to murder the British MP Airey Neave in 1979, as he drove away from the House of Commons car park. The third main category of bomb is the incendiary. This is an even smaller device which can be placed easily under inflammable materials in a warehouse or shop, with a small timing device attached to it. The device bursts into flame for long enough to start a fire in the target building.

Bomb detection and disposal has developed as an art since the early 1970s. The British Army, like other major armies of the world, already had Explosive Ordnance Disposal (EOD) personnel before the emergency in Northern Ireland witnessed the introduction of terrorist bombs in large numbers in 1971. They were mostly employed in disposing of Second World War German bombs. These teams have various detection and disposal aids available to them. In particular, remotely controlled vehicles capable of carrying and operating a variety of equipment necessary for the location and disposal of dangerous objects have been developed. These vehicles enable the Ammunition Technical Officer (ATO) to remain at a safe distance while he locates, identifies by TV camera and monitors a suspected bomb. If he decides that the object is too dangerous to be approached, he can attempt to disarm or destroy it by using various aids on the vehicle. Perhaps one of the best known of these remote EOD vehicles is Wheelbarrow, which has been developed and refined since the early days of the emergency, and continues in use today. It has a wide variety of 'add-on' elements so that the system can be adapted to deal with different types of target. Among its many attributes, Wheelbarrow has the ability to deal with petrol tankers, a favourite target of IRA bombers. It has a closed-circuit TV camera and monitor to allow remote surveillance, lights to illuminate the target and a shotgun to disrupt the firing mechanism of an explosive device.

Over the years, Wheelbarrow and other systems like it have saved many bomb disposal experts' lives.

In many circumstances a manual approach is necessary, either to prevent blast damage or because forensic evidence is required. In such cases the ATO will wear an EOD suit, which is designed to give some protection against fragments, blast and flames during the disarming of improvised explosive device (IEDs). It will also provide a measure of protection against larger devices at greater range. If a manual approach is made, the ATO will carry an inspection set consisting of probes, extension rods, mirrors, magnets, lock viewers and hooks and line. All of these items must be made from non-ferrous metals. Although remotely controlled vehicles are the safest method of dealing with explosive devices, manual approaches are often necessary.

Prevention by early detection is preferable to disposal later. Although most disposal equipment is manufactured in either the UK or the USA, detection equipment is designed and manufactured in Belgium, Canada, Finland, Germany, Switzerland, the UK and the USA. One of the main tasks of troops and police engaged in IS duties is the checking of vehicles and their occupants at vehicle check points (VCPs). Another frequent task is the searching of houses and waste ground. In the same way, airport security personnel have to keep a constant watch for attempts by terrorists to smuggle IEDs or weapons on to aeroplanes. Various devices have been developed to detect metal objects and explosive substances on the person or in luggage. Most explosives 'sniffers' will positively identify and indicate the presence of gelignite, dynamite, nitro-glycerine, nitro-benzine, DNT, TNT, RDX, PETN and other explosives.

Equipment apart, the ordinary soldier probably accounts for the greatest number of finds by using his eyes and common sense.

Major successes have also been achieved by trained 'sniffer' dogs and their handlers. Search techniques in a rural environment largely involve having an eye for the ground. Clearly it is not possible to search large areas of countryside comprehensively; it is necessary to put oneself in the mind of the individual hiding the arms, ammunition or explosives. Normally, anyone hiding something in the countryside will choose a suitable marker, such as a lone tree or a particularly prominent track junction. Often a search in the vicinity of such a 'marker' has produced results. Farm outbuildings, manure or silage heaps and culverts are popular hiding places. In buildings, any attic, floorboards or the inside of a false wall can conceal an illegal weapons cache.

This chapter covers a range of equipment in the bomb disposal and detection field, including remotely controlled bomb disposal

Left: Barringen Ionscan.

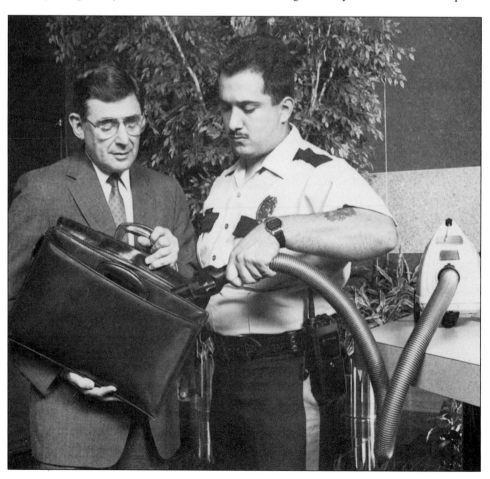

vehicles, bomb blankets, inspection sets, EOD suits, explosives 'sniffers', metal detectors and airport X-ray equipment. Conventional mine/metal detectors for use on the ground are not included, although these are used in rural IS situations.

CANADA

Barringen Ionscan

Ionscan can detect a wide variety of commercial and military explosives, including plastics, without the need to reprogramme the equipment for specific groups. The Ionscan is always in the most sensitive mode of operation, and provides a quick and positive indication, both visually and audibly, of the presence of explosives. The range of explosives detected by Ionscan include PETN, RDX, DNT, TNT, NG, HMX and TETRYL. During Ionscan's development, particular consideration was paid to ensuring the reliable detection of plastic explosives. Explosives of this type have extremely low vapour pressures. Most varieties of plastic explosives, such as Semtex A, Semtex H, C-4, PE1, PE4, Deta Sheet, etc., primarily consist of the explosive compounds RDX or PETN, or a combination of both. The Ionscan detects RDX and PETN by molecular clusters specific to each compound, which results in a specific and reliable (low false alarm) detection of plastic explosives.

Data: *sampling* continuous or discrete; *number of simultaneous detections* 8; *sampling rate* 10 samples per minute; *desorption/ detection time* 4sec; *calibration* automatic; *power requirement* 110V AC, 6 amps max, 220V AC, 3 amps max; *detector unit size* 50 x 45 x 30cm; *detector unit weight* 27kg; *pump unit size* 50 x 45 x 22cm; *pump unit weight* 24kg; *warm-up time* 30 min from cold start (1 min from standby).

Narcotics mode: *sensitivity* 5-15ng; *substances* all known controlled drugs; *IMS operating mode* positive.

Explosives mode: *sensitivity* 50-600pg; *substances* DNT, TNT, RDX, NG, PETN, Semtex, HMX, TETRYL; *IMS operating mode* negative.

EIRE

Kentree Hobo Remote EOD Robotic Vehicle

Developed from 1976 in response to the demand from the Irish Army for a remotely controlled EOD vehicle, Hobo is modular in construction to afford ease of maintenance and repair. The six wheels provide good manoeuvrability over difficult terrain, and a torsion system prevents the vehicle overturn-

Right: Kentree Hobo.

ing when negotiating obstacles exceeding the height of the wheels. The machine is controlled by cable or by radio via a console in a rugged transit case. All standard explosive ordnance disposal tools can be used, including a shotgun, disruptors, X-ray, a sniffer, a microphone, an acoustic detector, car towing, telescopic hook, etc. The updated L3A1 version has improved suspension and a greater variety of attachments.

Employment: Marketed by the British Royal Ordnance.

Data: *length* 1.47m; *width* 0.7m; *height* 0.88m; *reach* 1.5m; *weight* 228kg; *lifting capacity* 75kg (arm unextended), 30kg (arm extended); *speed* 0-4.8kph infinitely variable; *turning circle* within its own length; *maximum gradient* 45°; *rotation of turret/arm* 220° left/right; *power* 24V DC 55 amp-hours batteries; *endurance* 1-3hr on batteries alone; *cable length* 150m; *drive* 6-wheel independent electrically driven traction tyres.

Kentree Imp

The Imp miniature robotic vehicle is designed specifically for use in confined areas where access is denied to larger vehicles. It is ideal for use inside aircraft, trains, ships, underground railways, sports stadia, and in urban areas where access by stairs causes problems to less versatile remote control robots. The vehicle can be configured either as a four- or two-track vehicle, with the option of interchangeable wheels for added versatility. The whole vehicle is of modular construction for ease of maintenance and to give the operator the opportunity to configure the machine to suit individual situations from a simple surveillance task to a complicated manipulative function, handling or neutralising suspect packages. The whole unit is designed with ease of use and speed of adjustment in mind. A good example of this is the interchangeable top mounting plate, which can carry various arms, weapons, a mounting system, a baggage grab, cameras, pan and tilt, plus the multitude of other accessories available for this unit. Normal control is by radio link, allowing up to 90 minutes of continuous operation without battery charge. Cable operation can be used when a high degree of security is required, and

Below: Kentree Imp.

Right: Kentree
Vagabond.

additionally gives infinite operation capabilities.

Data: *weight* 65kg; *lifting capacity* 10kg; *drag capacity* 35kg; *drive* 2 or 4 track system from electric motors with worm drive gears; *speed* 20cm/s; *turning circle* within its own length; gradient 45°; *power* 12V DC battery pack 220/110V AC through umbilical cable for continual use or short link for battery charge.

Kentree Vagabond

The Vagabond is an example of how Kentree can employ the technology used in its range of remote control vehicles to convert standard production models for use in hazardous environments. The types of vehicle suitable for conversion are limitless, but in the case of the Vagabond a JCB 545 Material Handler was converted to handle large devices encountered by EOD personnel. The remote control equipment is fitted so as not to interfere with the normal functioning of the vehicles. The conversion kit or complete system can be supplied to the client's specification, and conversion includes all motor operations of the vehicle, including any specialised ancillary equipment added for specific functions, as well as camera functions for remote surveillance of the operations being carried out. Control of the vehicle can be either by umbilical cable or by radio link, giving ranges from 150m to 500m by cable and in excess of 1km line of sight by radio. Operation without an external power source for extended lengths of time is possible, as the remote control system is powered by the vehicle electrical power source and the duration is only limited by the vehicle's normal fuel reserves.

Employment: Several systems are in operation in a number of countries.

Data: *weight* 180kg; *drive* 6 DC motors (all wheels); *auxiliary motions* 6 DC motors; *claw lift capacity* 10kg; *arm extension* 2.4m; *arm swivel* 360°; *lift scoop capacity* 75kg; *television cameras* 3 on board, plus 1 remote; *umbilical control cable* 225m; *power* continuous-charging sealed batteries; *gun* 12-bore semi-automatic shotgun; *disruptors* self-installed by robot.

GERMANY

Meltron
EOD Suit MEL 2000

The helmet, which is made of ballistic Aramid, is shock-absorbing, fireproof, and self-extinguishing. The polycarbonate visor is fastened by quick-release tensioners. The helmet includes an air blower system, battery-powered, with charger, and a communication system. The jacket is a fully ballistic quick release design with side opening and an integrated high collar. It has pockets for chest and groin plates and a pocket for the air blower, to be fastened at either side. The trousers give complete protection to the leg and lower body parts. Zippers on both sides and an adjustable pair of braces permit easy dressing. Separate overboots protect the feet.

Ballistic Levels: *jacket body area* 530m/sec V50; *trousers/arms* 360m/sec V50; *helmet* 400m/sec V50; *visor* 700m/sec V50; *overboots* 360m/sec V50.

Weights: *helmet* 4.5kg; *chest/groin plates* 1.5kg; *jacket* 9.5kg; *trousers* 5.0kg; *power* 2.5kg; *total weight* 23.0kg; *padding size* 85 x 35 x 45cm.

Meltron Bomb Disposal Trailer MEL 600-2

If disarming at site is too risky, the bomb can be loaded into the bomb disposal trailer, which is coupled to the truck. It can be loaded by the hoist beam or any other auxiliary equipment which is carried inside the truck (hook-and-line-set, as well as ramps for the EOD remotely controlled vehicle).

Data: *length* 4.659m; *width* 2.4m; *height* 1.5m; *weight* 1,250kg.

Meltron Manipulator Vehicle System

The original concept of the manipulator vehicle system was to facilitate the transportation of remote controlled manipulator tools to the desired location by means of a highly manoeuvrable vehicle. Since then the vehicle has been extended and developed, and it is currently being used at nuclear plants, airports and areas where personnel safety is paramount. The MF3 and MF4 vehicles have a monocoque construction and feature differing chassis designs. The MF3 has four individually adjustable chain drives and the chassis can suit most requirements. The advantage of this system is that the vehicle can be driven over obstacles with a maximum height of 0.6m. The MF4 has two chain drive units with spring mounted track rollers. This vehicle is extremely compact

Left: Meltron EOD Suit MEL 2000.

Right: Meltron Bomb Disposal Trailer.

Below: Meltron Manipulator Vehicle System.

and is easily manoeuvrable in confined spaces. All operating instructions are transmitted either by radio control or by cable. Speed selection of the vehicle is determined by joystick. Each vehicle is equipped with a camera which allows the operator to study the subject and surrounding area. Picture and sound transmission can also be by radio or by cable. Radio transmissions are made on FTZ approved frequencies, which are ideally suited for use in buildings or in areas where normal communications are difficult.

Data: MF4 *length* (without manipulator) 1.3m; *width* (without manipulator) 0.6m; *weight* approx. 300kg; *climbing capacity* 32°; *speed stepless* 0-25m/min. **MF3** *length* (max/min) 2.26/0.94m; *width* 0.72m; *height* (normal/max) 0.4/1.08m; *climbing capacity* 52°; *speed stepless* 0-40m/min.

Available Accessories: TV-radio link, 2, 3, GHz or other frequencies; CCD camera including zoomobjective 12.5-75mm focus; drive cameras bw/colour; measurement device for gripper power, recovery device, window destroyer, diagnostic system for the electronic circuits, mounting device for Dynergit.

Unimex
Ferromex 120 Detector

The Feromex 120 is a very sensitive detector which detects ferromagnetic targets underground or in water. The device employs a passive method, and can be used for the detection of pipes, cable junctions, unexploded ammunition, sunken vehicles or wrecks. The limits of detection range depend upon the size, position and magnetic characteristics of the ferrous targets. Large targets such as bombs and parts of wrecks can be detected from a distance of approximately 6m or more. Ferromagnetic objects will cause a disturbance in the magnetic field of the earth which can be detected by a differential detection arrangement. The Ferromex 120 consists mainly of two magnetic sensors which are placed coaxially at a set distance inside the probe. As both are connected in a differential circuit, the influence of the earth's (homogenous) magnetic field will be suppressed. As soon as the probe comes within reach of a magnetic disturbance caused by a target, the sensors inside the probe will provide a bias in the circuit which is indicated by an audible and visual signal. The polarity and intensity of the target's magnetic field will be indicated.

Employment: German Bundeswehr and elsewhere in the world.

Data: *carrying case* 1.11m x 14.5cm x 27cm; *power supply unit* 9.5cm x 5.5cm x 31.5cm; *control unit* 9.5cm x 10cm x 26cm; *probe tube* 60cm long, 4.6cm diameter; *carrying tube* 1.035m long; *weight* 4.5kg; *locating range* 6m.

Unimex Electronic Stethoscope
UNEX500C

The electronic Stethoscope UNEX500C was designed for the EOD field, where it is necessary to detect mechanical clockwork fuses in objects suspected to contain explosives, such as letters, packages or 'lost property'. It is also used where weak sound waves need to

be detected. The principle of operation is simple. It is based on the amplification and selection of sound waves, which are transformed into an electric voltage by means of a sensitive impact sound microphone. This voltage is fed to an adjustable amplifier with variable arrangements of filters which suppress interference from ambient noise within certain limits. Since the amplitude (volume) and frequency (pitch) are infinitely variable, the audible signals can be adjusted to suit each requirement. The device is very easy to operate. The control elements are shockproof and located on the front panel of the electronics. They consist solely of the on/off operating switch and the twin infinitely variable adjusters for amplifications and frequency.

Data: *power supply* 1-piece 9V battery IEC 6F22 operating time approx. 15hr, 6 LR 61 alkaline battery approx. 20hr, NC battery 6hr; *special search* 1 unit battery 12V, /600 mA; *head* 6hr with normal ambient temperature; *temperature* -25°C + 60°C; *amplification* 11dB (700.000) at 4Hz approx.; *adjustable* F_1=2.5 - 5.796kHz; *filters* F_2 = 5.74 - 8.88kHz.

Unimex Rode

Rode (remote ordnance disposal equipment) is a third-generation EOD robot developed by Unimex Handels Gmbh of Munich in Germany. The vehicle has six drive wheels, each with an independent motor gearbox drive system, giving the vehicle maximum reliability and enormous agility. The all-wheel drive combined with articulated front and rear axles gives the vehicle an ability to climb objects which exceed its wheel heights. Objects such as railway tracks, ties,

kerbs and long grass, which frequently defeat other robots, can be crossed with ease. The 360° rotating turret carries a manipulating claw to a height of 3.13m and can reach down below its standing position to 1.015m. Rode can be equipped to carry a disrupter, a five-shot semi-automatic shotgun, door openers and other attachments. It is equipped with three cameras and two halogen floodlights that can be operated simultaneously, all as standard features. Cameras with auto iris focusing can be supplied as optional equipment. Rode can lift objects weighing over 80kg and transport them at a speed of 6.5kph. The pincer pressure can be regulated up to 30kg, ensuring a firm grip on the object which can only be released by a command from the operator. Rode can also pull a trailer weighing up to 800kg at a speed of 6.5kph, and can be fitted with extra attachments to open doors, car doors and windows. It is the only unit on the market today that has a 360° rotating turret which makes it possible to pick up any object from any place without having to manoeuvre the vehicle itself, which saves valuable time.

Data: *power* electric motors; *movement* 6 independent wheels (6 x 6) solid rubber tyres, with blocking device on sloping surface from 0 to 6.5kph forward and backward; *power supply* 2 x 1100 AH each maintenance-free, leakproof and rechargeable batteries, additionally a 220/240V net connected power unit; *length* 1.4m; *width* 0.67m; *height* 0.8m; *weight* 350kg; *range* 2hr in normal operating conditions; *cable length* 100m, extendible to 250m.

Vallon Bomb/Metal Detectors
Electronic Bomb Detector
Model MB 1710A

This equipment consists of an oscillator, a measuring amplifier, an automatic zero compensator, a power amplifier, a sensitivity adjuster, a function selector, a pilot lamp and an audible alarm loudspeaker, all integrated into a laminated plastic box. The acoustic signal will sound if the letter or parcel contains any suspicious metal components such as copper wires, a striker, mechanical

time-fuse devices or batteries necessary for the detonation of a bomb.

Data: *sensor zone* 22mm x 220mm; *voltage* 220V/50cps; *alarm* acoustic signal 500-2,500cps; *weight* 5kg.

Metal Detector Models
MH 1603, MH 1604 and MH 1607

The MH 1603 and 1604 were developed to provide security forces with a convenient metal detector capable of performing checks on persons and packages. They have been used to detect ammunition hidden in tree trunks, hedgerows, behind walls and in sim-

Below: Vallon Bomb/Metal Detector Model 1603.

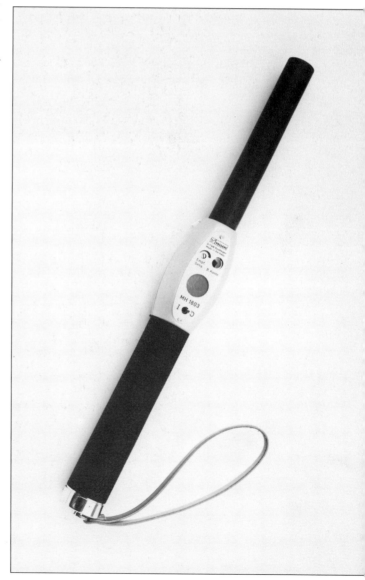

above: Vallon Bomb/Metal Detector Model ML 1750.

ilar places. The MH 1607 is used to screen envelopes to locate pieces of wire, mine ignition systems and other metal parts. The concentrated electromagnetic field of the detectors enables very exact pinpointing; even the course of a located metal wire can be determined.

Employment: German Federal Republic (Army, Lufthansa and Police).

Data: *length* 39cm (MH 1603), 40cm (MH 1604); 38cm (MH 1607); *weight* 0.5kg (MH 1603), 0.45kg (MH 1604), 0.41kg (MH 1607); *power* 9V battery.

Metal Detector Model ML 1750

This jeep-mounted mine detector is included because it is particularly suitable for IS operations. It would be largely irrelevant in conventional warfare, where a more blunt instrument such as a flail or dozer tank would be used; however, in an IS situation the ML 1750 would be ideal to clear tracks of metal-based anti-vehicle mines.

Data: *width of location* 1.60m; *weight of detecting coil* 43kg; *power supply* 12V; *current consumption* 3 amps.

Metal Detector Model MP 1781

Developed for use in airports, this equipment provides a visual alarm signal when any metal object passes through the gateway.

Variants: Model MP 1770 employs the same gate and footbridge but has a slightly more sophisticated electronics cabinet which indicates the part of the body where a metal object is secreted. Model MP 1783 indicates the type and size of the metal object.

Employment: German Federal Republic (Airport Authority, Lufthansa).

Data: *electronic cabinet weight* 14.5kg; *gate*

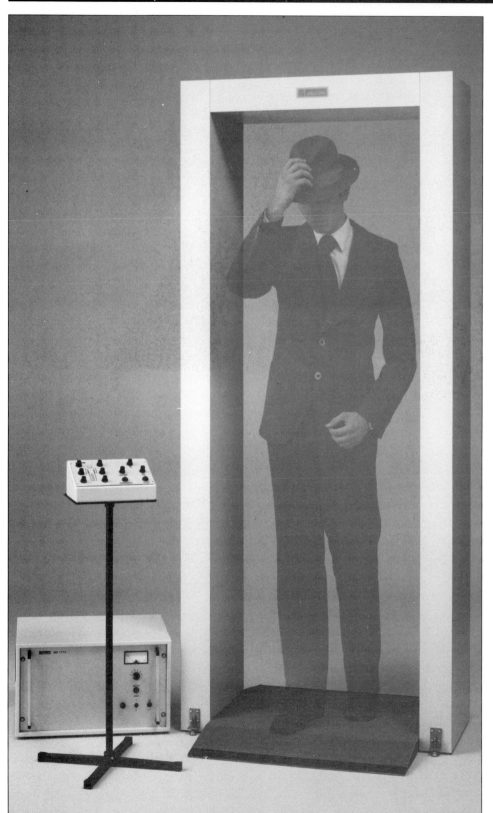

Left: Vallon Bomb/Metal Detector Model ML 1770

and footbridge weight 87kg; *cabinet depth* 28cm; *cabinet width* 49cm; *cabinet height* 18cm; *gate depth* 39cm; *gate width* 91cm; *gate height* 2.16m.

SWITZERLAND

Tig Bicord EOD Equipment
Anti-Magnetic Tool Set ASW-1

These tools are made of high-grade, anti-magnetic Beryllium.

Armoured EOD Van: A comprehensive package for civilian or military EOD experts, this carries the complete range of equipment necessary for a bomb, hostage or shoot-out situation, including the Garant 1 EOD robot vehicle.

Employment: in service with various European police forces.

Data: the vehicle (Type EOD/KFZ) can be supplied with the following equipment: 1 bomb protection blanket (type BSD-2); 2 bomb protection suits (BPS-1); 1 portable telephone equipment for the bomb protection suits (TTV-1); 1 portable EOD protection shield (PS-15); 2 bullet-proof vests (ANPO-1); 2 bullet-proof safety helmets (PSH-77); 2 mine detection protective suits (BPS-2-L); 1 mine detecting unit (ML); 1 set of anti-magnetic tools (ASW-1); 1 hook and line set (HLS); 1 defusing unit (EG-2); 1 defuser stand (STD-2); 1 defuser tripod (DRB-2); 1 fuse removing unit (ZAG-1); 1 portable X-ray equipment (RB-1); 1 portable developing unit (EWG-1); 1 stationary X-ray unit, 300kV (RN-2); 1 stationary developing unit (EWG-2); 1 explosives detecting unit (Explotest 100); 1 remote-controlled robot vehicle (Garant-1) with accessories; 2 track planks for the robot; 1 winching-down unit

Below: Tig Bicord Armoured EOD Van.

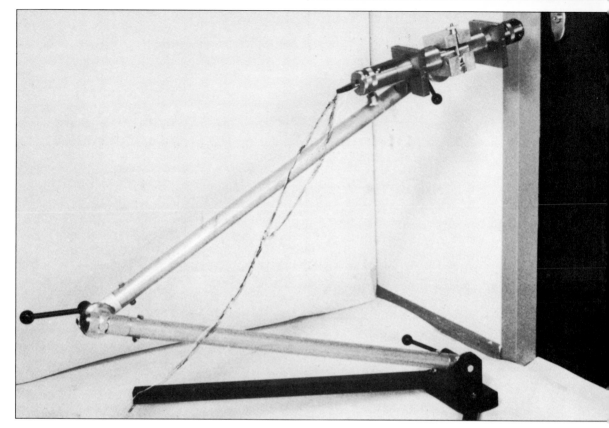

Above: Defuser/Disruptor Model EG-2.

(RE-1); 1 cable winding unit for the above (RE-WM); 1 portable power penetrator 12/220V (TSE); 1 set of electrical tools (SEW-1); 1 portable floodlight with tripod and 12V battery (TSBD-1); 1 cable drum with 200m cable (KTR-1); 1 inspection mirror (MIR-1); 1 inspection mirror (MIR-2); 1 siren (S-1); 1 blue light with magnetic base (BL-1).

Bomb Transport Trailer BOA-1

This enables a bomb to be removed from a location where an explosion would cause damage or casualties to a place where it can be dealt with in safety. Tig Bicord have also developed a technique to freeze an IED, and the trailer will keep the bomb frozen.

Defuser/Disrupter Model EG-2:

This is used to shoot the caps from tubular bombs, to destroy the detonators of unexploded grenades or bombs using a steel bolt or a water charge. It can also be used to shoot out locks. The Tig Bicord system is con-tained in three carrying cases, one for the defuser/disruptor and accessories, one for a folding stand, and a third for a folding tripod. The defuser/disruptor case also contains a suspension device for vertical shooting, a fixing cable with spring safety hook, a muzzle brake, an optical sighting mechanism, a detonator, a cable reel with 200m fuse cable, 50 propulsive charges, 50 powder ignitors, 20 steel bolts, 100 closing blanks, and 100 cup sleeves.

Explosives Detector Explotest-100

This portable explosives detector identifies most explosives and is particularly suitable for inspecting vehicles. The detector has an integrated battery, but can also be connected to a 12V or 24V power supply.

Garant-I EOD Robot

This large, wheeled and very powerful robot EOD vehicle can lift and tow suspect cars. It is also capable of lifting portable X-ray equipment to a target and returning with the

Right: Garant-I EOD robot.

Right: Tig Bicord EOD suit.

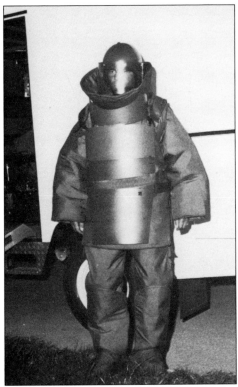

exposed film. Accessories include a towing hook, a cable drum, a large shovel with 75kg capacity, a small shovel and a remote control operating unit.

Employment: Various European police forces and EOD units.

Hook and Line Set (HLS)

The EOD expert is often confronted with a problem that can only be solved by moving parts of the bomb from its surroundings: to do this from a safe distance, hooks and line are used, with various accessories.

Tig Bicord Protective Garments and Equipment
Bomb Disposal Suit

Consisting of a protective helmet with wide-angle visor, front section, back protector panel and leg and foot protectors, this bomb disposal suit is made of extremely resistant material, which largely eliminates potential injuries while permitting good mobility. The front section incorporates an

additional two-section metal armour plate of special ballistic material designed to deflect the shock wave in case the bomb explodes. The high collar provides protection against neck injuries, while the back section has a pocket for a radio transceiver and bomb disposal tools. The titanium safety helmet can be equipped with earphones and a microphone so that contact with the EOD specialist can be maintained.

Safety Helmet PSH-77
Made of titanium, the PSH-77 comes in one size, with interior adjustment. It offers protection against bomb and grenade splinters and is claimed to be proof against 9mm Uzi submachine-gun rounds.

Variants: Visor VS-K-77 incorporates a wide-angled eye guard; visor VS-K-NV carries night vision equipment NV-2; a 12mm-thick transparent visor is also avail-

able, and this can be locked in raised or lowered positions. Facilities are inbuilt for the helmet to take headphones and a microphone.

UNITED KINGDOM

A.I.
Remotely Controlled Vehicle Ro-veh
The entire system works from either mains electricity or a portable generator, and the power is transmitted down the cable at only 65V. All of the video analog and operating signals are multiplexed down a single co-axial line. The combination of relatively high but safe power voltage and multiplexing on the co-axial line results in a very thin flexible cable (which is steel reinforced). Since there are no batteries at all, the vehicle is light and easy to manhandle; severing of the cable leaves Ro-veh inert and totally

Above: Ro-veh.

above: Dualscan.

safe. Momentary short-circuits during the cutting of the cable cannot fire the armaments, since that depends on receipt of digitally coded signals from the control module. The lightness of Ro-veh and the special attention paid to tread design results in a vehicle with exceptional stair-climbing ability. When Ro-veh is used on flat ground, the wheels can be fitted in a few minutes, giving a smoother ride and higher speed. The control console houses a video screen and all other controls: camera, armament (shotgun, disrupters, charge dropper, etc.), drive and boom controls. The armament is mounted on the superstructure. The standard boom arrangement folds away entirely within the length of the vehicle, but the modular construction using quick-fit connections allows any lengths or angles of boom to be constructed.

Employment: Various security agencies.

Data: *length* 1.12m; *width* 0.62m; *height* 0.37m (on tracks, without superstructure), 0.46m (on tracks, with superstructure folded); *reach* 2.06m (on tracks, with superstructure extended), 2.15m (on wheels, with superstructure extended); *arm movement* 180° (upper), 140° (lower); *turning radius* 0.65m (using neutral turn); *drive motors* two 95W (2 x ⅛hp); *speed* 26cm/sec (tracks), 44cm/sec (wheels).

Explosives Detector
Model 85 600 Dualscan

A second-generation walk-through explosives detector (or 'sniffing doorway'), this is both a metal detector and an explosives 'sniffer'. There are three models: 1. Walkthrough – people are tested sequentially without having to pause in the arch; the alarm comes *after* six seconds, so it is used ideally in this model when people are detained for at least 6 seconds by a subsequent security (e.g., documents) check. 2. Fast – red/green lights instruct people to remain in the arch for six seconds. 3. High sensitivity – test time is ten seconds, with electronic integration of results from a 100-segment trap.

Employment: Airports throughout the world.

Data: *overall height* 2.15m; *floor space required* 1.2m x 0.62m; *response time* 6 seconds from start of test, 10 seconds in high-sensitivity mode; *false alarm rate* less than 2%; *MTBF* better than 1,000hr.

Model 97 Portable Explosives Detector

The Model 97 is a fourth-generation unit. It will detect a wide variety of commercial and military explosives without the need to reprogramme the equipment for specific groups. Lightweight and simple to use, the Model 97 is contained in an unobtrusive attaché case. It is a non-contact instrument, which means that packages fitted with an anti-tamper device can still be checked without disturbing them. The Model 97 contains a unique real-time detection system that can rapidly discriminate between the vapours from an explosive and those produced by a similar non-explosive material. The results are instantaneous, as there is no tedious sample collection or slow analysis process in the system. The unit does not need to be purged clean once an explosive has been detected, and it is therefore ready to continue within a few seconds. The functioning of the detector cell is constantly monitored within the unit, which automatically compensates for changes in operating conditions, maintaining maximum performance.

Employment: In wide use throughout the world.

Data: *attaché case* (packed) 560mm wide x 520mm deep x 220mm high, *weight* 16.2kg; *response time* typically 2sec; *sensitivity* 1 part explosive vapour in 10° parts air; *detection* gas chromatography system.

Below: Model 97 Portable Explosives Detector.

Exfinder 152 Hand Held Explosives Vapour Detector

Based on the successful Exfinder range of ion mobility detectors, the Exfinder 152 is powered by 12V long-life rechargeable batteries, and can be used by non-technical personnel. The Exfinder 152 is simply turned on by depressing the 'on' button, and within a few seconds will automatically self-calibrate to achieve the optimum sensitivity. The instrument will give an audible and visual response to sampled air containing sufficient concentrations of explosives vapour. The tone of the audio response denotes the approximate concentration of explosives vapour present. The audio can be switched off, leaving the visual alarm visible only to the operator. Other indicators include the battery low-charge lamp, which alerts the operator to change the battery or to attach the mains/charger unit, and a fault lamp which shows that an internal fault is present. The Exfinder 152 is the ideal cost-effective screening device for many applications, including the screening of handbags, briefcases, people and open parcels.

Data: *detection principle* ion mobility; *response time* typically 1sec; *sensitivity* greater than 1 part of explosive vapour in 10° parts air by volume; *power supply* either 12V rechargeable nicad batteries or mains/charger unit, or both by direct couple or continuous operation; *battery life* 14hr continuous, 20+hr intermittent; *indicators* explosive alarm, audio, battery low, fault; *controls* instrument on/off, audio on/off; *dimensions and weights* hand unit 420 x 50 x 50mm, 680gms, case 470 x 280 x 80mm, 3.45kg, *packed for shipment* case 500 x 320 x 90mm, 3.70kg.

AB Precision Pigstick EOD Disrupter

The Pigstick EOD Disrupter is a large water-jet disrupter for dealing with soft-skinned improvised explosive devices such as parcel bombs and those contained in briefcases. It is

elow: Exfinder 152.

a multi-shot device capable of many firings without distortion of the body.

Data: Barrel *overall length* 485mm; *weight* 2.95kg. **Holdall** *overall size* 500mm x 300mm x 200mm; *material* canvas; *colour* olive green; *weight of kit* 4kg.

Variants: Improved EOD Disrupter for handling thicker-walled IEDs such as those in metal containers. The Needle EOD Disrupter is designed to disrupt small IEDs such as letter bombs.

ABL 1000 Recoilless De-Armer Disrupter

Developed as dual-role equipment to defeat the threat posed by more complex, better-protected IEDs and deal with unexploded ordnance (UXO), the ABL 1000 De-Armer Disrupter remains completely recoilless during operation. It uses a standard electricity-fired 0.5in cartridge. When used as a Disrupter, the ABL 1000 will be set up close to the suspect device and aimed at the firing circuit or detonator. On firing, it will project a water slug into the device, disrupting the firing circuit without causing detonation of the device's explosive contents. As a De-Armer, the ABL 1000 will project a variety of steel slugs into the fuses or pistols of air-dropped bombs and some land service ammunition. A bolster slug enables it to be used against other UXO as well as being effective against metal-cased IEDs.

Data: Disrupter *overall length* 515mm; *weight* 4.5kg.

De-Armer *overall length* 284mm; *weight* 3.5kg.

Container: *overall* 873mm x 428mm x 187mm; *material* aluminium; *colour* Nato green. *Weight of kit* 25kg.

Bristol Armour
Bomb Search and Disposal Suits

Type 12 Search Suit: This protective body armour system for explosives detection provides a high level of torso invulnerability

Above: Pigstick EOD Disrupter.

Right: ABL 1000 Recoilless De-Armer Disrupter.

system which delivers air at more than 400 litres per minute over the chest, legs, arms, back and face.

Ballistic Protection: The Bristol Armour Bomb Search and Disposal Suits give the following ballistic protection against a 17 gram (1.08g) steel fragment simulator: chest, groin and back (Search Suit) with plates fitted – V50>960m/sec; general body area not protected by plates – V50>500m/sec; lower legs and arms (Bomb Suit only) – V50>630m/sec; helmet (Bomb Suit only) – V50>312m/sec.

Far left: Bristol Armour Type 12 Search Suit.

Below: Bristol Armour Bomb Disposal Suit.

without restricting the wearer's movements. Complementary components can be selectively added to tailor the suit to the operator's specific requirement.

Bomb Disposal Suit: The Bomb Disposal Suit is a lightweight flexible composite armour suit giving maximum protection for explosive ordnance disposal personnel. The suit consists of a helmet (incorporating a visor, demister and radio transmitter), jacket, trousers, foot protectors, and ceramic plates for the protection of the chest and pelvic regions. To provide a more relaxed atmosphere in which to work, the suit can be used with a cooling

ght: Hadrian.

HADRIAN

Defence Systems Ltd Hadrian

The complete system consists of a remotely controlled vehicle with a range of operating accessories, a command console with an umbilical cable, and a power generator. The vehicle's performance comes from a special six-wheel design, which provides easy manoeuvrability over difficult terrain, long grass and obstacles. Each wheel has independent motor-gearbox drive for maximum traction and mobility and, unlike many tracked systems, the vehicle will continue to operate in the event of individual wheel or motor damage. Both front and rear axles swivel, and the vehicle can climb obstacles exceeding its own wheel height. Differential-wheel speed control on opposite sides allows the vehicle to turn on its own axis. Speed can be controlled from almost imperceptibly slow to 4kph.

Remote operation: Fitted to the vehicle chassis is a remotely operated arm containing a wrist and claw manipulator. At the end of the arm and wrist is a cleverly designed claw

capable of continuous rotation, allowing left- and right-hand screwing operations to be undertaken. It has a grip capacity up to 24cm. The claw has the unique capability of being able to pick up and fire a number of purpose designed disrupters, selecting and connecting them to the firing circuit without any requirement to return to the operator. Three closed-circuit television cameras mounted beside the wrist, gun and front axle allow the operator to view and manipulate objects from any direction in complete safety.

Accessories: The operating arm is arranged so that a 12-bore semi-automatic shotgun with rangefinder and sights (and floodlights) can be fitted permanently. Terminals are provided for a wide range of purpose-built accessories, including those for radioactive and chemical handling, firefighting, airport security activities, remote surveillance and defence operations. In addition to the arm accessories there are terminals and fittings on the front axle for a large variety of special tools and equipment. These include a large shovel capable of picking up and lifting larger objects. The operator has a clear view both of the front-mounted accessories and of where the vehicle is travelling via a CCTV camera mounted between the front wheels. Provision is also made for the mounting of headlamp on the front axles. Power for all of the accessories comes from the vehicle's own power supply. At the rear of the vehicle are attachment points for the fixing of a carrying hod. A specially designed umbilical cable control arm is also fitted to the rear axle. This pivots to keep the cable clear of the wheels and accessories during vehicle manoeuvring. (The claw can be used to pick up and untangle the cable if necessary.)

Employment: Several systems are in operation in a number of countries.

Data: *weight* 180kg; *drive* 6 DC motors (all wheels); *auxiliary motions* 6 DC motors; *claw lift capacity* 10kg; *arm extension* 2.4m; *arm swivel* 360°; *lift scoop capacity* 75kg; *television cameras* 3 on board, plus 1 remote; *umbilical control cable* 225m; *power* continuous charging sealed batteries; *gun* 12-bore semi-automatic shotgun; *disruptors* self-installed by robot.

Endoscan Top-Optic Endoscopes

Endoscan Top-Optic manufactures a range of rigid and flexible fibre-optic endoscopes and light-source boxes. These vary from micro-endoscopes of 1.5mm diameter to endoscopes of 10.3mm diameter. Working lengths vary from 130mm to 2,950mm. Fields of view vary from 30° to 70°. Endoscopes can have cameras or CCTV/Videos attached to them to secure a permanent photographic record.

Galt Composites
Galt Blast Container

Postal workers and post-room staff, especially those in sensitive jobs or locations, inevitably face the possibility of encountering parcel or letter bombs. Identifying suspicious items in the mail is vital, but even when this is successfully done there still remains the problem of how to minimise danger to people and property until bomb

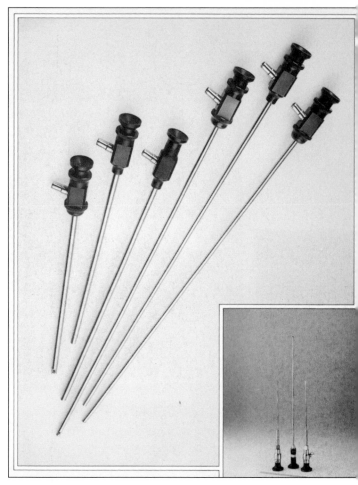

disposal experts arrive on the scene. Galt Composites has designed an armoured container suitable for any office or post-room, which will hold suspect packages until help arrives. The Galt Blast Container is constructed from GRP composite armour material, and is fitted with a fabric inner bag designed to support a package in an upright attitude, ready for X-ray inspection. This can be carried out without further handling of the suspect device because the container is transparent to X-rays even at very low, and therefore safer, pulse rates. Should a device detonate, the Blast Container will withstand the explosion and associated fragments from up to 8oz (225g) of commercial explosive, directing the force of the explosion upwards, where it will do the least damage. The container, which has been proved effective in a series of field trials, measures approximately

Above and opposite page, top, left and right: Examples of Endoscan Top-Optic Endoscopes.

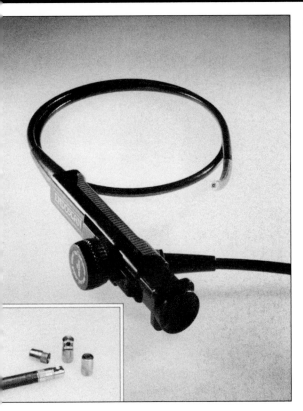

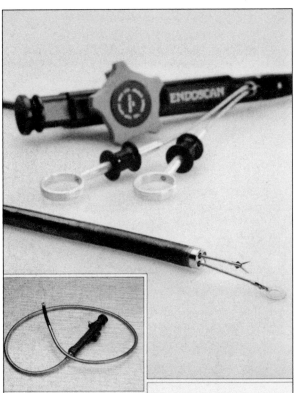

Right: Galt Blast Container.

100cm high by 50cm in diameter, and can be either permanently positioned or stored in a suitable site and rolled into place when required.

EOD Suit Mk 2 and EOD Helmet Mk3

Galt composites holds the sole licence from the UK MOD for both the EOD suit Mk 2 and the EOD Helmet Mk 3. The suit was developed by the MOD to provide the best combination of wearer protection and mobility. Well-proven in operational situations world-wide, particularly in Northern Ireland, it is NATO catalogued and has been adapted as standard issue throughout NATO. The suits are in service with military and civil

Right: Lightweight Body
Armour Ltd EOD Suit 9.

Right: Lightweight Body Armour Ltd EOD Suit 9.

authorities throughout the world. The Mk 3 helmet is also standard NATO issue. It has much better ballistic protection than its predecessor, the Mk2, plus a weight reduction from 4.7kg to 2.8kg. Cooling and ventilating equipment for the suit, and demisting and face ventilating equipment for the helmet, are also available.

Hunter Remote-Control EOD Vehicle (Series 3)

A joint Hunting Engineering and SAS Group venture, the remotely controlled Hunter robot was developed by experienced EOD officers to be as flexible and simple to operate as possible. Special features include an exceptional degree of control at slow speeds,

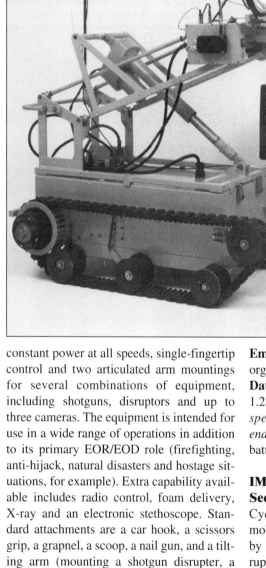

constant power at all speeds, single-fingertip control and two articulated arm mountings for several combinations of equipment, including shotguns, disruptors and up to three cameras. The equipment is intended for use in a wide range of operations in addition to its primary EOR/EOD role (firefighting, anti-hijack, natural disasters and hostage situations, for example). Extra capability available includes radio control, foam delivery, X-ray and an electronic stethoscope. Standard attachments are a car hook, a scissors grip, a grapnel, a scoop, a nail gun, and a tilting arm (mounting a shotgun disrupter, a window breaker, a charge dropper or a camera panning unit). The Series 3 includes the unique combined wheel and track TRAVADS system.

Employment: In use with many military organisations around the world.

Data: *weight* 115kg; *width* 0.65m; *length* 1.25m; *height* (with boom raised) 1.3m; *speed* 30m/min (approx.); *range* 100m; *endurance* about 2hr; *power supply* two 24V batteries.

IMVEC Cyclops Remote Controlled Security Vehicle

Cyclops, an extremely compact, highly mobile security vehicle, has been developed by IMVEC for the remote viewing and disruption of suspect EOD devices. It also has applications in areas hazardous to man, such as chemical, nuclear and smoke-filled environments. Its small size enables it to enter confined spaces in shops, ships, offices, trains, buses and aircraft. It is small enough to pass beneath chairs and desks, yet agile enough to negotiate kerbstones and staircases. The vehicle is highly manoeuvrable, can turn within its own length, and has sufficient reactive power to tow heavy packages away from vulnerable areas. Control signals and video reception are made through independent radio links, or multiplexed through a common trailing cable. Cyclops can be fitted with a lifting mechanism extendible to 1.2m in height, with a tilting head capable of carrying explosive disrupters and monochrome or colour TV cameras. It can also be supplied as a basic mobile platform which can be fitted with a variety of specialist equipment including a manipulative arm, thermal imaging equipment, mechanical handling and cutting devices, etc.

Employment: The French Navy has ordered Cyclops, and other French security services are either about to do so or have already done so. Manufacturing rights for Cyclops are being negotiated with companies in France and the USA.

Data (Cyclops Mk 3): *length* 750mm; *width* 360mm; *height* minimum (not including aerial) 240mm, maximum (ground to camera) 1,200mm; *ground clearance* 60mm; *speed range* 0 to 500mm/sec; *climbing ability* 40° slope; *power* rechargeable NiCad batteries; *vehicle weight* 18kg.

Morfax Wheelbarrow Remotely Controlled EOD Vehicle

Wheelbarrow Mk 7: This vehicle first saw operational service in 1972. It was developed to perform many of the functions that previously placed members of IS forces at considerable risk, and is capable of handling a variety of equipment necessary for the location and disposal of potentially dangerous objects. The vehicle is powered by two reversible electric motors, running off inboard 24V batteries. It carries vertical and horizontal booms for locating various manip-

Below: Cyclops.

ulating items. Wheelbarrow has a remotely controlled CCTV camera and panning head, allowing the operator to control his vehicle from a safe position using a TV monitor. Commands are transmitted to the vehicle by means of a detachable 100m eighteen-way control cable. The EOD operator can now attack virtually any IED he encounters, and if he runs out of time a machine is damaged, rather than a man killed. However, experience has shown that a Wheelbarrow is rarely totally destroyed in an explosion. The application of Wheelbarrow is not limited to EOD work. With the multi-purpose central mount (MPCM) it can carry and automatically fire a variety of weapons used in riot, hostage or 'shoot-out' situations. A comprehensive range of attachments are available.

Employment: Various US police forces, British Army.

Data: *weight* 195kg; *width* 0.69m; *length* 1.22m; *height* 0.82m (with boom folded); *speed* 33.5m/min; *range* 100m (standard cable and drum); *endurance* 2hr (mean); *power supply* two 12V 50amp-hr lead/acid batteries; *CCTV* single lens (2.10V 50Hz) supplied via an invertor; *monitor* 230mm model (12V DC or 240V 50Hz).

Wheelbarrow Super M: This is the logical development of the highly successful Morfax Wheelbarrow Mk 7 series, over 500 of which are in service in more than 50 countries throughout the world. Wheelbarrow Super M builds on some 15 years of operational use, and incorporates all of the improvements that this experience has shown to be desirable to increase versatility and performance. Super M is fitted with integral radio control as a standard feature. The Morfax Radio Control System (MRCS) not only gives greater range, but also provides increased manoeuvrability and versatility, particularly in operations in urban locations. The top speed of the vehicle has been increased by more than 50 per cent to 55m/min, whilst full control has been retained from the lowest 'creep' speed. The very wide range of accessories available

Right: Wheelbarrow Super M.

makes the Wheelbarrow Super M the most versatile EOD system in use. A telescopic boom with remote control of extension is now fitted as standard. New accessories include a modular weapon mounting system (MWMS) to provide multiple weapon capacity and a moveable arc of fire. A laser sighting system is also available. Accessories available for previous Mk 7 series of Wheelbarrow Super M include disruptors, a shot-

Right: Wheelbarrow Super M.

gun, a drum of firing cable, X-ray equipment, a car towing hook and an electro-mechanical grab. A CCD video camera is fitted as standard. Improved picture quality is provided by the use of auto-iris lenses, with viewing on a high-definition colour monitor. The monitor is housed in a rugged portable Ground Control Unit incorporating the data transmitter and video receiver. Surveillance facilities on Wheelbarrow Super M can be enhanced by the addition of a second, monochrome or colour CCD video camera. A special monochrome camera with zoom lens can be supplied, both zoom and focusing being controlled from the new hand control set.

Data: *average operational weight* 204kg; *width* 686mm; *length* 1,220mm; *height* (from ground to top of video camera, with boom horizontal and hamper vertical) 1,320mm; *lowest height above ground (using MWMS) of video camera lens* 65mm;

on-board power supply 2 x 12V, 70Ah lead/acid batteries; *speed* from creep to 55m/min; *video colour camera* CCD camera with auto-iris lens; *video monitor* 230mm colour screen, power supply from separate 12V lead/acid battery; *battery endurance* approximately 2 hr under normal operating conditions; after this, charging is necessary.

Morfax Wheelbarrow Mk 8 Radio Controlled EOD: The Wheelbarrow Mk 8 is the result of continuing development of the Wheelbarrow bomb disposal vehicles. The operator has an increased ability to adjust the vehicle's centre of gravity during operation, which improves stability when negotiating stairways. Maximum speed has been increased, and a telescopic boom is now fitted as standard. Many fixtures and accessories are similar to those used on the Mk 7 series. For instance, two video cameras can be fitted to the vehicle, one for independent general surveillance for driving, and the

Top right and below:
Wheelbarrow Mk 8.

hand-held control set operates the vehicle, offering multifunction display and facilities. At all times the operator is informed which functions are selected and available.

Data: *minimum height (telescopic boom stowed)* 94cm, *(telescopic boom deployed)* 137cm; *minimum width* 62cm; *minimum weight* 240kg; *weight of basic chassis and batteries* 195kg; *weight of top hamper* 28kg; *weight of telescopic boom* 17kg; *maximum ground clearance* 10cm; *speed* 0 to 1.67m/sec; *maximum climb* 45°; *turning circle* within vehicle axis; *duration* continuous usage approx 1hr, intermittent usage approx 2hr; *fording depth* 20cm.

Morfax Multi M: The Wheelbarrow MULTI M is an enhanced EOD vehicle based on the in-service Mk 8. Major enhancements resulting from design developments brought about by user feedback have produced significant performance benefits. These enhancements include:

other for more detailed investigation. Wheelbarrow Mk 8 is fitted with MRCS, the only such system approved by the British Ordnance Board, making operation as flexible as that of the radio-controlled Mk 7 series. A

Below: Morfax Multi M.

facilitate the remote manipulation of suspected explosive devices, as well as providing a means of gaining access to their location. The 100m line gives a safer distance between the operator and the device. The varied attachments enable the line to be securely fastened to all types of object used to make and conceal explosives.

Left and above: Morfax Mini M.

● New, electronically controlled, transmission system;

● New track system incorporating simplified drive tensioning and rubber tracks;

● Strengthened top hamper;

● Rationalised electronic package;

● Maintenance-free batteries;

● Optional battery management system;

● Remote battery condition indicator.

Morfax Mini M: This is a miniature portable and compact surveillance vehicle designed to penetrate areas inaccessible to its larger counterparts, the world-famous Morfax Wheelbarrow EOD vehicles.

Data: Tracked, fully radio-controlled, battery-operated vehicle. *Power* two sealed dry-fit rechargeable batteries giving an ample 2hr (approx.) working time between charges; *length* (camera in stowed position) 690mm; *height* (camera in stowed position) 290mm, (camera in maximum position) 1,665mm; *width* 370mm; *weight* 27kg; *camera pan* 340°; *camera tilt* 180°.

PW Allen
Hook and Line Set Mk 1
The original Hook and Line Set, this comprises a high-strength line and attachments to

Opposite page, bottom, and right and below right: Hook and Line Set Mk 1.

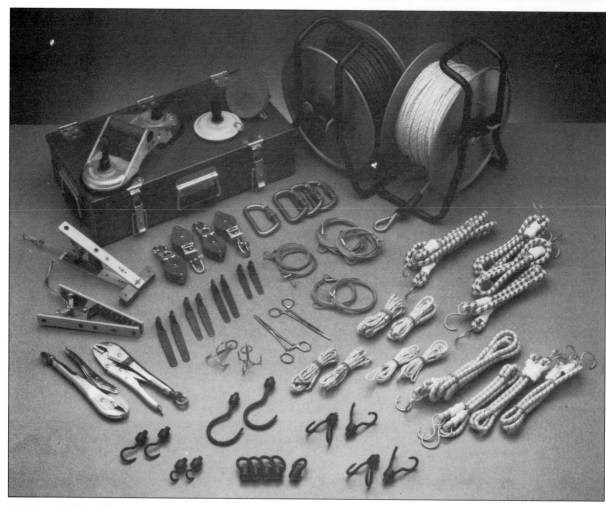

Hook and Line Set Mk 2: An enhanced Hook and Line Set that has been refined and updated to a new UK Ministry of Defence specification. The HAL Mk 2 has been extended to include a range of new components for dealing with the wide variety of improvised explosive devices now encountered. The comprehensive set includes two 120m lines to provide action at a distance, devices for attaching the line to all types of objects, and components for changing the direction of the line to give life, avoid obstacles or gain safe cover.

PW Allen Hook and Line Set Mk 3: A heavy-duty EOD Hook and Line Set approved by the UK Ministry of Defence for moving vehicles and heavy improvised explosive devices from sensitive or inaccessible locations. The HAL Mk 3 has been designed for use where the load limitations of the HAL Mk 1 or Mk 2 are likely to be exceeded. The wide range of attachments in the HAL Mk 3, including webbing strops, slings, hooks and shackles, enable the 150m towing line to be attached to a suspect vehicle or container quickly and securely with the minimum of disturbance. Snatch blocks allow the operator to change the direction of the line to gain cover for extra safety, or to operate in confined areas. Ground anchors enable the snatch blocks to be used where there are no natural anchorage points. All of the attachments are easily fitted and removed without tools, and can be packed into the accessory case for ease of transportation.

PW Allen EOD Tripod: Used with an Allen Hook and Line Set, the portable EOD Tripod can assist in the lifting and removal

Left and right: Hook and Line Set Mk 2.

Right: Hook and Line Set Mk 3.

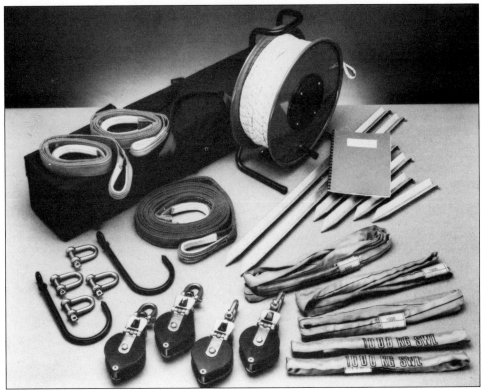

of heavy objects from difficult locations, such as car boots, manholes and culverts, from a position of safety. The Tripod has two-section telescopic legs that can be extended and locked to any one of four heights, enabling it to be used in areas of

Left: PW Allen EOD Tripod.

restricted height or on sloping ground. The head is fitted with leg splay stops that prevent the Tripod from collapsing under load, as well as two lifting eyes and a tethering eye. The self-levelling feet may be pegged to the ground for stability.

PW Allen Search Fibrescope Kit SF1: The ability to manoeuvre a fibrescope around bends and obstacles makes it a valuable search tool, providing visual access to awkward and inaccessible areas without costly damage or time-consuming disassembly. With a remotely controlled head, moveable by up to 120° in either direction, and a 90° viewing attachment, each fibrescope can give a complete 360° internal view of cavities through a 6 or 8mm-diameter hole. Illumination is provided from portable battery-powered light sources and transmitted to the fibrescope head through an integral fibreoptic light guide. For protection, the sheath is constructed of tough but flexible braided stainless steel.

PW Allen Search Fibrescope Kit SF2: A high specification fibrescope with a high-density image guide and a 75W tungsten halogen light source giving a brighter image with higher resolution. Fuel-proofed as standard, and available in 1m, 1.5m and 2m lengths. Packed in a foam carrying case, each kit includes a fibrescope, a light source and a rechargeable battery pack, providing a portable, lightweight search and inspection system of great versatility. A battery charger is supplied.

PW Allen SP86 Surveillance Periscope: A surveillance periscope for searching lifts and viewing over walls and obstacles from a

Below: PW Allen Search Fibrescope Kit SF2.

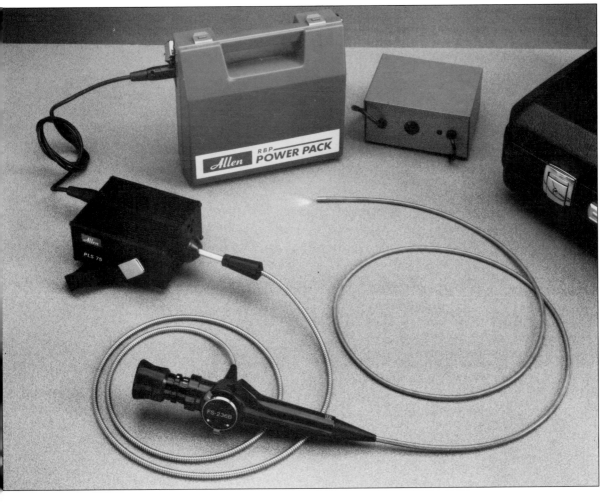

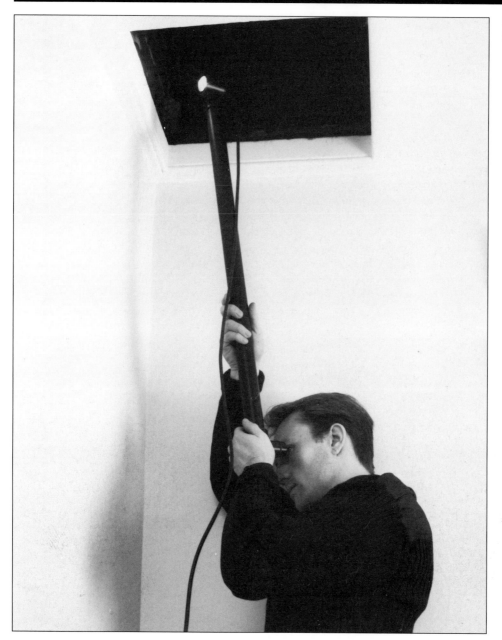

Left and right: SP86 Surveillance Periscope.

position of safety. The SP86 is lightweight and can be hand held with comfort or mounted on a tripod for continuous surveillance. An optional high-intensity, battery-powered light source can be fitted to the top of the periscope to provide brilliant illumination.

PW Allen Standard Search Endoscope: A portable endoscope kit for searching inaccessible areas of buildings, ships and vehicles. The robust fixed-focus endoscope can be used to inspect cavities and hollow structures internally through holes and gaps of 10mm diameter, with illumination provided by a bright 10W lamp protected within the tip. The endoscope is supplied with a lightweight battery pack which provides 2hr continuous use when fully charged, and a combined charger/AC power unit.

PW Allen Military Search Endoscope: The most versatile endoscope in the range. The SE30 is designed to assist ordnance and contraband search teams. Visual inspection

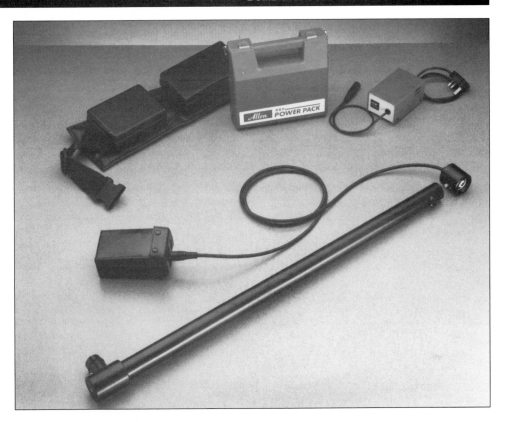

Right: SE30 Search Endoscope Kit.

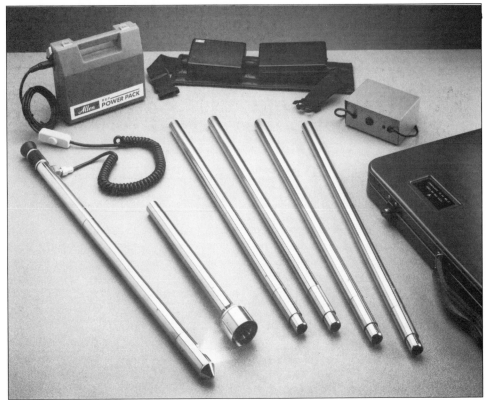

of inaccessible areas can be made with greater safety, without excessive damage to property, and often avoiding the movement of heavy loads. The high level of illumination from powerful tungsten halogen lamps contained in the endoscope head, and the large-diameter optics, ensure a high degree of visual clarity. Interchangeable heads provide wide-angle forward and side views to permit the complete internal inspection of deep cavities and large enclosed areas. The endoscope is in seven sections – one eyepiece tube, two objective tubes (one for forward viewing and one for side viewing) and four extension tubes all with self-locking taper connections – allowing the endoscope to be assembled in various lengths.

PW Allen SE737 Search Endoscope: A high-specification endoscope for use by military search teams. Constructed of tough 16-gauge stainless steel and protected in a waterproof and shockproof carrying case, the SE737 is designed to withstand adverse field conditions. Wide-angle forward and side views enable the SE737 to provide internal reconnaissance of buildings and enclosures through a 20mm-diameter hole.

PW Allen Search Inspection Kit SKM: A comprehensive kit containing a range of inspection mirrors and light probes, large

Right and below right:
A smaller endoscope of
6.65mm diameter, designated Interscope.

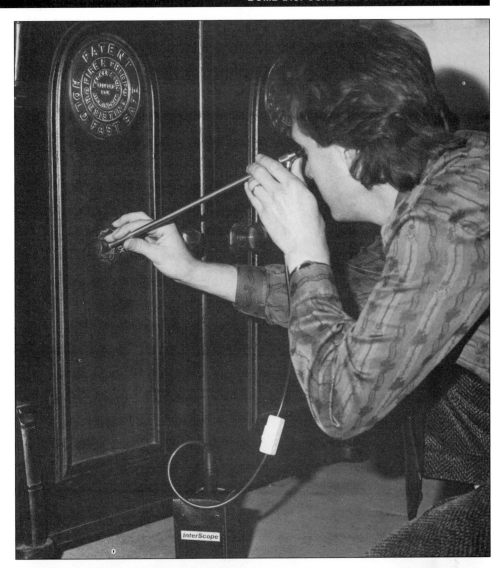

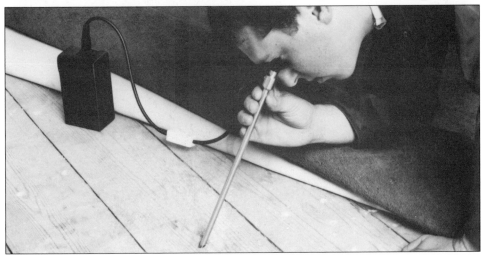

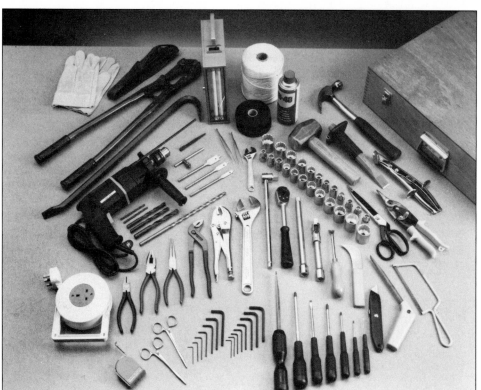

Above left: The PW Allen Search Inspection Kit SKM.

Left: PW Allen Search Tool Kit SKT/2.

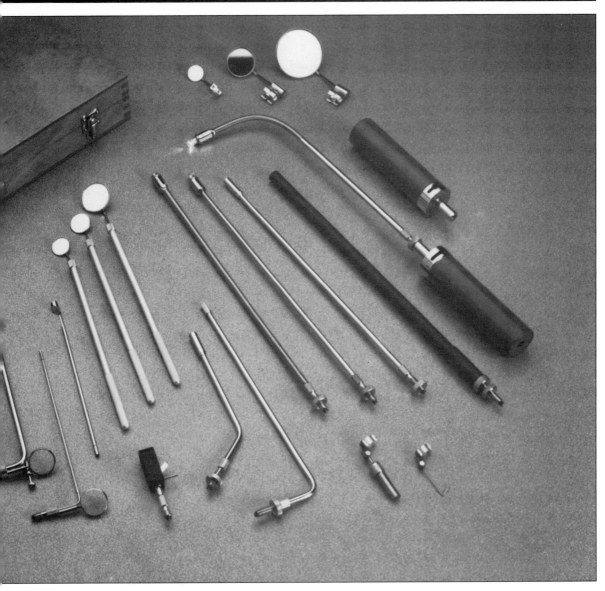

Above: The PW Allen Miniature EOD Set.

and miniature, an illuminated endoscope, a fluorescent hand lamp and two hand torches to facilitate the search for concealed articles. Designed to assist EOR, customs and scene of crime personnel, the SKM is supplied in a protective carrying case.

PW Allen Search Tool Kit SKT/2: A complete tool kit for search operations. The SKT/2 can be used alone or in conjunction with the SKM to provide physical or visual access to all types of containers and cavities. The kit contains a comprehensive selection of hand tools to dismantle equipment and machinery, and a range of cutters and saws to open gates and penetrate fences. When immediate visual inspection behind walls and panelling is required, the power drill enables inspection holes to be bored through all types of material and walls up to 250mm thick, allowing complete and rapid internal inspection with an endoscope or fibrescope. Supplied in two robust carrying cases.

PW Allen Miniature EOD Set: A selection of miniature mirrors and light probes to aid the internal inspection of all types of cavities, cases and containers through a small aperture with the minimum of damage and

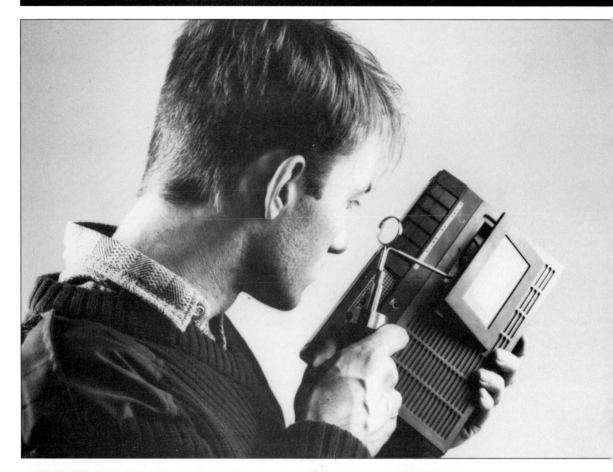

Above: The PW Allen Miniature Light Probe.

Left: The PW Allen Fluorescent Handlamp.

disturbance. Designed for EOR/EOD security and scene-of-crime search.

PW Allen Fluorescent Handlamp: Producing bright illumination over a wide area, the A33D is an ideal general-purpose search and inspection lantern. Constructed of steel with a tough acrylic window, it has been designed to withstand demanding military use. The lantern can be used handheld or freestanding, and will give 12hr continuous use before battery replacement becomes necessary.

PW Allen Search Mirrors
CEM and CEM/ILL telescopic type: Two lightweight telescopic inspection mirrors with and without illumination, providing a convenient means of searching inaccessible areas of buildings, ships and vehicles. The stem extends to 1,400mm and is fitted with an adjustable arm to give the perfect angle of view. When closed, the inspection mirror measures only 350mm, convenient for carrying and storage. A

ight: CEM and EM/ILL Telescopic ght Search Mirror in peration.

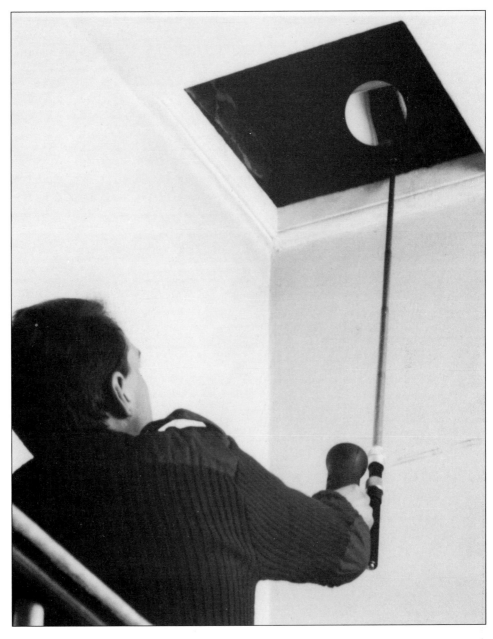

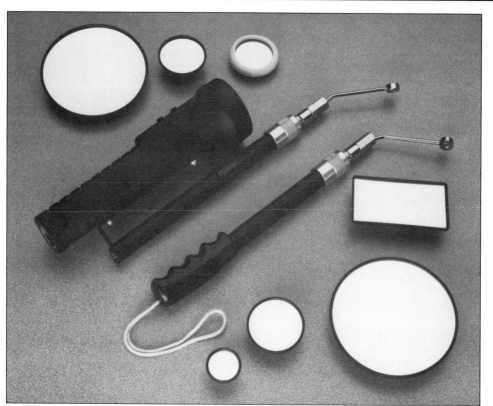

Left: CEM and CEM/ILL Telescopic Sight Search Mirror.

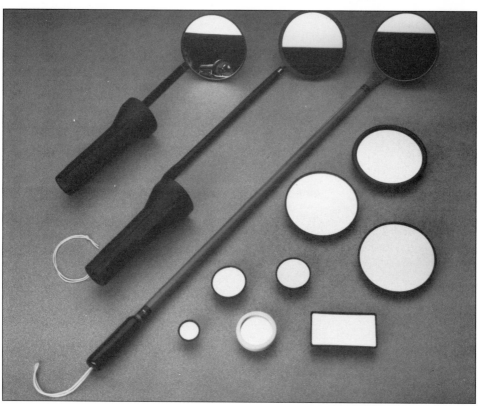

Left: The Fixed-length Search Mirrors.

Right: The Fixed-length Search Mirrors in operation.

wide range of mirrors in glass or stainless steel is available.

Fixed-length Search Mirrors

UCM/SMC short arm, with torch: An ideal mirror for checking wheel arches or overhead ledges. The stem is fitted with a watertight rubber torch and a standard 140mm diameter convex glass mirror (SMC).

UVSM/T portable vehicle search mirror, with torch: A portable illuminated vehicle search mirror designed with a longer stem, to enable convenient under-vehicle searches, and a ball-and-socket mirror joint to allow adjustment for the perfect angle of view. The stem is fitted with a 20'D' cell watertight rubber torch, which has a spare lamp enclosed in a protective end cap. The standard unit is supplied with a 140mm diameter

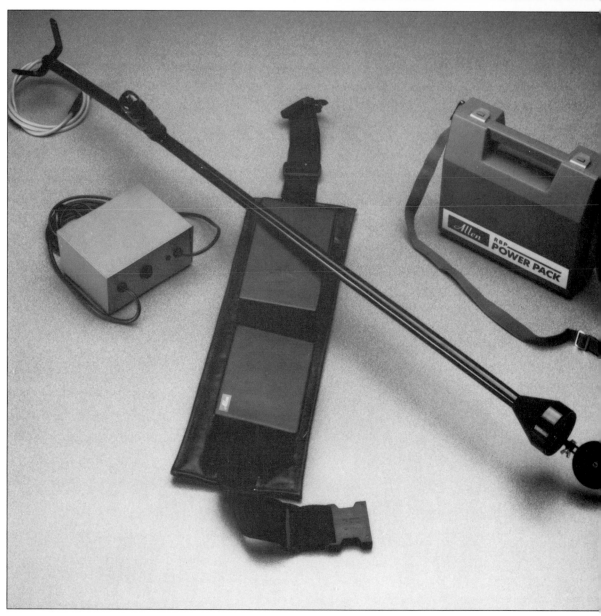

convex glass mirror with an extra protective rubber surround (SMC/X).

FSM/SMC long arm, without torch: A low-cost, unilluminated search mirror with a fixed length of 900mm. The angled mirror stem is fitted with a standard 140mm diameter convex glass mirror (SMC) to give a wide field of view, although any of the alternative mirrors in glass or stainless steel can be fitted instead.

Vehicle Search Mirror: A hand-held inspection mirror for searching the under-sides of vehicles. The shatterproof convex mirror provides a large field of view which is brightly illuminated by a powerful 55W tungsten halogen lamp. The mirror is fitted to the shaft on a double-jointed arm, allowing adjustment for angle. With a handgrip and upper arm cradle, the mirror can be controlled perfectly with one hand. The VSM is lightweight, highly manoeuvrable and can be used for long periods without fatigue. It is powered by a 12V rechargeable battery belt or shoulder pack.

bove: The VSM Light
Weight Vehicle Search
Mirror.

bove right: The VSM
ight Weight Vehicle
earch Mirror in opera-
on.

Vehicle Search Mirror Trolley Model (pictured overleaf): A robust illuminated inspection mirror mounted on castors, for searching the undersides of vehicles. The large convex mirror ensures a wide field of view, and the energy-efficient fluorescent light source provides bright illumination. A two-position light switch mounted on the handle grip permits continuous use or brief inspections, further extending battery life. Fitted with a 2m flying lead, the light source can also be unclipped to allow the search of vehicle inte-

riors. Two versions of the search mirror are available. The VMBD/2 is powered by 'D' cell batteries (disposable or rechargeable), which are concealed in the handle. The VM8, supplied with an 8m cable, can be used with an external 12V source, such as a car battery, or mains power using the transformer VMT.

Pocket Vehicle Search Mirror: The CMT is a truly compact vehicle search mirror and torch, designed to fit a pocket or handbag. With a unique telescopic handle that is com-

Left and below left:
Vehicle Search Mirror
Trolley Model.

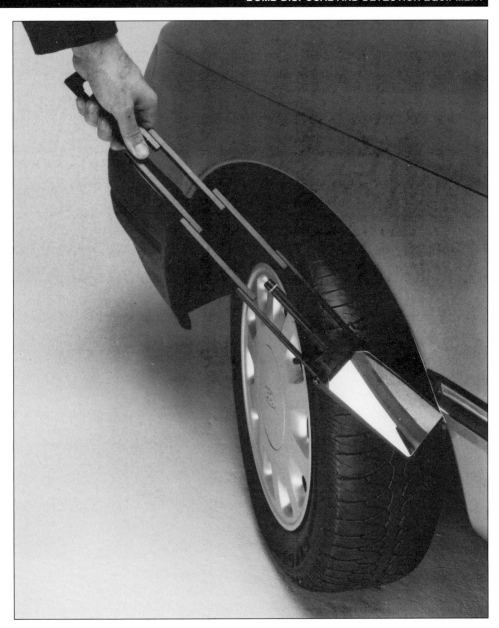

pletely rigid when extended, and an integral torch that can be used when the mirror is open or closed, the CMT is a valuable aid to personal security.

Paladin Anomaly Locator

The majority of IEDs are attached to vehicles using a strong magnet, such as a marine magnet. The Paladin Anomaly Locator (PAL) will identify, quickly and precisely, any such magnet that has been attached to a vehicle. Although every vehicle has 'natu-ral magnetic fields' emanating from springs, exhaust pipe etc., the detector will, depending on the relative field strengths, differentiate between these magnetic fields and those introduced to the vehicle. The PAL, with its telescopic probe, enables the user to check his vehicle for any magnets within minutes. Once the PAL has identi-fied an anomaly, the small powerful torch, supplied with it, can be used to highlight the area under suspicion. The main features of the PAL are:

● Will detect a marine magnet up to 38.1cm away;

● Fits comfortably into a pocket, handbag or briefcase;

● A telescopic probe which extends the reach to over 45.72cm, allowing ease of scanning of all of the underneath of a car;

● Audio indication of the presence of a magnetic field;

● A headphone socket for covert operation;

● Its own power source (PP3 9V battery), giving up to 300 typical searches, plus a battery test facility;

● Supplied with the locator is a Solitaire 7.62cm torch which attaches to a key ring, ensuring a light source at all times.

UNITED STATES

Remotec ANDROS

Andros is a small but powerful US-manufactured remote controlled vehicle designed for EOD disposal. It can be fitted with a shotgun disrupter, a laser sight, a water disrupter, cameras, x-ray equipment and a charge-dropper. Its unique track system achieves unusual mobility.

Data: *size* 43.2cm wide x 81.3cm high x 76.2cm long (114.3cm long with tracks horizontal); *weight* 249.7kg standard unit – 317.8kg with on-board reel, wrist pitch and shoulder rotate; *speed* variable 2.5 to 76.2cm/sec; *climbing ability* 45°

stairs/slopes, 0.6m-high ledge and 0.6m-wide ditch; *manoeuvrability* turns on centre with 180° turns in 1.06m-wide hall; *surfaces* operates on all types of wet or dry surfaces; *environment* operates in all types of weather (-29°C to 50°C).

Variants: Andros Mark VI or Little Andros is only 43.2cm wide and ideal for travelling down the aisle of an aircraft. It is capable of making a neutral turn within its own radius.

Data: *size* 43.2cm wide x 81.3cm high x 76.2cm long (114.3cm long with tracks horizontal); *weight* 90.8kg standard unit; *speed* variable 2.5 to 30.5cm/sec; *climbing ability* 45° stairs/slopes, 30.5cm-high ledge, and 45.7cm-wide ditch; *manoeuvrability* turns on centre with 180° turns in 45.7cm-wide hall; *surfaces* operates on all types of wet or dry surfaces; *environment* operates in all types of weather (-17.8°C to 50°C).

Right: Andros.

ANDROS

ANDROS is an all-terrain, multi-tracked, remote controlled vehicle specially designed for use in hostile environments. Assigned to police or military agencies it is adept at bomb disposal and invaluable in hostage and terrorist situations. A lengthy list of options allows each unit to be customized for specific tasks including: Lifesaving, fire-fighting, ordnance deployment, and others.

4

Anti-Riot Weapons and Equipment

This book is concerned primarily with the fight against terrorism, and the equipment and weapons necessary for the defeat of the gunman and bomber. However, terrorist situations often arise out of (or are associated with) civil unrest. Large and often violent crowds are now commonplace almost everywhere in the world. In the USA, race riots in the 1960s, and later, posed serious threats to law and order. A recent example was the rioting in Los Angeles in the spring of 1992, following the acquittal of three policemen for beating a black car driver. Belgium, Holland, France (in particular the student riots of 1968), West Germany and even Switzerland have all experienced serious street violence during the 1970s and 1980s. In South America, India and in parts of South East Asia riots are almost endemic. In South Africa, black protests on the streets have continued relentlessly ever since Sharpeville. A recent tragic example was Boipatong in June 1992, and another was Ciskei in September of the same year.

The Japanese take their riots very seriously. Students manage to equip themselves very nearly as well as the police, which leads to pitched and prolonged battles over relatively minor issues, such as the siting of an airport or the closure of a road. In Great Britain recently there have been the Bristol, Toxteth and Brixton race riots and the miners' strike of 1984/5 and, more recently, the anti-poll-tax riots of 1990 and 1991. In Northern Ireland riots and street violence of varying intensity have continued since 1969.

It is, of course, the right of every citizen in a democratic society to protest peacefully and by means of organised marches and meetings. Sometimes, however, such gatherings get out of hand and have to be controlled by the police. There is no suggestion that such disturbances in any way equate to terrorist activity. Anti-riot weapons and equipment, however, are manufactured by the same companies that produce other types of IS equipment. They should, therefore, be included in this book. Anti-riot weapons and equipment include 'tear' (CS) gas grenades and launchers, PVC rubber projectiles, tear gas generators, various aerosol CS gas dispensers, riot shotguns, batons and shock-sticks, riot shields, helmets and limb protection equipment.

In a riot it is usually preferable for troops or police to maintain a reasonable distance between themselves and the crowd. This prevents the security forces being overwhelmed or outflanked, and tempers tend to remain cooler if a sensible distance between the two sides is maintained. This is not always possible and, when close contact is unavoidable, the most common means of crowd control is the wooden baton or truncheon. It is not intended to cover batons in this chapter, except for a recent development of the baton, the shockstick, which gives an uncomfortable, though not dangerous, electric shock. It resembles a rolled-up umbrella, and when the cover is removed and the stick switched on it emits a loud crackling noise. At the same time blue static sparks flash up and down the spiral element.

CS grenades can be thrown by hand or fired from a variety of anti-riot weapons, including shotguns, grenade launchers and conventional rifles. Many of these anti-riot weapons can also fire anti-riot projectiles of various sizes and materials. Both rubber and PVC projectiles are available, and are designed to counter petrol bombers or stone-throwing crowds up to a range of about 60m and to cause no more than bruising or shock. They should not be used at very close range. Baton rounds do have the advantage of being selective, while CS smoke is not: in extreme situations CS gas is a very effective crowd disperser, but affects bystanders, adults and children and (if they are not equipped with gas masks) rioters and security forces alike. Crowds all over the world have become adept at wearing wet handkerchiefs over their faces to combat the effects of the gas, and have learned to throw or kick the grenades back at the security forces. Nevertheless, CS gas is an extremely effective way of dispersing a crowd. The gas causes extreme discomfort to the eyes, nose and breathing passages, yet has no serious or lasting effects. It can also be dispensed from a grenade, by means of an aerosol spray, or from a vehicle-mounted or hand-held generator.

Shotguns are also used in some riot situations to fire lightweight polyethylene pellets, which at about 35m are not able to penetrate a sheet of newspaper, but at 3-15m have an impressive deterrent effect.

The Metropolitan Police in London have invested in expensive anti-riot equipment in recent years. This includes public order surveillance vehicles nicknamed 'hoolivans', which are Ford Transit vans, each containing two television cameras and a 35mm photographic system mounted on a periscope and backed up by a pair of video monitors. The vans have been used for monitoring football crowds, and are useful for VIP escort and security duties. They have also developed evidence-gathering cameras, which are mounted on tripods and capable of providing both still photographs and videos, and these have proved to be an effective deterrent to football violence. These cameras are especially designed to produce high-quality pictures even in poor light. The London Metropolitan Police also have helicopters equipped with television cameras, which they can use in riot situations if necessary, while protected vans with reinforced corners and window grills carry officers to the scene of a riot. Communication during riots is a major problem, and the 'Met' has 10,000 two-way radios to enable police units to keep in touch. Powerful searchlights are also necessary after dark for taking photographs and enabling officers to see what is happening. (See separate sections dealing with vehicles, surveillance systems and communication systems).

Police forces around the world use varying degrees of force to dispense a riot. In some countries the army is automatically called upon; elsewhere, as in the UK, the Police are used and the army is only called in as a last resort. Many countries have formed special 'third force' organisations to deal with riots and other IS problems. Examples are the Compagnie Républicaine de Sécurité (CRS) in France and the Federal Border Guard in West Germany. (Had such an impartial and well-disciplined force existed in Northern Ireland in 1969, would it have been necessary to call in the army?) The philosophy of the CRS in France is diametrically opposed to the British approach of minimum force. In France, maximum force is used at an early stage to demonstrate to the rioter that the authorities 'mean business', and this is intended to deter further misbehaviour. The CRS put down the May 1968 student riots in Paris ruthlessly. The German police use much the same tactics. The British, on the other hand, have always used only the necessary degree of force to meet a given situation, and have escalated their reaction as necessary. There are arguments in terms of pure efficiency for both approaches.

The Japanese riot squad, the Kidotai, are the most heavily armoured riot police in the world. They also need to be fit enough to operate inside a $14^{1}/_{2}$lb uniform while carrying a 12lb aluminium shield. Their equipment includes wooden truncheons, polycarbonate helmets, wicker-and-metal shields, tear gas guns, truck-mounted smoke dispensers, water cannon, extending towers that can fill occupied buildings with tear gas, and nets strung on long poles for intercepting missiles.

America's anti-riot squads vary from State to State. In Washington, specially trained police are organised in ten-man civil disturbance units, and they are armed with a helmet visor, an 0.38 revolver, tear gas, a 3ft-long riot stick and crowd-dispersing grenades. The National Guard, which reinforces the police, carries rifles, shotguns and riot batons.

In France, both Gendarmerie and CRS carry transparent shields and are armed with rubber truncheons, 9mm submachine-guns, 9mm automatic pistols, 7.5mm carbines and tear gas grenades.

Whatever methods are used by troops or police in riot situations, they will to some extent rely on the type of equipment illustrated in this chapter. No attempt has been made to provide comprehensive cover of anti-riot equipment in service throughout the world – one CS grenade looks much like another. Rather, a representative cross-section of the main categories of anti-riot equipment has been chosen.

FRANCE

Alsatex
Gas Grenade Equipment
Persistent Effect Grenades: These two grenades, 56mm in diameter, 200mm long and weighing 285g (hand grenade) and 250g (rifle grenade), are either thrown or can be projected by rifle up to 100m. They produce a persistent and invisible tear gas cloud.

Flash or Stun Bomb: This grenade contains a pyrotechnic composition creating a flash effect on detonation. It can be used to achieve surprise and shock action in a hostage situation. It is 56mm in diameter, 120mm long and weighs approximately 190g.

Offensive Tear Grenade: 51mm x 140mm and weighing some 120g, this grenade does not discharge in trajectory. It has a 2.5sec delay when thrown, and produces an explosion on impact without fragmentation. The tear gas emission is instantaneous.

Model F4 Grenades: The Alsatex model F4 grenades are 56mm x 160mm and weigh 160g, 125g and 175g. They are rifle or hand instantaneous CS tear grenades, composed of two interlocking parts, the head separating from the base during trajectory.

Employment: French Army, Gendarmerie and CRS, and several other overseas armies and police forces.

Gendarmerie Zig-Zag Grenade: The Zig-Zag grenades are 56mm in diameter, up to 252mm long and weigh up to 320g. They are tear gas grenades designed for use in urban areas, their main characteristic being a cylin-

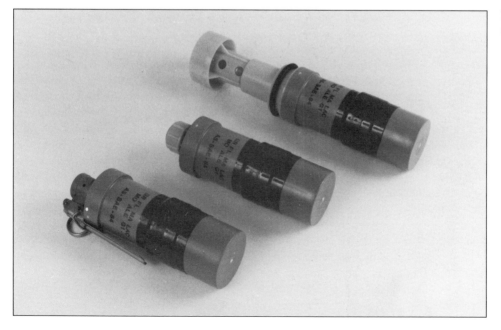

Left: Alsatex Zig-Zag Grenade.

drical jacket including a nozzle, which produces jerky propulsion in the air and random jumping on the ground, making the grenade unpredictable and uncatchable. One grenade covers a surface area of 100m².

Tear Gas Dispensers

Individual Tear Gas Dispenser: With a diameter of 35mm, a height of 100mm and a weight of 50g, the individual tear gas dispenser delivers a jet of tear gas to a range of 4m. Various container sizes are available, as well as different concentrations of tear gas.

1 Litre or 2 Litre Tear Gas Dispenser: The 1 and 2 litre dispensers deliver a CS gas solution to a range of 12m. The 1 litre dispenser has a diameter of 80mm, a length of 400mm and a weight of 2.5kg. The 2 litre dispenser has a diameter of 100mm, a length

of 460mm and a weight of 3.8kg. The 2 litre dispenser differs from the 1 litre version in having a carrying handle and an additional safety pin.

Back Pack dispenser: With a 10m minimum range, this has a diameter of 370mm, a length of 750mm and a weight of 18kg (powder loaded), 21.5kg (liquid loaded) or 16-20kg (gel loaded).

Tear Gas Grenade Launchers

Alsatex manufactures a variety of Tear Gas Grenade launchers to project its various types of grenade. These include sleeves mounted on 5.56mm and 7.62mm calibre rifles to project a grenade 100m or 200m (if grenades are fitted with plastic fins). A device based on the MAS 36 rifle can fire grenades 100-350m at a rate of six rounds per minute. The total weight of this device is 21kg. A grenade

Below: Alsatex Tear Gas Dispensers.

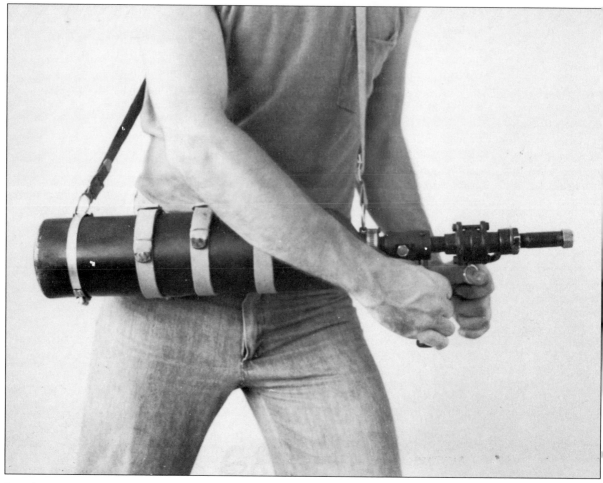

launcher based on the MR 73 revolver can launch grenades 100-350m at a rate of twelve rounds per minute. Total weight is 17kg.

Grenade Projector Armoured Cowling
Developed for the Berliet Gendarmerie IS vehicle, this can also be fitted to other IS vehicles. It allows troops to launch CS grenades from within an armoured vehicle by engaging a grenade launcher in the device. It consists of a mechanically welded armoured cowling, which can be fixed to the Berliet Gendarmerie's forward right hatch. Portholes can be fixed to the cowling if desired, for observation and aiming. The cowling and its mounting device are a water-tight assembly.
Employment: France (Gendarmerie).
Data: *armament* shortened MAS 36-51 rifle firing F4 grenades; *rate of fire* 6 rounds per

minute; *firing angle* +25° to +55° (elevation), ±50° (azimuth); *weight* 75kg; *range* 200m.

ISRAEL

Ispra Israel Product Research Company
Projectojet CS Fog Projector
This tear gas generator was developed in Israel as a weapon for use against groups of violent agitators in narrow streets and alleys. It is a highly effective method of CS gas dispensation, has a range of 15m in still air, and will neutralise in five seconds any person within 3m either side of the line of fire. It weighs less than 9kg and is rechargeable.
Employment: Believed to be in use with Israeli Armed Forces.

Above: Projectojet CS Fog Projector.

Israel Military Industries
Rubber Ammunition

The rubber ammunition is packed in an aluminium launching container holding 15 cylindrical rubber plugs. The launching container is fitted with an adapter tube which slips easily over the flash suppressor (or grenade launcher adapter) on the launching rifle. The rubber projectiles are ejected from the launching container by the gasses from the ballistic launching cartridge (as used for firing rifle grenades). After firing, the launching container remains on the rifle and can be easily removed by hand. The cloud of projectiles hits the demonstrators, causing them pain and scattering them.

Right: Israel Military Industries Rubber Ammunition.

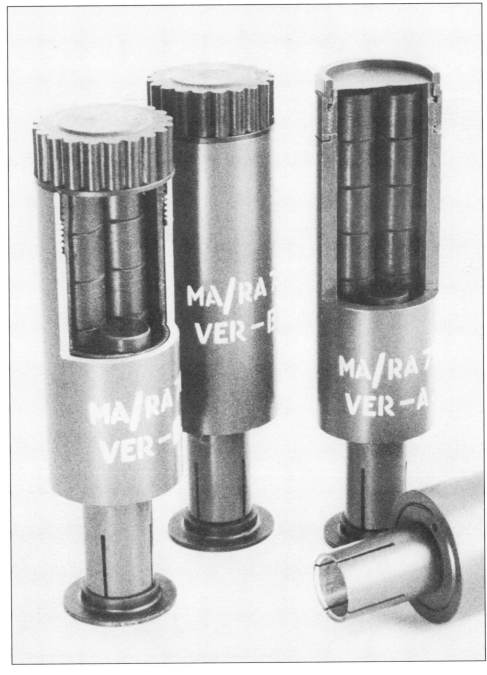

Israel Military Industries Rubber Ammunition

Version	Launching container	Hitting Energy	Effective Ranges (m) for rifles		
			M16 5.56mm	Galil 5.56mm	Galil or FN 7.62mm
A	MA/RA 77	Low	30-50	40-40	50-70
	MA/RA 82	Medium	40-70	50-70	60-90
	MA/RA 83	High	40-70	50-70	60-90
B	MA/RA 78	Low	30-50	40-60	50-70
	MA/RA 84	Medium	40-70	50-70	60-90
	MA/RA 85	High	40-70	50-70	60-90

SINGAPORE

CIS 40 GL Grenade Launcher

The CIS 40 GL is a shoulder-fired, multi-purpose grenade launcher. Owing to its modular design it can also be easily adapted to fit a wide range of assault rifles. The grenade launcher is a single-shot, breech-loaded lightweight weapon. A wide range of 40mm grenade cartridges can be launched to 350mm with considerable accuracy.

Data: *calibre* 40mm; *length of launcher* (with stock) 655mm; *length of barrel*

Left: CIS 40 GL Grenade Launcher.

Right: Arwen 37 Riot Control Weapon System.

305mm; *weight* unloaded, with stock 2.05kg, without stock 1.70kg, loaded 2.27kg; *trigger pull* 4.0kg; *ammunition* practice, HE, HEDP, Illum; *action* breakopen, single-shot; *muzzle velocity* 71m/sec; *maximum range* 400m.

UNITED KINGDOM

Arwen 37 Riot Control Weapon System

The Arwen 37 has a five-round capacity using the revolver principle. It can be fired from the left or right shoulder at the rapid fire rate (five rounds in 4 seconds) or the sustained fire rate (twelve rounds per minute). Ammunition for the Arwen 37 includes:

● AR1, a plastic baton round delivering a non-lethal body blow;

● AR2, a multi-source irritant smoke (CS);

● AR3, a frangible-nosed irritant (CS)

baton round combining a body blow with a discreet dose of irritant;

● AR4, a multi-source smoke screen;

● AR5, a barricade penetrator with irritant (CS).

Data: Arwen 37, *calibre* 37mm; *type of action* revolver; *capacity* 5 rounds; *rifling* 5-groove; *weight* 3.1kg (3.8kg loaded with 5 rounds); *length* 76.2-83.8cm; *rate of fire* (5 rounds) 60 rounds/min.

Arwen Ace Anti-Riot Weapon

This single-shot weapon fires the complete range of purpose-designed Arwen ammunition; AR1, which deals a non-lethal blow; AR2, which lays down a carpet of irritant smoke; AR3, which combines a body blow with a 'discreet' dose of irritant; AR4, which dispenses screening smoke; and AR5, a barricade penetrator. Loading is achieved through a single aperture,

Left: Arwen Ace.

eliminating the need for a break action.
Data: *calibre* 37mm; *rifling* 5-groove;
weight 2.1kg; *length* 69cm–77cm adjustable
(6 positions); *rate of fire* 12 rounds/min;
sighting self-illuminated optical; *normal
operating ranges* 20–100m (AR1), 85–95m
(AR2), 2–50m (AR3), 85–95m (AR4),
2–80m (AR5).

Hayley and Weller Pyrotechnics
Hayley and Weller of Draycort, England,
also manufactures a range of anti-riot
pyrotechnic equipment.
Hand Grenades: Three variations of hand
grenade are the E160 Mk 2, the N201 Mk 3
and the N25, all of which contain CS gas.
Each emits CS gas for 20-25sec. They vary in
weight from 445g to 630g. The time from
throw to start of emission of CS gas is 2-4sec.
66mm Vehicle Discharge Grenades: A
variety of grenades which can be discharged
from any 66mm launcher, standard on the

Left and right: A selection of Hayley and Weller hand grenades.

majority of armoured vehicles throughout the western world, are available. These include smoke, phosphorous, CS and fragmentation grenades. The smoke and phosphorous grenades are designed to screen the movement of vehicles or troops; the 66mm CS grenades burst in the air, dispensing 23 sub-munitions. The fragmentation grenade airbursts 100m from the vehicle and produces a 360° pattern of low-velocity fragments for use against personnel. Obviously such a weapon cannot be used in anti-riot sit-

uations, but it might be suitable in an anti-terrorist situation.

38mm cartridges: Hayley and Weller manufactures baton, CS and dye-dispersant 38mm cartridges.

Hilton Gun Company
MPRG 83

The MPRG 83 is a multi-purpose gun capable of firing a range of differing types and sizes of ammunition. The gun is supplied with 38mm, 25mm and 12-bore barrels, and

a 5.56mm rifle barrel. A 40mm rifled barrel for firing a 40mm grenade is also available. **Data:** *overall length* rifle 827.5mm, pistol 284mm; *weight* 38mm rifle 2.5kg, 38mm pistol 1.5kg, 25mm pistol 1.7kg, 12-gauge rifle 2.8kg.

HG40 Grenade Launcher

The HG40 adds an extra dimension to the firepower capabilities of the ordinary infantryman's rifle. It is a grenade launcher designed to be fitted to standard infantry rifles such as the British SA80, and provides

Below: Hilton MPRG 83.

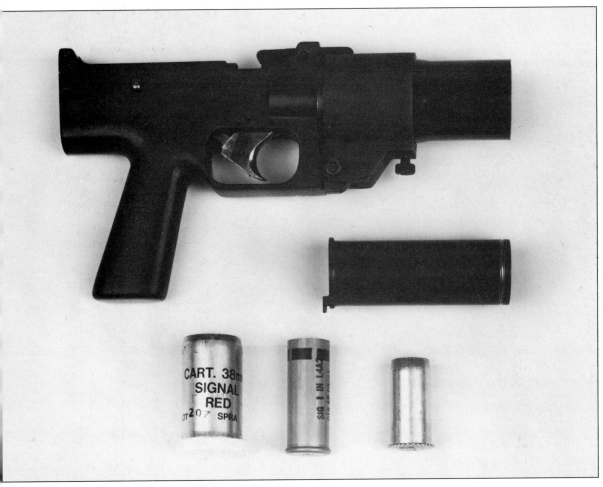

the foot soldier with the capability of firing 40mm-calibre grenades accurately up to a maximum range of 375m. A simple clamping mechanism enables the HG40 barrel with its supporting bracket and trigger action housing to be quickly and easily removed without the need to dismantle the clamps. The grenade launcher is a single-shot weapon with a break-action, swing-down barrel for loading.

Data: *barrel length* 310mm; *total length* 388mm; *width* 70mm; *height* 142mm;

Right: Hilton HG40.

weight 1.5kg; *feed* single shot; *mode of fire* single shot; *muzzle velocity* approx. 75mm/sec.

Royal Small Arms Factory Anti-Riot Weapons
RSAF Grenade Launcher

Designed specifically as a portable launcher for the British L11 Bursting CS Grenade, the Royal Small Arms Factory (Enfield) weapon is light and easy to handle. Power is provided by two standard torch batteries, and a large number of grenades can be fired before replacement is necessary. The CS bursting grenade distributes approximately 23 smoke pellets over an area of approximately 25m diameter just before impact with the ground, providing a number of gas sources rather than a single plume.

Employment: British Army.
Data: *length* 69.5cm (overall); *weight* 2.7kg (launcher), 550g (grenade); *maximum range* 100m.

Above: RSAF Grenade Launcher.

Below: Shockstick SA121.

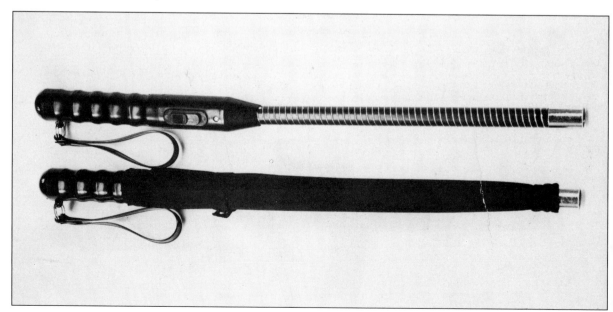

SAS Developments Shockstick SA121

The Shockstick, or protective staff, resembles a rolled umbrella in appearance. However, the resemblance ends there. When switched on it emits a powerful charge of 6,000–7,000V, but it does not burn or cause an injury. This is due to the very low milli-amp rating (a maximum of 8.3mA), and a wiring system localises the shock – the recipient does not get a through-body current, and the shock is entirely confined to the small surface area with which the stick makes actual contact. The stick is designed to emit a loud crackling noise, accompanied by blue static sparks flashing up and down the spiral element. This warns an assailant that he is confronted by something less innocuous than it appears. If he ignores this warning and grasps the stick, or is touched by it, he will be instantly repelled by the electric shock, but without suffering any harm or damage.
Data: *length* 57.8cm; *weight* 0.54kg (including batteries).

Schermuly Multi-Purpose Riot Gun 2000

The Schermuly MPRG 2000 is a logical progression of the tried and proven Schermuly 38mm multi purpose Gun. The gun has a single chamber that will accept all standard 37/38mm ammunition, including the long penetrating and muzzle blast type cartridges. A rifle barrel option is also available to provide even greater accuracy. Accessories include a 12-gauge adapter and a grenade launcher. The latter enables the user to deploy CS and smoke grenades at long range.
Data: *calibre* 37/38mm; *weight* 2.7kg; *length* 820mm; *sight range* 50/100/150m.

Schermuly Lightweight Respirator S/61

This protective respirator differs from most respirators in that the filter is situated to the left side of the face, where it is least in the way, and allows the wearer a clear field of vision, particularly when using an anti-riot

Below: Schermuly Multi-Purpose Riot Gun 2000, here seen with its signal pistol variant.

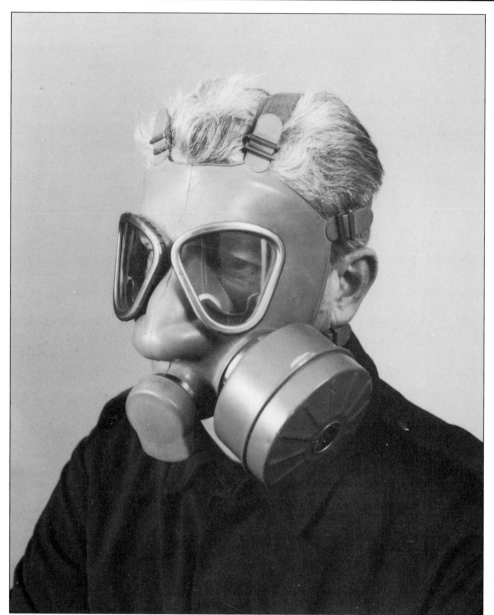

gun. An inner mask prevents the vision glass misting over. The S/61 weighs 575g. This respirator is typical of many manufactured in Europe, the United States and elsewhere.

SES Excalibur Mk 2

The Excalibur Multi-shot Riot Gun is a shoulder-fired weapon employing the well-proven revolver action. The five-round cylinder is chambered to accept 37/38mm cartridges of the standard rimmed-base type up to 120mm long from a variety of manu-

facturers worldwide. The weapon will also fire 37/38mm standard to short-length signal and flare cartridges. Excalibur is essentially simple in design, robust in construction and very easy to operate and maintain to suit the demanding operational requirements of law enforcement agencies. It is capable of a high rate of accurate fire, five rounds being fired as fast as the trigger can be operated, and produces negligible recoil with standard ammunition. Enabling a single user to engage several targets outside stone-throw-

Below and right:
Excalibur Mk 2.

ing range, Excalibur is far more effective than a single-shot break-open riot gun. It also enables a very rapid build-up of CS or screening smoke to be produced and sustained.

Data: *calibre* 37/38mm; *weight* 4.3kg; *length* with butt spacer 790mm, without spacer 753mm; *cross-section H* 210mm; *cross-section W* 120mm; *sights* 50, 100m and 150mm; *materials* high-tensile alloy, stainless steel and polymer plastic; *ammunition* all standard 37/38mm cartridges up to 120mm length; *chamber* 5-shot.

Wallop Industries Pyrotechnics
Wallop Industries of Andover, England, produces a whole range of pyrotechnic products designed for riot control purposes. These include smoke and CS hand grenades, various shotgun cartridges with riot control applications, 37/88mm baton rounds and

37/38mm CS cartridges, hand-held flares, a 2in mortar illuminating round and a rocket launching device.

UNITED STATES

Smith & Wesson Anti-Riot Equipment Chemical Mace Non-Lethal Weapons

In 1965 these were made available to police forces in the USA by Smith & Wesson. Now, over 400,000 Chemical Mace Non-lethal Weapons are in service with 4,000 police departments in the USA. All types are easily reloaded with a spare cartridge.

Employment: Various US police forces.
Data: *length* from 10.1cm (Mk III) to 16.5cm (Mk V); *diameter* from 23mm (Mk III) to 58mm (Mk IX); *range* (in still air) from 3–4m (Mk III) to 8m (Mk IX); *contents* from 20 (Mk III) to 60 (Mk IX) one-second bursts; *formulation* CN; *weights* from 40g (Mk III) to 300g (Mk IX).

CN and CS Gas Grenades

Smith & Wesson has developed a comprehensive range of grenades using both CN and CS. In particular, the Rubber Ball Grenade is worthy of special mention. This innovative grenade virtually eliminates the possibility of throwback and minimises the chance of injury.

Employment: Various US police forces.
Data: *overall length* from 11.8cm (Rubber Ball No. 15) to 15.2cm (Continuous Discharge No. 2); *diameter* from 60mm (Continuous Discharge No. 3) to 84mm (Rubber Ball No. 15); *range* 30m (Mighty Midget No. 98, 50m); *burning time* between 15 and 50sec (Blast Dispersion No. 5 instantaneous only); *delay* 1–2sec (Blast Dispersion No. 5 and Mighty Midget No. 98, 3sec).

Gas Guns and Grenade Launchers

37mm Gas and Flare Pistol: This pistol is designed to fire all Smith & Wesson 37mm

Above: A selection of Wallop Industries Pyrotechnics products.

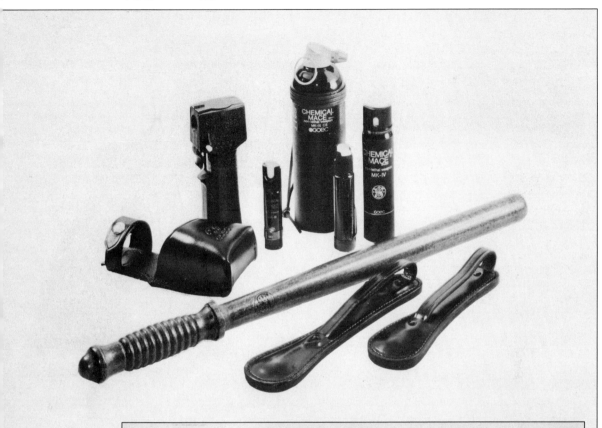

Above: Smith & Wesson Chemical Mace. Non-Lethal Weapons.

Right: Smith & Wesson Rubber Ball No.15 CS Gas Grenade.

159

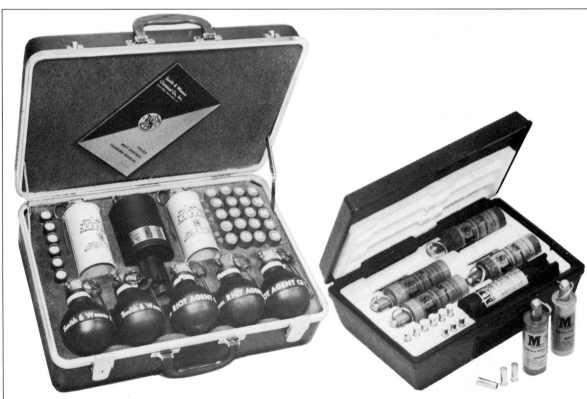

Left: Smith & Wesson 37mm Gas Gun and Flare Pistol.

Opposite page, bottom: Smith & Wesson Shotgun tear gas kit (left) and Model 103 Mighty Midget Grenade Kit (right).

Below: Smith & Wesson Portable Riot Control Kit.

projectiles (except for Tru-flite penetrating projectiles).

37mm Shoulder Gas Gun: This gun will fire all 37mm projectiles. The barrel is detachable, the weight is under 2.7kg and the length is 73.7cm.

Riot Control Kits

Shotgun Tear Gas Kit: The addition of a chemical munitions capability makes the 12-bore shotgun a highly effective non-lethal weapons system. This Smith &

Wesson shotgun Tear Gas kit contains a variety of CS or CN Tear Gas grenades, a 12-bore grenade launcher, and 20 Tru-flite Barricade projectiles.

Mighty Midget Grenade Kit: This is a lightweight composite kit which contains 12 Mighty Midget grenades, either CS or CN, 12 Mighty Midget .38 special launching cartridges and a universal revolver launcher to fit any .38 Special or .357 Magnum revolver. The kit, which measures 19.2 x 29.2 x 9cm, weighs just 2.27kg.

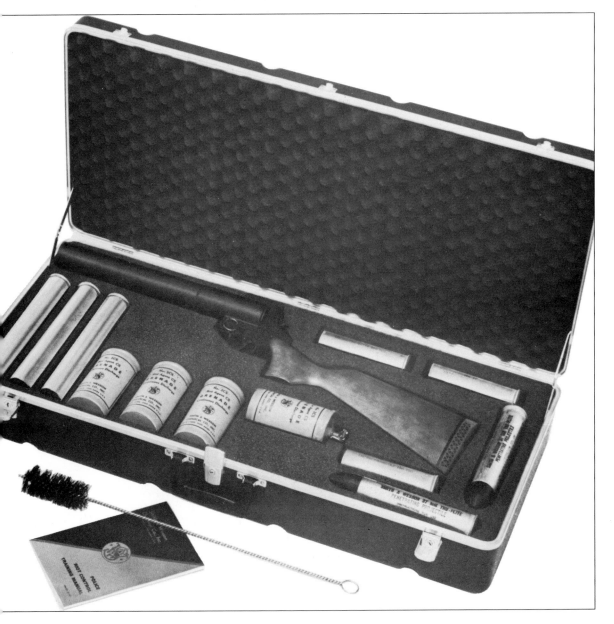

5

Body Armour and Shields

Body Armour is normally designed to protect only the most vulnerable parts of the body, namely the chest and back. It is not feasible to provide adequate protection for the head, except for the special case of bomb disposal, in which every attempt is made to provide maximum protection for all parts of the body. The more comprehensive, but cumbersome, bomb disposal suits inevitably affect vision. Armour can be provided for the arms and legs, but this inevitably slows down movement.

A wide range of body armour is now on the market. It varies from lightweight concealable undervests, designed to provide protection against low-velocity ammunition fired from submachine-guns and handguns, to heavier vests designed to stop high-velocity rounds. Nowhere has the art of manufacturing bullet-proof vests reached the level attained in the United States, where virtually every policeman (and even some private citizens) wear them. Special vests have been developed for women. It is due mainly to the emergency in Northern Ireland that there are also many UK manufacturers of body armour. Other manufacturers in Belgium, Germany, Israel and Switzerland have since produced their own versions.

Conventional military helmets proved inadequate in IS situations. They were too heavy, offered insufficient protection and, in some cases, were difficult to keep securely on the head when the wearer was being jostled in a crowd, acting as a member of a 'snatch' squad, jumping in and out of vehicles or was involved in a number of demanding IS situations. Various manufacturers in the United States, the United Kingdom, Switzerland, Germany, Belgium and other

Western countries have therefore produced a range of helmets to offer a much higher degree of protection. In some cases they are constructed of high-quality Titanium; most have visors of some sort to provide at least protection against stones, and some provide protection against low-velocity rounds. All are much closer-fitting and secured by chin-straps; some have built-in microphones and earphones connected to a two-way portable radio set. Some are designed to allow the use of respirators under an armoured visor, while others permit the attachment of night vision aids to the helmet itself, leaving the hands free for driving a vehicle, holding a weapon or flying an aircraft. In short, IS helmets are highly sophisticated and a long way removed from the conventional infantryman's 'battle bowler'.

There are basically two types of shield: one is designed to be used in a riot situation and must therefore cope with stones, bricks and bottles; the other is proof against bullets. Most riot shields are constructed of polycarbonate and are both shatterproof and fire resistant. The German company Rheinstahl, for instance (which makes the Marder MICV), also makes a variety of bullet-proof shields that incorporate pistol and vision ports. There are more cumbersome casemates for use in hijack or shoot-out situations: these are on wheels, and offer complete protection against 7.62mm rounds while remaining towable and manoeuvrable by the men they are protecting. Other ingenious ideas include bullet-proof clipboards. Although only proof against handguns, such devices afford a chance of survival for a gate security man who, for example, is checking a vehicle when the occupant produces a handgun at close range and without warning in order to force an entry.

Protection is also provided by shatter-resistant film, bullet-resistant laminate, bullet-resistant glass, bomb curtains and other types of body armour. Bombs cause flying glass which can cause widespread injury. It is possible to apply a form of adhesive to glass that holds shattered glass together. Similarly, a laminate can be applied to car or house windows to withstand strikes by 7.62mm rounds from a range of 10m. Cars are in particular need of protection: violent attacks on VIP cars and security vehicles are increasing in frequency and ferocity all over the world. Here, the glass is of crucial importance. Road vehicles, especially saloons, must have adequate visibility: unprotected windows make a VIP passenger highly and unnecessarily vulnerable. However, car windows can be manufactured to offer a high degree of protection against handguns, shotguns and other weapons, and can be curved and framed so that, when fitted, they are visually quite indistinguishable from ordinary glass.

Very simple precautions in government buildings, which are vulnerable to terrorist attack, can be achieved. Clearly it is not possible, except at enormous expense, to fit bullet-proof glass to every window in a large government building. A far cheaper solution is to hang anti-bomb curtains – simple mesh curtains weighted at the bottom to catch any glass that is blown inwards by the force of the explosion from a bomb placed outside the building. Body armour additional to helmets, shields, bullet-proof vests and 'flak' jackets is also available. Indeed, in theory there is no limit to the amount of armour that can be provided for IS security personnel. Another option is 'variable' body armour. This is basically a light protective jacket with large pockets at the front and rear into which heavy metal plates are inserted according to the degree of protection required. Weight considerations make it likely that such equipment would be more usually worn by vehicle-borne troops or those deployed in a semi-static role, such as manning a checkpoint.

But in practice there is a limit to the amount of protection that can be realistically achieved for a soldier or policeman who is expected to be mobile, agile and able to react to a variety of situations. In the final analysis, it is not possible to guarantee immunity from a high-velocity rifle in competent hands, but it is possible to provide complete protection against many threats, and to increase the overall chance of survival in most situations.

UNITED KINGDOM

Bristol Armour
Lightweight Glass Reinforced
Opaque Armour panels

Bristol Armour opaque panels are fibre reinforced composite structures specially designed for toughness and excellent resistance to low- and high-velocity projectile impacts. These products are currently being supplied for banks and building societies, military vehicles, civilian vehicles and equipment protection. Nine standard grades are manufactured by Meggitt Composites to protect against most threat levels, including handguns, shotguns, grenades and high-velocity military rifles. Two standard panels are available – 2,000 x 1,000mm or 2,440 x 1,220mm. Panels can be supplied cut and machined to customers' dimensions/drawings.

Tolerances: Standard panels are manufactured to the following tolerances: *weight* +6%; *thickness* +1mm; *width/length* +2mm; *flatness* maximum gap of 1.5mm when laid horizontal on a flat surface.

The armour will resist multiple impacts at a pitch greater than six times the projectile diameter for threats quoted. For lower-order threats the armour will stop two impacts on the same spot and strikes close to the panel edge.

Type 10 Armour Vest

This Bristol Armour Vest is contoured and shaped for optimum comfort and protection. It has been designed to be worn unobtrusively under a shirt or jacket and to allow maximum freedom of movement.

Left: Bristol Armour Type 10 Armour vest.

Type 10 Armour Vest

Size	Chest Size Range	Protection Area	Total Weight (kg)	
			K8DS	K16DS
Small	86 – 94cm	0.31m^2	1.45	2.65
Regular	94 – 105cm	0.33m^2	1.60	2.95
Large	105 – 115cm	0.42m^2	2.15	3.90

Data: There are two grades of protection, K8DS (for maximum concealment) and K16Ds. (See table above.)

Type 11 Armour Jacket

The slimline Type 11 Bristol Armour Jacket for use by police and security forces allows discreet yet effective armoured protection from a range of threats. This externally-worn jacket affords excellent protection and impressive mobility owing to its lightweight modular construction, which also makes it suitable for use in a variety of climatic conditions.

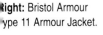

Right: Bristol Armour Type 11 Armour Jacket.

Type 18 Armour Jacket

Designed in co-operation with military and special forces, the Type 18 jacket incorporates a number of features to enhance operational performance levels, such as a standard collar protector, an optional front pelvic

Type 18 Armour Jacket

Size	Chest Size	Protected Area
Small	85 - 105cm	0.38m^2
Regular	95 -115cm	0.43m^2
Large	195 - 125cm	0.45m^2

Left: Bristol Armour Type 18 Armour Jacket.

Opposite page: Deenside Body protective Equipment. Left: Womens Breast Protector. Right: Forearm/Elbow Guard Mk I.

protection panel and 'non-slip' shoulder rifle butt pads which are all designed so as not to inhibit the wearer's movements. The Type 18 is available with a variety of removable outer jackets in harmony with the user's particular requirements, including olive drab and camouflaged versions.

Double-curvature ceramic insert places provide extra protection against up to 7.62mm armour piercing rounds.

Type 21 Armour Jacket: Bristol Armour's new Type 21 jacket meets the increasing need for light flexible personal armour for easy deployment. This front-opening jacket has been designed for use by both military and police forces. The Type 21 jacket can incorporate any of Bristol Armour's wide range of flexible inserts, and in addition incorporates a high level of protection against high-velocity rifle fire using any of the Bristol Armour ceramic plates.

Deenside Body Protective Equipment
Deenside Protective equipment produces a wide range of protective equipment to protect the vulnerable areas of the body from impact by projectiles in riot control situations. The company also produces protective equipment for police horses. The range includes knife-resistant vests, protective vests, kneeling pads, women's breast protectors, and guards for shins, knees, thighs, groin, shoulders, forearms, elbows, upper arms and hands. Deenside also produces

Type 21 Armour Jacket

Size	Chest Size	Protected Area
Small	86 – 96cm	0.38m^2
Regular	96 – 112cm	0.42m^2
Large	112 – 128cm	0.45m^2

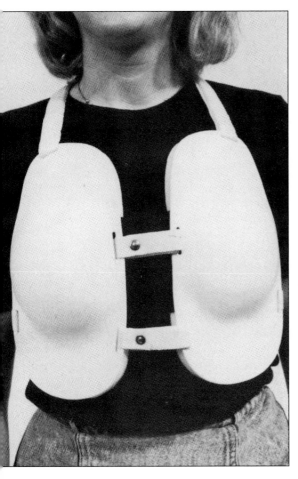

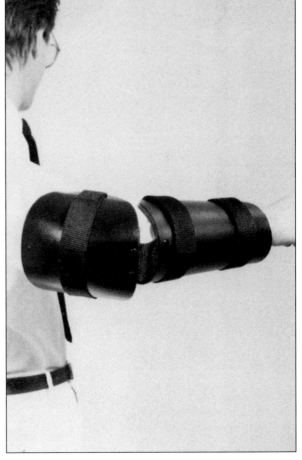

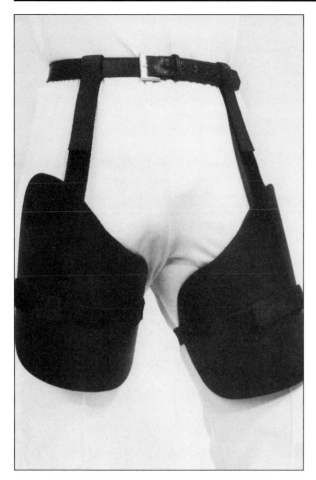

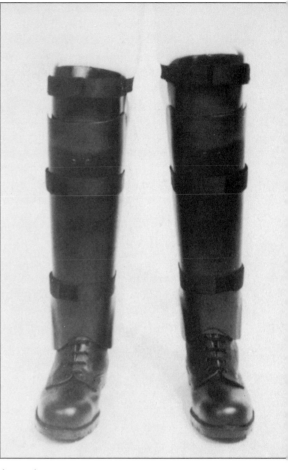

Above: Deenside Body Protective Equipment. Left: Thigh Guard Mk II. Right: Shin/Knee Guard Mk II.

nose guards, visors, knee guards and cannon bone guards for horses.

Dowty Armourshield

Dowty Armourshield provides a whole range of body armour to suit different circumstances: concealed body armour (series CBA), law enforcement 'standard' body armour (series SBA), police body armour (Series PBA), ballistic protective shields (Series BPS), female body armour (FBA), knife resistant armour (KRA), discreet body armour (Series DBA), and protective screens and blankets and ballistic bags (Series BPB). Dowty Armourshield equipment includes a patented system of trauma attenuation, the blunt trauma shield. Even when a bullet is stopped from penetrating the body, it can cause a deep depression in the armour materials and transfer a large amount of shock energy–blunt trauma – to the wearer. This can incapacitate the wearer or even prove fatal. Dowty Armourshield also offers a wide range of multi-curved ceramic composite plates to allow an immediate upgrade of soft body armour to help protect against high-velocity-rifle threats. These weigh between 2 and 3.2kg.

Galt Composites
British Army Body Armour Mk 2

Galt Composites is an MOD licensed manufacturer of Mk 2 Body Armour. This is designed to provide the combat soldier with the best combination of protection and fighting mobility, and is worn as discreet armour below combat smocks. Multiple layers of Kevlar 20 provide all-round protection against fragments and medium-velocity bullets. Separate armour plates can be inserted front and rear to cover vital areas against high-velocity small-arms fire.

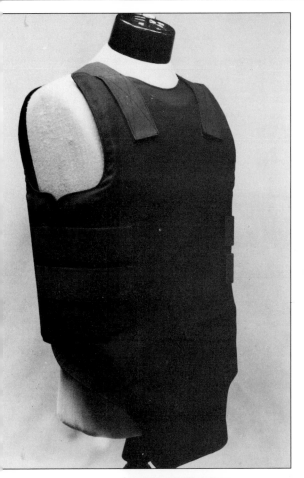

Above: Dowty Armourshield Ultra Light Soft Body Armour.

Above right: Dowty Armourshield Armoured Clipboard.

Right: Dowty Armourshield Lightweight Flexible Screen.

Left: Dowty Armour-shield Rigid High Velocity Screen.

Below, left and right: Dowty Armourshield Shield.

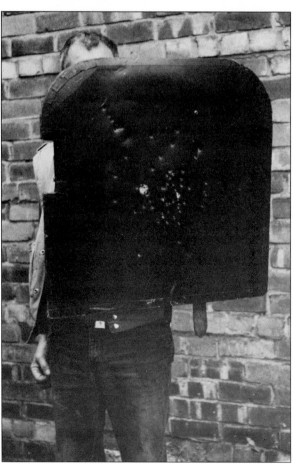

ICL Technical Plastics Ltd

ICL Technical Plastics produces body armour and shields of unusual quality. They are used by police forces throughout the UK.

Shields: ICL Tech shields are manufactured from Lexan Polycarbonate, and are annealed to relieve manufacturing stress in order to improve resistance to petrol attack.

Limb Protection: ICL Tech also manufactures arm guards, arm/elbow guards, thigh guards and shin and knee guards. They are flame-retardant for up to at least 20sec of exposure to intense flames, lightweight, and allow considerable mobility.

Below: ICL Plastics shield, head and body armour.

Lightweight Body Armour Garments and Equipment

All products use the Tetranike armour system, consisting of resistive laminated materials. Products range from protective vests, EOD suits, helmets and shields to composite armour materials for vehicle, boats, aircraft and equipment.

Armoured Clip-Board: An ordinary clip-board that doubles as a mini-shield. A rigid handle is fitted to the back.

Data: *weight* 1.2kg; *dimensions* 385mm x 310mm.

Helmets: Model APH4 provides protection from shell fragments; APH6 defeats up to 9mm NATO ammunition, as does the Police Helmet PPH. Various chinstraps can be fitted, as well as visors, neck guards and camouflage nets.

Weights: APH4 1kg; APH6 1.4kg; PPH 1.4kg; standard visor 250g; ballistic visor 1kg; neck protector 500g (APH4 320g).

Siege Shield: This is a body-length shield fitted with carrying handles and an observation window in bullet-resistant nil-spall glass. It can be folded for use in restricted spaces.

Data: *weight* 12kg; *height* 1.83m (extended), 1.15m (folded); *width* 0.58m.

Police Protective Helmet (PPH)

The PPH is of one-piece, high-impact-resistant Tetranike armour system construction, offering a protection level up to standard 9mm NATO ammunition fired from military handguns. It is fitted with an adjustable headband for exact sizing and a drawstring system to provide correct depth of fit. Chinstraps may be specified with two-, three- or four-point mounting systems, and include a chincup and quick-release fastening as standard. Visors and neck protectors are available to provide protection levels against threats ranging from thrown missiles to standard 9mm NATO ammunition. An alternative shell configuration with a lower rear profile may also be specified.

Employment: In service with police forces in the UK and other countries.

Data: *weights* helmet 1.4kg, standard visor 0.25kg, ballistic visor 1.0kg, neck protector 0.5kg.

Ministry of Defence Body Armour Internal Security Combat Helmet

The British Army has developed a type of internal security helmet known as the IS Combat Helmet. The helmet, which is made of composite material and incorporates a visor plus a new type of chinstrap liner, is

Opposite page:
Lightweight Body Armour
Police Protective Helmet.

Below: Ministry of
Defence Body Armour
Internal Security Helmet.

Below right: PG
Products Riot Control
Equipment.

lighter, more comfortable, more secure and gives a higher degree of ballistic protection than the general-issue Mk 4 steel helmet. The wearer can also hear a great deal more easily than with the enclosed-type HART currently in service. The polycarbonate visor is readily detachable, and a helmet cover can be added for operations in a rural environment.
Employment: British Army.
Weight: helmet 1.41kg; visor 0.41kg.

PG Products Riot Control Equipment
Riot Helmets: The SAR 20 and the SAR 30 form the basis of the Riot Helmet range. Both helmets are manufactured from injec-

tion-moulded ABS, and they are available in white, black and light blue. The shell is fully lined for comfort and protection, and is fitted with an adjustable chin-strip and a chincup. Audio plugs are fitted to each side of the helmet as standard. The SAR 20 has a detachable nape protector for easier maintenance, while the SAR 30 has a permanent nape protector fixed to the inner edge of the shell, offering wider protection to the neck. Both helmets have a 3mm-thick high-impact clear polycarbonate visor mounted on an aluminium carrier which has a close fit to the aluminium support frame, forming a seal to prevent liquids entering the face area. The

visor is fitted with ratchet mechanisms to allow it to be lifted when not in use. The latest SAR 90 helmet includes a pair of audio plugs to aid the hearing of commands.

Riot Shields: The riot shields are all made from high-impact clear polycarbonate, and they are fitted with ABS/plastazote comfort pads to provide additional protection to the user. A variety of handle configurations are available, from heavyweight webbing to aluminium handles, sleeved in rigid tubing to increase comfort and grip.

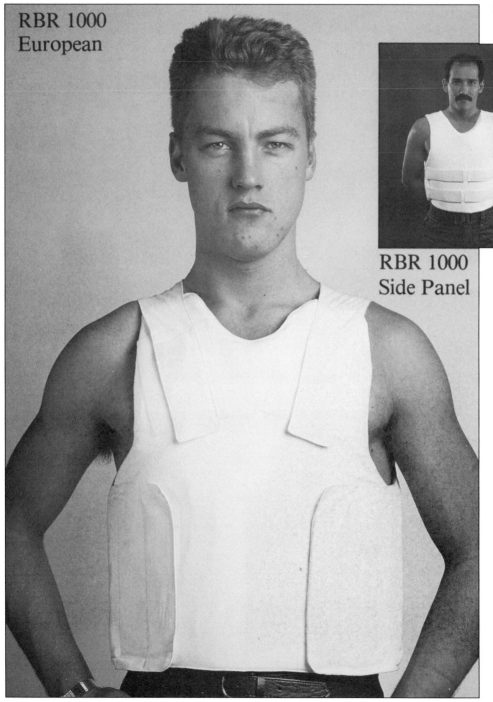

RBR 1000 European

RBR 1000 Side Panel

Left: RBR 1000.

Right: PG Products Riot Control Equipment, showing helmet and shield.

Below: RBR 2000.

RBR 2000

Riot Suits: A range of riot suits are manufactured to meet individual customer requirements, in fire-resistant cotton, nomex, or customer specified material. The standard suit has a stand-up collar with a velcro flap, zip closure, chest and waist pockets, epaulettes, knitted cuffs and velcro closure at the ankles.

Arm and Leg Protectors: The arm and leg protectors are lightweight, providing high levels of protection to exposed limbs. They are constructed in foam-lined plastic with fire-resistant outer covers in navy blue, with two webbing straps with velcro to close. Each item is shaped to fit the arm or leg, maximising protection and retaining full movement.

Accessories: Riot batons, handcuffs and gloves are available to complement the range of riot control equipment.

RBR High Technology Body Armour

RBR (Armour) Ltd produces a range of soft body armour, hard body armour based on ceramic plates, ballistic helmets, ballistic shields, vehicle armour, EOD suits, IED (search) suits, bomb blankets and anti-riot equipment. Examples of RBR equipment are given below.

RBR 1000 'European' concealed undervest: Weighing between 1.45 and 2.8kg, depending on the style, this provides protection against low-velocity rounds and, when up-armouring plates are inserted, against high-velocity rounds.

RBR 2000 Police and Military overvest: Weighing between 1.4 and 3.3kg, this provides the same degree of protection as the RBR 1000.

RBR 2003 Police overvest: 'Peardrop' ceramic plates form an integral part of this garment. Consequently it has the ability to stop 7.62mm and 5.56mm ball ammunition at 10m. It weighs 8.8kg.

RBR 3000 military overvest: Weighing between 2.2 and 4.1kg, this provides protection against low-velocity rounds and fragments and, when up-armouring plates are inserted, against high-velocity rounds.

RBR 8001 search suit: This provides V50

protection against a 17-grain fragment of 455m/sec. The expression V50 is the average of the velocities recorded from six impacts, consisting of the three lowest velocities for complete penetration and the three highest velocities for partial penetration, provided the spread is not greater than 40m/sec.

RBR Ballistic combat helmet: A composite ballistic helmet for use by parachute and ground troops. The S4 version weighs 1.25kg, can stop a gun round and provides V50 protection against a 17-grain fragment at 585m/sec.

Employment: Sri Lankan Navy, Luxem-

Right: RBR 3001.

Left: RBR 8001.

bourg Gendarmerie (4 contracts), Luxembourg Police (5 contracts), Luxembourg Prison Service, Belgian Gendarmerie, Belgian Police (5 contracts), Belgian Customs, Pakistan Sind Police, Pakistan Punjab Police (2 contracts), Pakistan Baluchistan Police, Indian Manipur Province Police, Indian Police Consolidated Contract, United Kingdom Police, Northern Ireland Police (4 contracts), Turkish Gendarmerie, Spanish National Police (4 contracts), Tanzanian Army, New Zealand Army (trial quantity), Saudi Arabian National Guard, Saudi Arabia Special Security Forces, Australian Army (trial quantity), Bangladesh Dhaka Police, Finnish Army, Portugal G.N.R., Portugal Guarda Fiscal, Pakistan Army, Indian Army, Indian Special Forces, Indian Navy (two contracts), Pakistan Air Force (Helmets), Kuwait Special Forces, Finland Special Forces, United Kingdom Customs & Excise, Belgian Security Companies, United Nations P.K. Force (Helmets), Pakistan Gilgit Police, Swedish Army (Helmets), North American Police, Australian Army (Helmets), Singapore Marine Police.

Security Equipment Supplies Body Armour

Like many other manufacturers, SES of Andover, Hampshire, uses Kevlar in its garments, building layers to increase ballistic protection, and ceramic tile inserts further increase effectiveness. Customised armour is available in addition to the basic patterns, which include the following.

EOD Suit Mk 4

In service in Europe, the Middle East and the Far East, this suit features overboots that protect the feet and ankles, a blast deflection plate covering the chest and groin area, and a fully air-cooled ballistic helmet with integral visor and built-in microphone and earphones.

Data: *weights* 7kg (jacket), 2.5kg (trousers and overboots), 4.5kg (chest and groin), 1kg (cooling fan), 1.5kg (cooling fan battery), 4.5kg (helmet); *cooling fan running time* 8hr; *cool air flow* 180 litres per minute; *ballistic levels* from 360m/sec V50 (trousers, arms and overboots) to 700m/sec V50 (visor).

Below: Security Equipment Supplies EOD Suit Mk 4.

Ambassador Model: Designed to be worn over uniform by police and military personnel, this garment protects front, back and sides, and a groin protector can be fitted. More than 14,000 of these jackets are in service.

Assault Jacket: Offers total protection to the upper area of the body, with large adjustable sides and collar adjustment; magazine pouches come as an optional extra.

Flak Jacket: Primarily designed for military use, this jacket features patterned stop patches at the shoulders to aid weapons grasp.

SWAT Model: A fully adjustable jacket that offers maximum protection area while allowing unrestricted movement.

Diplomat: This is designed to be worn under a shirt, and offers good protection for the user while concealing the fact that body armour is being worn.

Anti-Knife Jacket: Based on the Diplomat model, this offers protection against stiletto knife attack. The anti-knife insert has a light-weight lamellar metal section fronting the Kevlar packs at the front and back of the jacket.

Left: Security Equipment Supplies Flak Jacket.

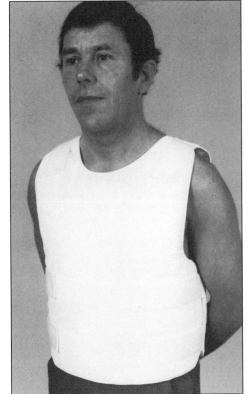

Above: Security Equipment Supplies Ambassador Model.

Above right: Security Equipment Supplies SWAT Model.

Right: Security Equipment Supplies Diplomat Model.

Waistcoat: This looks identical to a normal cloth garment.

Immediate Response Jacket: Designed for specialised forces, this is a lightweight (1.5kg) garment that makes use of nylon netting material to remain cool in tropical climates.

UNITED STATES

American Body Armor Equipment Inc. Protective Garments and Equipment

American Body Armor Equipment Incorporated of Fernandina Beach, Florida, provides a comprehensive range of body armour, facemasks, helmets, shields, barrier blankets and EOD suits. It also manufactures bomb handling equipment and letter bomb suppression pouches.

Vests: Two female vests are available, the Contour Style and Side Coverage Style. They provide protection against rounds up to and including 9mm calibre. Two male vests are available, with protection similar to the female vests.

Armitron Body Armor: Armitron provides one-piece 'soft body armour' protection against 9mm and .44 Magnum projectiles. This is a most impressive performance, since no metal plates are incorporated. It is most suitable for police on undercover work.

Tactical Jacket: A conventional flak jacket with good protection against low-velocity rounds and shrapnel. To upgrade the jacket, a ceramic plate can be inserted into the front and/or rear pockets of the vest, and this will provide protection against projectiles up to and including 7.62mm and 5.56mm.

Tactical Assault Vest: The Tactical Assault Vest offers similar protection to the Tactical Jacket, but is less bulky and can be worn more easily with load-bearing equipment. Ceramic plates can also be inserted.

High Coverage Tactical Armor: This armour provides comprehensive protection against handguns, shotguns and submachine-guns and, with the addition of the 'ceramic throw over', against rifles.

Model AK-47 Lightweight Military Body Armor: This armour is designed for military use, and is one of the lightest vests available that, with ceramic plates, can defeat high-velocity rifles. It weighs 2.65kg. The 25cm x 30cm ceramic plate weighs another 3.63kg.

TAC-100R Tactical Facemask, TAC-22R Tactical Helmet and TAC-300R Tactical Protective Shield: The Facemask protects the face from most handguns, shotguns and submachine-guns, giving valuable protection and a strong psychological advantage. The mask is constructed of Kevlar. If a round hits the mask, the amount of energy transferred to the head and neck is claimed to be comparable to the impact received from a good punch to the head. It weighs 0.57kg. It is best worn with the Kevlar TAC-200R helmet, weighing 1.71kg, and the TAC-300R Tactical Protective shield, 83cm x 48.5cm, weight 5.45kg.

Riot Vest: This comes in three versions, Model 210 for protection against handguns and weighing 3.63kg; Model 310 for better protection against handguns and weighing 4.54kg; and Model 620 for protection against up to .30 calibre rifles and weighing 8.18kg.

Armor of America Protective Garments Sacramento Vest

Developed by Armor of America of Beverly Hills, California, the Sacramento Vest is designed for use by police and SWAT teams. It can hold chest and back panels of any grade of hard armour. A sleeveless garment, reinforced with ballistic nylon felt that acts as a shock absorber when hit by rocks and bottles, it is also ideal for crowd control. Without an insert, the Sacramento Vest can stop 9mm submachine-gun fire at 8m and weighs 4.08kg (SAC AHP Version). A Sacramento Armor Shield insert weighing an additional 2.88kg will stop a 7.62mm NATO round at 8m. The garment also protects the neck, spine and groin.

Employment: Various US SWAT teams and police forces.

Tactical Vest

Without a hard armour insert, this vest can stop a 9mm submachine-gun round at 8m. With an insert the Tactical Vest can stop up to 30.06 AP. The vest is available in two versions, the AJ weighing 4.54kg, and the AHP weighing 2.72kg.

Employment: Various US police forces.

Undershirt Armoured Vest

Armor of America has developed a range of lightweight vests for undershirt wear. These provide protection against most handguns and include Armor-Hide (1.1kg), Super Armor-Hide (1.7kg), Super Armor-Hide Countour (1.81kg), Armor-Hide Super Contour + P (1.5kg) and Ultra-thin (0.89kg). The Armor-Hide range offers slightly differing

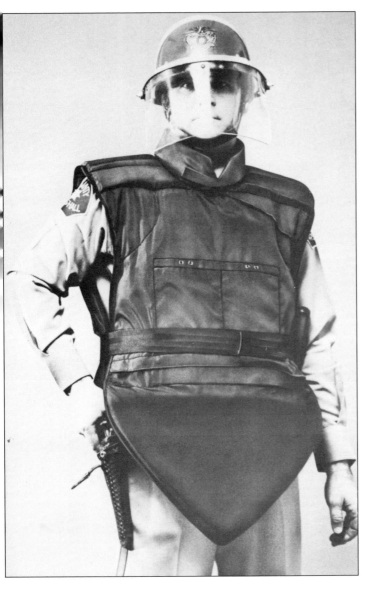

Below: Armor of America Protective Garments Sacramento Vest.

levels of protection, but all are of the same basic design.
Employment: Various US police forces.

Woman's Vest

Designed for policewomen, this vest can stop virtually all handgun rounds, including .38 calibre, 9mm HP and .41 Magnum. It weighs 0.91kg and is available in sizes 32, 34, 36 and 38.
Variants: The women's vest is available in a version providing a slightly higher degree of protection against 9mm FMJ (USA) and weighing 1.1kg.
Employment: Various US police forces.

Second Chance Body Armor

Second Chance Body Armor is thought to have saved the lives of over 500 US policemen to date.

Command Jac Assault Vest: Provides complete torso protection against .30 US carbine and all known handgun rounds. An armour plate is an optional insert for protection against AP rifle fire. The jacket is suitable for police and SWAT team wear.

Hardcorps II: Hardcorps II is available in one standard size, 32cm x 38cm. The soft ballistic panels (without metal inserts) offer protection from shell fragments, handguns and shotgun parabellum. Also available is a contoured 25cm x 33cm armour plate assembly that provides protection against high-velocity AP rounds. The same plate can be inserted for back protection. Hardcorps II (without the plate) weighs 1.8kg; the insert is 4.9kg.

Hardcorps III: An all-purpose body armour system offering the wearer 80.4cm^2 front and back protection from shell fragmentation, handguns and shotguns. There are three frontal inserts and an optional back guard insert. These provide protection against high-velocity rounds. Hardcorps III without the plate weighs 2.47kg; with frontal plates the total weight is 8.38kg.

Hardcorps IV: A logical development of Hardcorps III, with an extra front panel. It has the same level of ballistic performance.

Concealable Armour: For use by VIPs and police, this affords protection against handguns. With the K30 plate inserted there is additional protection against high-velocity weapons.

Employment: Second Chance Body Armor is used by some 50 police departments in the USA, including the San Francisco, Detroit and Chicago Police, the Texas, Ohio, Massachusetts Police Departments, the Michigan State Police, and the FBI.

Right: Second Chance also manufactures a female vest, illustrated here.

6
Surveillance, Security and Perimeter Protection Equipment

Surveillance equipment, though important in conventional warfare, is especially so in IS conditions. In modern warfare image intensification (II), infra red (IR), and thermal imaging (TI) weapon sights are commonplace in order to facilitate the 24-hour battle. Although night and all-weather sights are important in rural IS situations, surveillance aids, as opposed to weapon sights, are particularly important for observation posts (OPs) that may be keeping watch on a target for days on end. Time spent in surveillance is seldom wasted, and often pays dividends out of all proportion to the effort involved. Indeed, a successful operation is often preceded by hours, weeks or even months of painstaking surveillance. Telescopes are a basic aid for daylight static observation tasks. These often have a zoom facility, which has proved highly effective. The basic range of IS night viewing aids has been augmented in many armies with hand-held II surveillance equipment.

White light illumination at night is equally important, particularly in a search operation. Search or bomb disposal teams are now able to use 20K candlepower torches for night illumination. Helicopters are also able to illuminate the ground with searchlights such as Nightsun.

Cameras are, of course, a vital tool in IS operations. To secure convictions it is often necessary to have photographic evidence, for instance of an illegal weapon in its hiding place before removal for forensic tests. Appraisal of an IED can be made using a TV camera and remote monitor. In Northern Ireland something like one man in every eight is equipped with a camera for the purpose of securing evidence. (It is not proposed to feature cameras as such in this chapter.) Another fascinating use of camera equipment for IS purposes is the remarkable air-to-ground surveillance and reconnaissance system known as Heli-Tele. The system consists of a colour TV camera mounted on a helicopter, a microwave link with multi-range aerials, and a number of display units both in the helicopter and at a ground station to which the camera transmits a 'real-time' picture.

Radar also has an IS application. Infantry has long used short-range portable surveillance radars in conventional warfare. Examples are the French Thomson-CSF Olifant 2 radar and the British Marconi Elliott ZB98 radar. This type of equipment, although primarily designed for use in conventional warfare, is especially suitable for surveillance of a border, extending the zone observed by a patrol, or even surveillance of boat traffic in river – all possible IS tasks in a rural environment. Another application of radar for a specifically IS task is Claribel, a British development. This is an active radar surveillance device that indicates to within a 30° arc the direction from which a sniper has fired. Vehicles or static OPs can be fitted with sensors. If fired at, the system provides audio warning that a shot has been fired and a visual indication to identify the 30° arc from which the shot came. In a built-up area it is virtually impossible for an unequipped observer to tell from which direction a shot has been fired, as the 'crack and thump' of a high-velocity rifle echoes and re-echoes off the walls of the buildings.

Perimeter protection has become a growth industry since military and government installations have, in recent years, become more prone to sabotage, espionage and plain vandalism. The airport, the nuclear plant, the oil terminal, the power station, the armaments store, the radar site, the ordnance factory, the communications centre, the ruler in his palace, the general in his headquarters or the politician in his seat of government – all of these are vulnerable targets, and in many cases more vulnerable than they need to be. Terrorist organisations worldwide have demonstrated their ability to attack the infrastructure of the state. Intruder alarms provide varying degrees of security. The main aims of a perimeter protection system are to provide the earliest possible detection of intruders; to maximise reaction time; to ensure security against overcoming the system by tampering; to give a low (preferably negligible) false alarm rate; to ensure relia-

bility over long periods as well as ease of installation; and ideally to provide protection in depth.

Perimeter protection can be provided by microwave/IR fences, tripwire/differential-force systems, acoustic, seismic or magnetic sensors, or by radar or TV surveillance. Often a combination of these systems is the best answer. Sensors can provide protection in a number of ways. They can detect an intruder crossing a line, they can detect attempts to climb or interfere with fences or walls, and they can sense interference with windows. Additionally or alternatively, they can be used to provide focal protection so that the presence of a person in a room is indicated. Most perimeter protection systems are connected to a central control or station,

Below: A surveillance operative gathering photographic evidence.

Above: A typical target under surveillance.

thus keeping to a minimum the manpower required to monitor them. Ideally, any security system installed should perform the following functions:

● Deter an intruder from entering;

● Detect a security threat before it happens;

● Sense an intrusion when it takes place and pinpoint where it has occurred;

● Locate the intruder so as to determine the nature of the threat;

● Respond to the threat and neutralise it.

A large establishment will be covered by a multi-camera installation with the control unit in one central location. The only time it should be necessary to go to the camera head is when a sensor tube needs changing, which is normally only once in several thousand hours of operation. The type and method of use of the camera vary depending on the site and the required system parameters. The first main consideration in designing any system is to determine what is to be viewed and why. Having established this, the site is surveyed so that the type of cameras and their locations may be decided upon. In some instances, when it is required to have continuous surveillance of the whole perimeter, it is necessary to position fixed cameras with fixed fields of view at regular intervals all round the site. On a rectangular site, for example, the cameras should be divided into four groups, one for each side, and each

Above: The same target as shown on the opposite page magnified many times.

group would be allocated its own picture monitor. The pictures from the cameras could be selected for viewing on the appropriate monitors by manual selection, or they could be made to sequence automatically, the sequencing switch having a manual override. As the cameras are fixed, there are no remote controls, so the system is kept simple. It has a high security integrity, as any one camera will cover part of the next camera's field of view and, if a camera fails, all is not lost. It does mean, however, that a relatively large number of cameras may be required, and the cameras are restricted to viewing only one area; there is therefore some inflexibility.

An alternative type of installation uses remotely controlled cameras. With this arrangement a camera can be remotely positioned to view any required area within defined limits. The cameras are mounted on pan-and-tilt heads and controlled from a remote point by means of a simple joystick. Associated with this type of installation, it is normal to fit a zoom lens which is also remotely controlled. In use, the camera is made to pan around and tilt up and down to observe any given area of the perimeter, with the lens at a wide angle. When it is considered that an area needs closer inspection, the zoom lens is brought into operation to give a close-up view of the suspect area. The advantages of this type of system are that it is very flexible, large areas can be viewed with one camera, and close-up views can be obtained. On a one-for-one basis this is more expensive, but, generally, fewer cameras are used, to the point where its overall capital cost is lower than that for fixed cameras. On the other hand, it is a more complex system, with remote-control circuits, associated cabling and more unit parts required to make the whole. A clever intruder could aim to be where the camera was not pointing. The system's integrity could be seriously affected by failure of any one function or camera, unless fully compensating camera positions were designed-in.

There is another vulnerable aspect to a system using only television cameras; it relies on a man to monitor the pictures continually. This can be a tedious operation, and, in the case of movable cameras, they may not be viewing the right areas, so an intrusion may go undetected. For a large installation the many viewing screens required would complicate the matter. This problem is overcome by employing a system that *automatically* detects the presence of an intruder. This can be achieved by use of geophones (seismic microphones), or by the use of infra-red beams. A security system could include either of these or a combination of them. Geophones will detect the presence of an intruder by sensing the vibrations set up by his activity. The wide variety of methods of geophone deployment allows their use in many roles; on fences (more usually), in paths or buried directly in the ground. The sensitivity of a geophone is such that virtually any activity in its vicinity will cause sufficient vibration to provide a working signal to the system. Even so, it is a robust and wholly passive device.

Geophones are employed in multiple arrays. There is interconnecting wiring between each geophone unit within the array, and from the array to the control units. It is usual to mount geophones on chain-link perimeter fences, on alternate fence panels approximately 6m apart. The fence is divided into sectors, each of which can be up to 150m in length and employ 25 geophones. The length of the sector will depend upon the application and the overall system configuration. Up to eight sectors can be accommodated in one control unit, and several control units may be housed in a single equipment rack. The geophone itself is a seismic detector that, when mounted on a fence, operates in the vertical plane. It consists of a finely balanced coil suspended within a magnetic field. Any movement of this coil induces a voltage proportional to the amplitude and frequency of the movement. The induced voltage is detected in the control unit, where any significant change is signalled as an alarm. A single small movement would not be significant, but a series of small movements, such as an intruder sawing gently through the wire, would be detected and signalled as an alarm.

Infra-red systems constitute the third main category of surveillance systems. An infra-red source (the transmitter) provides a cone of infra-red light which illuminates the infra-red receiver. No visible light is emitted by the transmitter, and each one can generally illuminate more than a single receiver. Both transmitter and receiver are optically focused so that a relatively narrow beam exists between them. The receiver will respond to either an increase or a decrease in the received signal. The infra-red beams will operate in all weather conditions where the transmitter can be seen visually from the receiver. Generally, multiple beams are deployed to form a fence of infra-red. This fence can be of any height and with inter-beam spacing to suit the circumstances. Infra-red transmitters and receivers are normally mounted in a specially constructed pillar. The standard configuration is for each pillar to be fitted with the transmitter, sending out a cone of non-visible infra-red light, and six receivers equally placed over a height of 2.5m. The pillars are faced in metal, with apertures of black acrylic through which the beams are transmitted or received. Infra-red pillars are installed facing each other, and the normal operating distance between them is up to 100m.

When an intruder disturbs the infra-red beams, causing a significant rate of change in received beam intensity, the signal processing circuit will generate an alarm. Where multiple beams are deployed in a stack or fence formation, the alarm will be delayed when only one beam is broken, as opposed to the virtually immediate alarm when all beams are broken simultaneously; by this means, false alarms (induced by birds flying through the beams or the intrusion of small animals) are reduced to a minimum. However, an intruder will be detected, even if he attempts to roll through the bottom beam. Changes of beam intensity by the onset of rain, fog or snow are automatically sensed by the processing circuits, and loss of system sensitivity is countered within the control unit. Similarly, if an attempt is made to introduce an external source of infra-red light, an alarm will be generated.

Both the CCTV and intruder alarm systems used on their own can have disadvantages. An intruder may be undetected by a camera system, while an intruder alarm system merely detects an intrusion without verifying the nature or extent of the threat. If the two systems are used together, they complement each other. As automatic intruder alarms are monitored continuously by electronic control circuits, they possess a 'long watch' capability. Even so, there are drawbacks in using a security system comprised solely of automatic intruder alarms. The cost-effectiveness of such systems can only be assessed by the user in terms of minimising false alarms. A television camera does not give false information – even if the camera were to be 'shot out' it would tell you something!

The method of combining the two types of system can vary from being simple to sophisticated. A simple method would be to rely on the security guard to respond to the intruder detection alarm by selecting the relevant camera for picture display on the monitor and, in the case of remotely controlled cameras, to point the camera to the area indicated and then verify the type and extent of the intrusion. A sophisticated method would be to use the intruder detection alarm to switch the relevant picture on to a picture monitor automatically, and, in the case of remotely controlled cameras, the camera would be made to point automatically to the intruded area. The detection system would have priority over a manual or sequencing switch, and the picture would be held until the alarm was reset or another alarm was signalled. Such a system meets all the require-

ments of a perimeter protection. It detects a threat: one guard using the television cameras can effectively patrol the whole area without moving from his monitor screens and, by their use, can detect any suspicious activity outside the fence. It senses an intrusion: the intruder alarm system will signal an alarm immediately an illegal attempt is made to enter the premises, and the television system will verify the nature of the threat. It locates the intruder: the intruder alarm system will give a broad indication of the area where the intrusion is taking place, and the television system will locate the exact position. It responds to and neutralises the threat: because the guard has seen the intrusion on the television, he will know how many people are involved and whether they are armed, so he can use his judgement as to whether to send a patrolman to chase off or apprehend the intruder, or call on the services of security forces. Further, he can effectively monitor the progress of his patrolman and call for extra assistance if required. So a television and intruder alarm system can perform all the functions required for a security system. And it will be appreciated that all this can be achieved with a very small staff. Having said this, no system can entirely compensate for armed guards, particularly in a developed terrorist situation.

All perimeter protection systems must include some fence or barrier to delay or impede the progress of the intruder towards his target. It is not the intention of this section to include comprehensive coverage of fencing, barriers or gates, but some examples of the more sophisticated types of gates, fences and anti-intruder automatic road blocks are included.

Finally, when considering any system, the amount of light available at night must be considered. Lighting is the lifeblood of television, and the amount of light available determines what type of sensor tube should be deployed. The most commonly used sensor tube is the Vidicon; for most applications, there is nothing that does the job quite so well. The Vidicon is reasonably priced, readily available and has a good life

Left: Perimeter fencing outside Parliament in London.

Right: Fencing around Parliament designed to prevent intruders climbing onto the roof.

Far right: More security fencing around Parliament.

expectancy. It can be used in such a way that the camera automatically adjusts to give a constant level of picture for changes in the illumination of the scene. Using a Vidicon, the average minimum incident illumination required would be 20 lumens per square foot. This assumes an average scene, and includes a factor for deterioration of the lighting units due to age as well as occlusion from rain, dust and snow. This is, of course, higher than is used for normal security lighting, but it does have its advantages. It acts as a deterrent; intruders do not like to be seen – darkness is their best ally. Pictures can be

obtained with lower levels of illumination, but they will not be of such high quality. In some instances, installations can operate with light levels of between 1 and 5 lumens per square foot, but the pictures tend to be ill-defined. In this case the Vidicon is being made to work very hard, which will shorten its life as well as having other side-effects.

For lighting levels above 1 lumen per square foot but no higher than 5 lumens per square foot, a more sensitive tube is called for. Such a tube is the silicon diode array Vidicon. This is a more expensive tube (in the order of five times as expensive as the normal Vidicon), and cannot be operated automatically within the camera. To achieve a constant picture level output, a special type of lens is required; this in turn costs more than a conventional lens, whether zoom or fixed. By automatic electronic sampling of the picture signal, the aperture setting of the lens regulates itself using a servo motor. This process is continuous, and by using this technique the picture signal is maintained at a constant level. These lenses are usually fitted with a neutral-density filter, which, when used in conjunction with the iris, enables the camera to maintain a constant level of picture signal from dim to very bright lighting conditions.

To operate in lighting levels below 1 lumen per square foot, a more specialised type of sensor tube is required. There are several different types available, but one thing they have in common is that they are all very expensive, and usually the cost of such a system is not justified within the scope of normal security work. Generally, this kind of system is restricted to military applications.

If the availability of light is a problem, there are alternative solutions, one of which is to fit searchlights on the camera panning head so that the camera is always viewing an illuminated area. The 'throw length' of the light path must be taken into account, and this can restrict the effective range of the camera. An intruder would obviously know where the camera was pointing. Because of the visible light beam, this cannot be seriously considered a primary detection system. A solution to this – and, coincidentally, to another problem – is the use of infra-red light. Some sites, for various reasons, cannot have a highly-lit security area. (The reasons could be that they are in the middle of a res-

idential area, where the local residents would object to brightly-lit premises nearby, or the site owners may not wish to advertise the existence of a security site.) Under the circumstances, use can be made of a silicon diode array Vidicon, a version of which is highly sensitive to the infra-red content of light. For such applications, a cluster of searchlights is fitted to the panning head so that they move and point where the camera points. These lights are enclosed in two special housings, one mounted on each side of the camera. The front of the housing is fitted with visible light-absorbing, or infra-red pass filters. Thus the only light to shine through is infra-red, which is not visible to the human eye. This is termed a covert light source. The range of these lights is in the order of 200m, and an intruder can be illuminated and detected without knowing it. Such a system will operate satisfactorily in normal daylight, the lights being required only at night.

Perimeter protection has many aspects, and one short chapter cannot possibly do it full justice. However, it is hoped that the examples in the following pages of the wide

Below: Ernst Leitz Canada Optical Sight.

range of equipment available will serve to illustrate the scope, sophistication and complexity of this form of protection against terrorism.

CANADA

Ernst Leitz Canada Optical Sight

The Leitz Optical Sight has been developed by Leitz Canada to be the primary sighting system for a variety of small-arms. The sight will significantly improve hit probability, particularly at longer ranges and in poor visibility, and will shorten target engagement times. The optical sight is second-generation and designed for use in all adverse weather conditions. It has proved effective for use on machine-guns as well as rifles, permitting the tracer and fall of shot to be clearly seen at extended ranges and under low ambient light. Today, its prime use is with the M16 and MINIMI. As an integrated component of the next generation of advanced combat rifles the sight attests to Leitz Canada's commitment to product development and optical excellence.

Data: *magnification* 3.5X; *field of view* 7°; *apparent field of view* 24.5°; *entrance pupil diameter* 28mm; *exit pupil diameter* 8mm; *dimensions* 160mm long x 72mm high x 55mm wide; *weight* sight 350g, mount 290g.

DENMARK

JAI 736 SIT Low Level Surveillance Camera System

The JAI 736 Gated SIT TV camera is a low-light-level (LLL) camera mounted with a special camera tube and a high-voltage switching circuit. By gating the image intensifier part of the SIT tube the operator can electronically control ultra-short exposure times. This enables any movement or action to be frozen for instant control or identification. The gate time is selectable from 20 microseconds to 2 milliseconds, and the 'continuous' mode provides the LLL performance of the SIT camera. In 'slope' mode the gate time will continuously change around the gate time selected, to ensure that the pictures are correctly exposed. The JAI 736 can be used to identify terrorists entering a secure zone.

Below: JAI 736 SIT, manportable version.

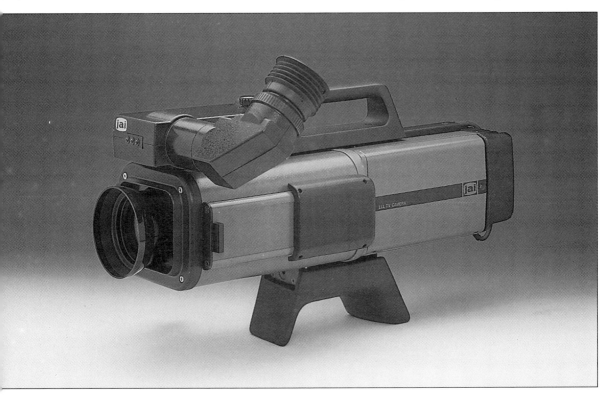

Data: *exposure time* 20 microseconds to 2 milliseconds in 8 steps for high flexibility; 20 MHZ video amplifier bandwidth; wide light control range of 1:4 x 10 12; Ni-Cad battery or Mains (110/120V - 220/240V 50/60Mc.

JAI 733 SIT/743 ISIT tc Camera

Nighthawk: Nighthawk cameras operate under all light conditions – the SIT from full sunlight to moonlight, and the ISIT down to starlight conditions. The special design of the JAI EHT unit provides ultimate protection for the sensitive camera tube, via automatic control of the camera's shutdown. This protection feature is further enhanced by the unique JAI ND spot filter in the lens. For increased picture stability the Nighthawk series is equipped with an outstanding back-focus design that efficiently negates adjust-

JAI 733 SIT/743 ISIT tc Camera

	733 SIT	743 ISIT
Sensitivity (100% contrast, 300 lines resolution)	6×10^{-5} lux	8×10^{-6} lux
Resolution (at 6×10^{-5} lux)	300 lines	480 lines
Resolution (at 8×10^{-6} lux)	Not useable	300 lines
Resolution (daylight conditions) (without lens)	700 lines	600 lines
Power requirements	12 Volt DC nominal (10,5 Volt–17 Volt)	
Power consumption	0.8 amps (without lens)	
Power supply	12 Volt DC, 24 Volt DC or 220/240 Volt AC	
Dimensions	L = 394, B = 153, H = 127mm (with PSU)	
Weight	5.5kgs inclusive power supply	

ments resulting from changes in the ambient temperature.

GERMANY

Elkosta Perimeter Protection Equipment

Elkosta of Salzgitter produces gates, railings, barriers, turnstiles, road blocks and fencing.

Gates: Elkosta produces a variety of gates to aid security. These include sliding gates, telescopic sliding gates, hinged gates, centrally pivoted gates and lowering gates. They can be operated manually or by electro-mechanical or electro-hydraulic drive units. All Elkosta gates are manufactured from high-quality steel and are galvanised and plastic coated. They are all immensely strong and can be opened or shut quickly. They are, therefore, designed with security in mind.

Entrance Barriers and Road Blocks: Elkosta manufactures conventional entrance barriers, some of which are lowered, and others that rise into position from underground housings. Where it may be necessary to guarantee preventing vehicle access or egress, electro-hydraulic or electro-mechanical road blocks with a resistance to impact in excess of 120KN are ideal. Visible and acoustic safety equipment signal the movement of the barrier out of the road and into a blocking position.

Turnstiles, Railings and Fencing: Turnstiles incorporating a coded access system, a palisade and welded mesh fences are available.

Below: Example of Elkosta Perimeter Gates.

Left and right:
Examples of Elkosta
Perimeter Gates and
Entrance Barriers.

SWITZERLAND

Wild Leitz Forward Observation and Reconnaissance Thermal Imaging System

This system is specially designed for military and paramilitary use. Its large and selectable field of view, its high target resolution and long range make it ideally suitable to observation, reconnaissance and surveillance tasks. Mist and smoke do not substantially reduce performance.

Data: *wavelength* 8-12μm; *detector* CMT (cadmium, mercury, telluride); *number of detector elements* 24; *cooling system* Joule-Thomson, 77K; *temperature resolution (NETP)* approx. 0.1K; *geometric resolution* 0.8 mrad/0.2 mrad; *field of view* 19 x 9°/4.7 x 2.2°; *image display* large viewing lens (TV as option); *nominal voltage* 7.2V; *power consumption* approx. 3W; *weight* (without bottle and battery) approx. 11kg; *dimensions* approx. 40cm long x 23cm wide x 29cm high; *range* (at standard atmosphere, 293K based on the Nato-target size), detection approx. 6km, recognition approx. 2km, identification ≥1km.

UNITED KINGDOM

Claribel Hostile Fire Indicator

Developed for the British Army as a means of determining the source of fire aimed at patrols or observation posts, Claribel is a low-powered X-band CW radar system. It provides 360° coverage in all weathers, and picks up missiles of all velocities except stones, bricks, etc. Comprising four radar

Below: Wild Leitz Thermal Imager.

heads, commander's and crew's displays, a central processor unit, an orientation unit and a power supply, the equipment can be fitted in Land Rovers, APCs or even saloon cars, in the last case invisibly located in the body-work. After the tracking data has been processed, the direction of fire is indicated on a simple electro-luminescent clockface display. This visual warning is supplemented by an audible alarm. The system will indicate the positions of two separate snipers firing simultaneously. Should the vehicle driver take evasive action, the in-built orientation system correspondingly updates the information display. Powered by lead/acid batteries, the Claribel system can operate for eight hours between charges.

Variants: a man-portable variant known as Aries houses the radar heads in a specially

designed flak jacket; the processor unit is carried in a pouch on the belt, and the display on a watchface at the wrist.

Davin Optical Night Vision Systems Modulux 130

Intended primarily for night-time photography, Modulux comprises a set of rugged, compatible modules that can be assembled and installed into a wide range of systems to give the best configuration for any given set of circumstances. Offering unrivalled performance based on a choice of first- or second-generation high-resolution, low-distortion image intensifiers, Modulux permits users to view and/or record images that have been amplified by a factor of at least 100,000 times. The system is totally compatible with most popular commercially available SLR

Below: Davin Optical Modulux 130.

cameras and lenses.

Data: *image intensifier tube gain* x150,000; *weight* (with batteries) 2.1kg; *monocular lens* magnification x70 focusing range; *binocular lens* magnification x3.5.

Minilux

Minilux has been developed to provide a cost-effective second-generation night viewer that has the added capability of being used with 35mm SLR cameras or CCTV systems. Minilux is light and compact, and together with the specially designed eyepiece and relay lenses is capable of producing high-

quality images at remarkably low cost. When used as a direct observation unit, the unique eyepiece design produces a 40° viewing angle with a very comfortable flat field image. The system magnification is typically x3 with a 75mm objective lens.

Data: intensifier type 18mm second generation; *resolution* typically 30m lp/mm; *gain* typically x20,000; *supply voltage* 2-3.5V; *supply current* 18mA; *power supply* 2 x AAA batteries; *system magnification* x3 (with a 75mm lens); *eye relief* 20mm for full field of view; *field of view eyepiece* 40°; *hours of operation* 40hr approx.

Left: Davin Optical Minilux.

Above: Davin Optical
Minimodulux

Minimodulux

The Minimodulux has been designed to fulfil the role of a small, compact night vision system capable of being used as a hand-held night viewer or for photography and filming at night. The image intensifier tube incorporated into the Minimodulux is a combined first- and second-generation tube offering high performance coupled to small size and low weight. Ideal for covert operations, the Minimodulux uses 1-inch C-mount lenses for operational versatility, or will accept 35mm commercial camera lenses via adapters. In photographic or filming mode, an optical relay lens is used to maximise image transmission and frame exposure, and adapters for 35mm SLR and 1-inch C-mount CCTV/CCD cameras are supplied. The Minimodulux has full flash protection, automatic brightness control and bright light suppression, allowing the unit to operate in rural and urban environments. Powered by AA-size batteries, the Minimodulux offers superior performance over second-generation equipment without an increase in size or weight. A variable gain control allows the user to adjust the gain to suit operational requirements.

Employment: British Army, police forces and various overseas customers.

Data: 18mm, two-stage image intensifier with proximity focused MCP wafer first stage and electrostatically focused distortion corrected second stage incorporating full flash protection, automatic brightness control and variable gain control; *output resolution* 32 1p/mm; *gain* 310,000 x; *EBI* 0.1 μ lux; *screen brightness* 60 Cd/M^2; *batteries* 2 x AA Alkaline Cell; *length and weight* (excluding camera and lens), observation 120mm (1.1kg), photography 169mm (1.6kg), filming 205mm (1.6kg).

Spylux

Spylux has been designed as a low-cost but effective night viewer capable of operating in urban and rural areas at night. The first-generation image intensifier tube incorporated in Spylux is carefully selected to give a high-resolution, low noise image enabling target acquisition at ranges of greater than 200m at low light levels. Unlike most first-generation systems, Spylux can operate in urban areas with minimal interference from bright light sources. The unit has an overall magnification of 2.5 using the 75mm objective lens supplied, and its design allows alternative lenses to be fitted to increase magnification to suit the operational requirement. Spylux is small and compact, weighing 0.85kg, and is therefore ideal for covert operations and general purpose use. The body is sheathed in a PVC sleeve to allow comfortable handling. The unit is powered by AA-size batteries giving up to 90 hours' use.

Employment: British Army, British police forces, various overseas customers.

Data: first-generation, single-stage image intensifier with automatic brightness control; *output resolution* 100 lp/mm; *luminance gain* 400 cd/m^2/lux; *equivalent background illumination* 0.2 μ lux; *supply voltage* 2-5V; *overall weight with lens* 0.85kg; *overall length with lens* 150mm; *power supply* 2 x AA batteries; *hours of operation* 30-90hr; *magnification with 75mm lens* x2.5.

Dragon Portable Searchlight

Dragon searchlights are in service with every police force in the United Kingdom and with defence and security agencies worldwide. The 100W is the most powerful filament available, giving exceptionally large area high-intensity long-range illumination in excess of 1km, coupled with wide-angle peripheral light – ideal for riot control and special duties owing to its brilliance and colour rendition. It has a continuous duration

Below: Davin Optical Spylux.

of approximately 46 minutes. The unit is designed for combat use under the most arduous conditions, all components being housed in a hardened waterproof PVC carcass, and it can be used hands-free for riot control and other operations. A range of special charges is available to suit any requirement, i.e. high speed, vehicle, airframe or multi-outlet. It can be powered by any 12V vehicle for unlimited-duration lighting.

Employment: UK and many other police forces, British MOD.

Data: *length* 38cm; *case diameter* 10cm; *head diameter* 15.25cm; *weight* (with battery) 3,75kg; *light output* 250,000CP (100W), 180,000CP (50W); *duration of full charge* 46min (100W), 80min (50W); *battery type* Ni-Cad; *battery storage life* 10 years; *service life* (operational) approx. 6 years+; *charger type* constant current; *charge time* 10-12 hours; *high-speed charger* constant current with sensory circuit; *charge time* 1hr to operational condition, 4hr or less for *full* recharge.

Fenceguard Perimeter Protection System
Fenceguard FG310 and FG311
Fenceguard FG310 is an outdoor microwave intruder sensor designed to provide complete round-the-clock perimeter surveillance. It is especially suited to high-risk applications such as power stations, government establishments and petro-chemical plants. Its detection sensitivity may be set to one of five levels, and on high sensitivity it will detect belly crawling intruders and will deter even the trained saboteur. It is recommended for sites with permanent on-site personnel backed up by physical security such as chain-link fencing and additional security equipment such as a CCTV surveillance system.

Below: Dragon Portable Searchlight.

Above: GEC Marconi thermal video camera.

Left: A thermal imaging picture.

Above: GEC Marconi thermal video camera in second generation casing.

The secure perimeter is made up of a number of links. Each link consists of a transmitter and a receiver which can be located up to 150m apart. Intruders are detected when they pass through a cigar-shaped beam which is formed between the transmitter and the receiver. FG310 links are located around the perimeter of the site, with overlaps to ensure continuous coverage. Four switch-selectable modulation channels are provided to prevent interference between adjacent units. The vertical antenna array provides greater sensitivity in the horizontal plane, so that heavy rain or falling leaves will not trigger an alarm. In addition, circuits are incorporated to minimise false alarms from radio frequency interference, birds flying through the beam, and small animals crossing the sensitive zone. FG310 has an in-built test facility which simplifies installation and field service. It confirms that the equipment is operating correctly and, if not, indicates where the problem lies. Modular construction allows rapid field replacement of individual sub-assemblies which are available as

spares that can be stocked on site.

The FG310 has been designed to blend into the background, and will operate under a wide range of environmental and climatic conditions.

Model FG311 has all the features of the FG310 with the additional capability of remote test. This permits all of the links in an installation to be simultaneously tested from a central point.

Data: *frequency* X Band (actual frequency to suit local regulations); *range* self setting 20 to 150m; *operating temperature* -35°C to +60°C; *power supply* 13 to 60V DC (negative earth) 200mA per link; *height* 137cm; *diameter* 32cm; *weight of each transmitter or receiver* 28kg; *packed weight of 1 link* (one transmitter and one receiver) 64kg.

GEC-Marconi
Pyroelectric Surveillance Head PSH 711

The PSH711 passive infra-red surveillance head is a small lightweight pyroelectric sensor unit consisting of a stainless steel body

Left and below left:
GEC-Marconi PSH 711.

housing a germanium lens, a single element compensated detector and a high-quality low noise amplifier. Designed for outdoor and indoor use, it is fully weatherproof. The outer surface of the custom designed germanium lens is hard carbon coated to give durability in harsh environments. A separate processing unit in a weatherproof housing contains all of the processing electronics. The input connection is via a weatherproof connector, and the output is via two 4mm terminals. The output may be connected to an audible alarm or to a suitable radio transmitter.

Data: Sensor Head *diameter* 24.5mm; *length* 116mm; *field of view at 50m* 2.2m x 0.65; *supply voltage* 6V to 9V; *supply current* (quiescent) <200A; *settling time after switch-on* <60sec; *output impedance* 0.3k; *operating temperature* -20°C to +50°C; *storage temperature* -20°C to +60°C. **Processing Unit** *length* 125mm; *width*

80mm; *depth* 57mm; *weight* (excluding battery) 750g; *battery* 9V MN1604 or equivalent; *relay output* 250mA, 200V DC, 3W max non-reactive load.

Connection Cable: 3-core screened cable with connectors; standard lengths available – 2m, 5m and 10m.

System performance: *target to background temperature difference* >2°C (assuming black body within the range -10°C to 50°C); *target size at 50m* >0.5m^2 within the field of view; *target velocity* 0.2ms^{-1} to 5ms^{-1} horizontal component normal to the line of sight; *target to sensor distance* 1m to >50m in clear weather conditions; *dead time after alarm* 2sec.

Pyroelectric Surveillance Head PSH 812

The PSH 812 is an upgraded long-range version of the well established PSH 711 device. The stainless steel body houses a germanium

Below: GEC-Marconi PSH 812.

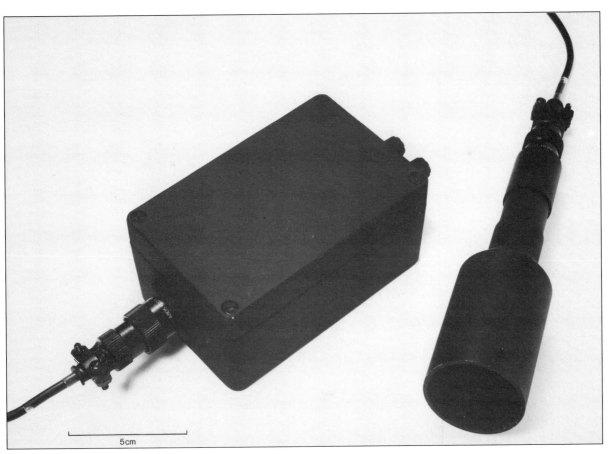

lens, a single-element compensated detector and a high-quality low noise amplifier. The head has been designed for indoor and outdoor use and is fully weatherproof, the outer surface of the custom-designed germanium lens being hard carbon coated to give excellent durability in harsh environments. Power supply and output connections are provided via a weatherproof connector. This device uses the same processing unit and connecting cable as the PSH711, ensuring full compatibility. Performance depends on weather conditions as well as target and background temperatures and emissivities, but human targets can normally be detected at ranges up to 100m, with 120m or more being achieved in good conditions. Typical battery life is over 3 months.

Data: Sensor Head *maximum diameter* (excluding sight) 46mm; *length* (excluding connector) 170mm; *weight* 380g; *field of view at 100m* 4m x 1.2m; *supply voltage* 6V to 9V; *supply current* (quiescent) <200A; *settling time after switch-on* <60sec; *output impedance* 0.3k; *operating temperature* -10°C to +50°C.

Processing Unit *length* 125mm; *width* 80mm; *depth* 57mm; *weight* (excluding battery) 750g; *battery* 9V MN1604; *relay output* 250mA, 200V 3W max d.v.

Connection Cable 3-core screened cable with connectors; standard lengths available – 2m, 5m and 10m.

System performance: The system will detect a target with greater than 95% probability under the following conditions: *target to background temperature difference* >2°C (assuming black body within the range -10°C to +50°C); *target size at 100m* >0.5m² within the field of view; *target velocity* 0.2ms⁻¹ to 5ms⁻¹ horizontal component normal to the line of sight; *target to sensor distance* 1m to >50m in clear weather conditions; *dead time after alarm* 2sec.

Pyroelectric Surveillance Head PSH 613

The PSH 613 is a miniature short-range equivalent of the well established PSH711. It has been a prime design requirement for the device head to be small and easily hidden; this has been accomplished by moving the high-performance preamplifier into a separate small 'in line' unit connected to the head by a short cable. A longer cable makes the final connection to the processor box, which is the same as that supplied with the PSH 711. This device will be suitable for a variety of indoor and outdoor applications, although the optical system will not withstand prolonged contact with water. It is envisaged that multiple-element and narrow-angle verisons will become available for specialised applications.

Data:
Sensor Head *diameter* 14.5mm; *length* (excluding connector) 52mm; *effective minimum length for installation* 130mm. *Cable length for preamplifier* 500mm; *field of view at 15m* 1m x 1m.

Preamplifier Module *dimensions* 30 x 35 x 88mm; *effective minimum length for installation* 160mm; *cable length for processor* 2m standard.

System Performance: The system will detect a target with greater than 95% probability under the following conditions: *target to background temperature difference* >2°C; *maximum range* 15m; *target size at 15m* >0.3m.

GEC-Marconi PIM 100.100 Thermal Video Camera

The PIM 100.100 is a lightweight camera employing an array of 10,000 detection elements. The performance of this compact, hand-held battery powered unit rivals that of other equipment, but requires no cooling of opto-mechanical manning mechanisms.

Data: Square array of pyroelectric infra-red detectors hybridised to a silicon multiplexer array; *number of elements* 10,000; *element pitch* 100μm x 100μm; *readout technology* switched MOSFET array with integral x8 inverting amplifier and multiplexer; *control inputs* clock and field initiate pulse; *operating frequency* 10Hz to 751Hz frame rate.

Geoquip Guardwire Protection System

Geoquip's Guardwire protection systems are based upon a revolutionary new sensor

Right: GEC-Marconi PSH 613.

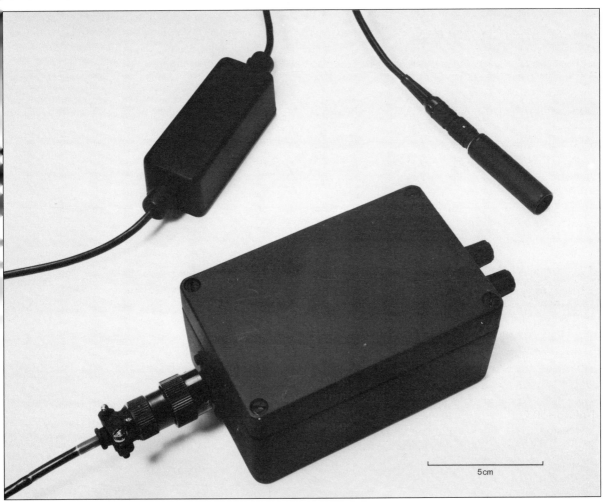

5 cm

cable, developed by Geoquip specifically for this purpose. The linear induction principle of the Guardwire cable overcomes most problems inherent in earlier systems using co-axial cables, results in a cleaner signal over a greatly extended length of cable, and allows greater flexibility in locating the control equipment. The cable can be used in a number of ways, depending on the application, the area to be protected and the availability of security guards. It can be attached to fencing, walls, pipelines, roofs, skylights etc. For aggressive situations, military applications of high-security protection of essential infrastructure services such as water, electricity, gas or oil, enhanced physical measures may be required.

Guardwire Sensortape: Combines the physical barrier of razor-sharp stainless steel barbs with the sensitivity of the Guardwire sensor cable, hidden and protected in the heart of the barbed tape. Any attempt to cut through or move the Sensortape barrier will be reported by the alarm system. The barrier itself will then delay the attackers long enough for defence forces to reach the scene. Special systems are available for fast deployment during riots, or as temporary barriers.

Guardian Intruder Detection System

Guardian is a self-contained, battery-powered intruder detection system specifically designed for applications where portability and rapid deployment are required and where an AC power source is not readily available. The protection of parked military, commercial and private aircraft against unauthorised

Left, top and bottom:
Guardian Intruder
Detection System

access is obviously of vital importance. While security controls of parking area perimeters, where used, are an important first line of defence, they cannot guarantee protection against determined professionals. Only security measures taken in the immediate vicinity of the parked aircraft can provide the necessary protection. At the same time, it is obviously out of the question, on grounds of both cost and available manpower, to guard every aircraft individually, particularly – as is often the case – when they are dispersed over large areas and in isolated locations.

The Guardian uses a passive infra-red detection system to sense IR (heat) energy radiating from people, vehicles or other objects moving into its field of view. A very-wide-angle lens, with 300° coverage, focuses the IR energy on to the sensors, which, through the associated electronic circuits, generate an alarm signal. This signal is used for different purposes in the two basic Guardian models:

Guardian I; a top-mounted light flashes and a high-powered klaxon sounds.

Guardian II; a built-in radio transmitter sends a coded signal to a remote receiver which indicates which detector has been alarmed.

Data: *detector range* Type 01 2m, Type 02 5m, Type 03 10m; *coverage* 300°; *internal power* 12V DC 10 Ah sealed lead-acid battery giving approx 100hr operation, in-built charger for 240/110V AC supply; *construction* all electronics housed in weatherproof container within standard plastic cone; *dimensions* (approx.) 1m high, base 500mm square; *weight* approx. 15kg.

International Security Services Perimeter Protection Equipment

Citadel Barbed Tape: Unlike barbed wire, which consists of twisted wire interwoven with single pointed barbs, barbed tape has a sharp-edged strip of extruded steel die-stamped into razor-like barbs at 25mm to 100mm intervals. Hand-holds are thus denied the intruder. There are two types: Barbed Tape Concertina, in which the tape is around a high tensile steel core, and Barbed Tape Obstacle, which is manufactured without the core. The former is intended for permanent sites, the latter as a re-usable riot control barrier. ISS also makes the Citadel Instant Barrier, a helical, long barbed tape concertina joined by lengths of high-tensile wire housed in an aluminium container for speedy deployment and recovery. This makes 30m of 1,015mm diameter obstruction. Citadel Rota-Barb is a 'cheval de frise' rotary-mounted tape system. ISS also supplies security doors, complete fencing systems and vehicle barriers, including Citadel Auto Stop and Truck Stop, which are sur-

Below: International Security Services Perimeter Protection. Short and Medium Barbed Tape (left). Long Barbed Tape (right).

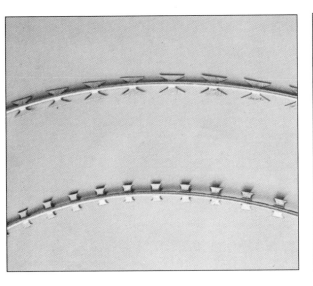

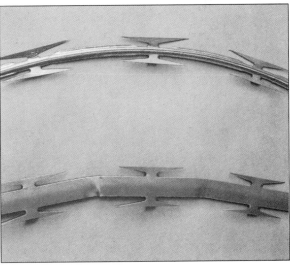

Left: International Security Services Perimeter Protection.

face mounted 'sleeping policemen' type flip-up obstructions intended to impale an intruding vehicle.

Lion Helmet Torch

This helmet torch is suitable for police, EOD teams, search teams and house entry or assault teams. It has variable focus and spot and wide beam use, and an endurance of 6/7 hours with a standard bulb or 2/3 hours with halogen.

Employment: British MOD, police forces.
Data: *weight* 100g without batteries; *range* approx. 80m.

Nitech X-cell Portable Lighting
The G00H Sabre

The G00H sabre portable rechargeable torch is designed for military and police use. It can operate continuously for 70 minutes, and can be charged directly either from mains (AC line) or any low-voltage (vehicle supply) between 8 and 30V. It is extremely robust, and is designed to float beam-up in water. An infra-red filter is available.

Employment: British MOD, various police forces.

Data: *weight* 1.11g; *dimensions* 210 x 124 x 135mm; *beam output* 500,000CP; *continuous*

Right: Lion Helmet
Torch.

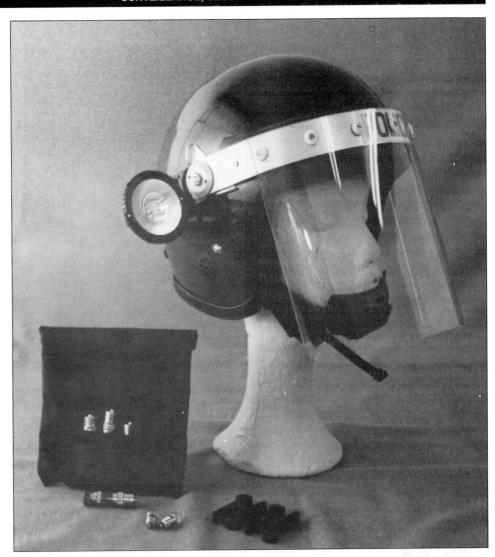

Right: Nitech Portable
Light.

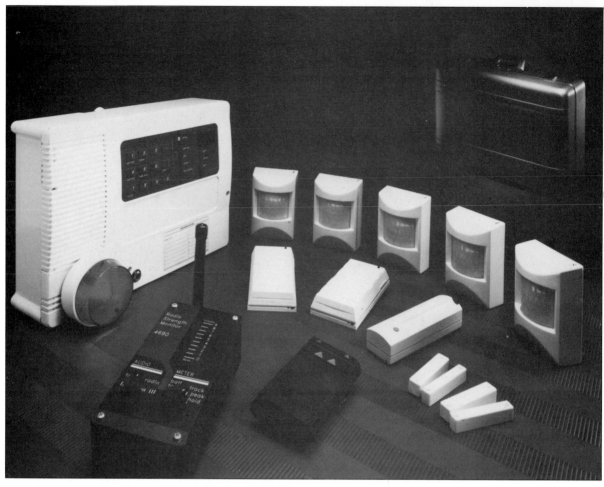

operating time 70min; *maximum recharge time* 16-18hr; *environmental tolerance* -40°C to +60°C; *resistance* impact, water, most chemicals; *recharge cycles* up to 3,000.

Paladin Portable Protector

The Paladin Protector has been specifically designed as a portable self-contained alarm system for those requiring an extra level of protection. It comes complete in its own case and can be activated immediately. The Protector consists of a control unit and eight sensors. Each of the sensors has its own intruder code. If any of them are activated they transmit that code to the control unit, which is continually monitoring each sensor. If more than one sensor is activated at the same time, the control unit will automatically scroll each unit on a display, giving an immediate visual warning of the breaches in security.

Provided the position of each unit has been recorded, it also gives the operator the location of any breach. Apart from a visual display, the control unit will warn of a breach of security by way of a flashing light and an audible tone. As circumstances might require silent monitoring, the audible tone can be switched off or listened to via headphones. The sensors will transmit up to 45.75m, depending on the location.

Pilkington Passive Night Vision Devices
Eagle Long Range Hand Held Night Vision Device

Eagle is a lightweight, long-range passive night device. It features a catadioptric lens configuration and houses a second-generation, micro channel plate image-intensifier tube which affords very high gain within

Above: Paladin Portable Protector.

Right: Pilkington Eagle Long Range Hand Held Night Vision Device

tight constraints of dimension and weight. The equipment weighs under 4kg, yet offers the range capability of first-generation systems weighing over 20kg. The system can recognise a man-sized target at 500m in starlight 10^{-3} lux conditions. The system is completely passive (undetectable), and security eyepads on the binocular eyepiece prevent any stray light from illuminating the user's face. The eyepiece allows simultaneous bioptic viewing, thus providing a large degree of user comfort.

Employment: Eagle has been sold to several customers worldwide.

Snipe Individual Weapon Sight

Snipe is a compact, lightweight night sight designed to meet a demanding military specification for weapon-aiming sights. Featuring the latest advanced technology in electro-optics, Snipe has a catadioptric lens configuration and an 18mm micro channel plate image-intensifier tube. With power derived from two 1.5V commercially available batteries, Snipe affords a very high gain and a field of view of 15°, with overall magnification of x2.3. A feature of the second-generation tube is that bright sources of light such as muzzle flashes or headlights become localised in the image and do not cause a washed-out view. The wide field of view permits quick target acquisition, and Snipe is adaptable to a large number of weapons. An adjustable internal aiming graticule is incorporated; this can be illuminated to assist vision when viewing objects of varying contrast.

Left: Snipe Individual Weapon Sight

Employment: Snipe is in service with the British Army and several armies worldwide.

Pilkington Fibre Optic Senors

Optical fibre material has been used commercially for over 20 years, and is now well established. However, one lesser-known application is that pioneered by Pilkington Security Systems, in which optical fibre serves as a sensor for intruder detection. This possibly offers the ultimate level of reliability, freedom from false alarms and high probability of intruder detection. Weather changes, windborne litter, small animals and long grass do not trigger false alarms. Because the system is based on light transmission rather than electrical, it is not possible to bypass it by bridging or tapping. Immunity to radio frequencies, electrical interference, noise and vibration are also qualities of optical-fibre-based security, which has been adopted by governments and industrial/commercial operations worldwide.

Plessey Perimeter Protection System 3PS

This is an intruder detection system that relies on special co-axial cable that can be concealed on a perimeter wall or buried in the ground. If an intruder enters the area near the cable an alarm is triggered. Unlike many beam-breaking systems, detection is effected by the whole body of the intruder, thus giving a better discrimination against birds and small animals. When used in open ground, the equipment can be completely concealed by being buried at depths of up to 0.5m. Irregular local topography presents no prob-

lems. The system comprises an electronic driver unit connected to a pair of radiating co-axial cables, each up to 200m long, separated by approximately 2m. The cable pair is arranged to follow the perimeter or boundary of the site to be protected. Movement of an intruder in the vicinity of the cable triggers an alarm, which is indicated at a control centre. One of the cables is connected to a low-power r.f. transmitter, the other to a receiver. The movement of human intruders disturbs the r.f. field established between the cables such that an imbalance occurs. This generates the alarm signal.

The 3PS cable pair can follow the lie-of-the-land and does not depend upon line-of-sight conditions. It can ideally be concealed by being buried or hidden behind the walls, and is thus difficult to detect. Cables can be laid under road surfaces or concrete. The cable pair can follow changes in direction, and thus the full 200m length can be used irrespective of the number of corners there may be on the perimeter. This compares favourably with systems that depend on a clear line of sight between transmitter and receiver units. For sites where the total perimeter exceeds 200m, two or more

Above: Quartz Halogen Search-Lites.

sets and associated cables can be used in tandem to provide full boundary protection. Each sector provides independent alarm indications at the control centre without electrical interaction between equipment.
Data: *dimensions of drive unit* 20cm x 15cm x 10cm; *weight of drive unit* 2.5kg; *selector length* up to 200m; *detector dimensions* 1.2m high x 3m wide.

Quartz Halogen Search-Lites

This portable searchlight system is ideal for house siege or ambush situations. It has a range in excess of 1 mile and is five times more powerful than a car headlight. It is operated either off a 12V vehicle supply or a nitech 12V shoulder mounted power pack. There are two versions, the SL1 and SL2.
Data: *dimensions* 210 x 120mm (SL1), 270 x 160mm (SL2); *power pack* 195 x 190 x 78mm.

Power-lite Torches Power-lite torches come in four models, all suitable for military or police use.

Racal CLASSIC Remote Ground Sensor System RGS 2740

Racal-SES and the Royal Signals and Radar Establishment (RSRE) successfully conclud-

Power-lite Torches

Model	Weight (with batteries)	Candlepower	Dimensions	Batteries
PL1	115g	10,000	145mm x 20mm	2 x AA supplied
PL2	485g	30,000	260mm x 33mm	2 x D cell not supplied
PL3	610g	50,000	320mm x 33mm	3 x D cell not supplied
PL5	825g	70,000	450mm x 33mm	5 x D cell not supplied

Above: Power-lite Torches.

ed Project LASS (Local Area Sensor System), which detects, classifies and remotely displays 'target' information on personnel and wheeled and tracked vehicles. Extensive trials in association with RSRE proved this ground sensor system to be highly effective and discriminating in its target classification, with a low false-alarm rate unequalled by similar equipment. CLASSIC (Covert Local Area Sensor System for Intrusion Classification), is an extension of LASS, offering deployment flexibility and additional sensor (e.g., infra-red) capability. The basic system consists of two main units, the sensor and the monitor. Sensor units, up to eight of which may be used with each monitor, are designed to be hand-emplaced at strategic points where there is the likelihood of personnel and/or vehicle intrusion. Each sensor is coupled to a transducer, either a geophone or an infra-red detector. The unit contains signal processing circuitry, which classifies the input and broadcasts a tone-coded message

by means of a built-in VHF FM transmitter. The monitor unit receives the VHF FM signal, decodes the data and presents the information on an LED display to show sensor identification, type and frequency of intrusion. To extend the range of the sensor transmission, a relay unit is available to receive and retransmit signals from the sensor unit; this is of particular value in areas of poor direct radio propagation. CLASSIC is a modular system incorporating a range of optional accessories, including alternative antennas and battery units, transducers/pressure pad switches and a hard-copy printer to meet the requirements of a wide range of ground sensor applications.

Simrad GN Night Vision Goggles
The GN1 Night Vision Goggles are based on a new unique patented design incorporating a folded optical path. This results in an extremely compact and lightweight piece of equipment. The depth is half that of other

221

Above: Simrad GN1 Night Vision Goggles.

existing goggles, dramatically reducing strain on the neck muscles. The GN1 is worn with a lightweight face mask. A dovetail enables the GN1 to be clipped on to the face mask or helmet. This mounting system also ensures that the distance between the face and the goggles can be adjusted for optimum viewing over the field of view. An add-on eyepiece prism system, providing dual vision, is optional. With this system the GN1 will provide combined day and night vision, allowing easy reading of instruments for vehicle drivers and pilots.

Data: Optical *objective lens focal length* 26mm, *relative aperture* f/1; *magnification* x1; *field of view* 40°; *focusing range* 20cm to infinity; *eyepiece dioptre adjustment* +2 to -6 diopters; *eye relief distance* 20mm; *high contrast resolution* 1.5mrad. **Physical** (incl. batteries, excl. mask) *weight* 390g; *width* 157.5mm; *height* 72mm; *depth* 58mm.

Thorn EMI Security Devices
Watermark Magnetics

Plastic cards with conventionally encoded magnetic strips have become universally accepted over the past twenty years, and during this time the encoding technique for storing information has changed very little. Using readily available modern technology it is now relatively easy and cheap for criminals to alter or copy the encoded data on the ubiquitous plastic card. As valuable encoded data becomes more vulnerable, so the number of fraud attacks increases, and it is now generally agreed that the current level of fraud has reached an unacceptable level. Watermark Magnetics tape contains encoded information that is permanently bonded into the magnetic oxide coating. It cannot be copied or altered without destroying its structure. By developing a system to read the Watermark Magnetics encoding, Thorn

Above: Thorn EMI Watermark Magnetics.

EMI has enhanced the security features of Watermark Magnetics. This reading system will destroy most fraudulent attempts to simulate Watermark Magnetics, and it also checks for two undisclosed parameters found only in genuine Watermark Magnetics tape.

Employment: Several UK police forces, British Telecom, UK government establishments and the British Central Electricity Generating Board.

UNITED STATES

Javelin Electronics Night Vision Equipment
Model 220

Javelin Electronics of Los Angeles, California, has developed Model 220 for use with TV and photographic cameras, and for mounting on rifles. The equipment can be mounted on a tripod and used with a binocular viewer, enabling the operator to use both eyes during long surveillance duties.

Variants: Model 221 is essentially the same as 220, but incorporates a focal plane iris to reduce the field of view and eliminate bright lights from the edge of a scene, which makes it more suitable for use in an urban area.

Employment: Numerous US police departments, Army, Navy, Air Force, FBI, Secret Service, CIA, Australia, Brazil, Canada, Chile, Colombia, Ecuador, France, Iraq, Italy, Japan, Kuwait, Malaysia, Mexico, Panama, Philippines, Puerto Rico, Taiwan, Switzerland, Venezuela, West Germany, Zambia.

Data: *length* 21.5cm; *diameter* 6.7cm; *weight* 1.3kg; *intensifier gain* x50,000.

Model 222

A second-generation night viewing device

that, because of its light weight, is particularly suitable for attachment to cameras.

Employment: As Model 220.

Data: *length* 10.8cm; *weight* 0.95kg; *intensifier gain* x45,000.

Model 223

Designed specifically for military and police applications, this model is currently in use in many countries. It can be adapted to fit almost any rifle, and can be used for observation in the field and for aiming a weapon at night.

Employment: As for Javelin Model 220.

Data: *length* 33cm; *diameter* 9.9cm; *weight* 1.87kg; *intensifier gain* x50,000.

Model 226

This has a binocular viewer on a swinging door-type mount, with an optional adjacent swinging door for attachment of a TV or photographic camera. The advantage of this arrangement is that a target can be watched by means of a binocular viewer, and then within seconds the doors can be changed to position a camera to photograph the scene.

Employment: As for Javelin Model 220.

Data: *length* 45.7cm; *diameter* 10.2cm; *weight* 6.1kg; *intensifier gain* x100,000.

Model 229

This is capable of locating and identifying targets at ranges in excess of 1,000m. The

Right: Cohu 4910 Surveillance Camera.

Below: Javelin Model 223 Night Vision Device.

target can be pinpointed by reading the co-ordinates on the azimuth and elevation scales on the base of the device. Model 229 is particularly suitable for use in observation posts in urban or rural areas.

Employment: US Army, US Coastguard, and armies throughout the world.

Data: *length* 83.8cm; *diameter* 26cm; *weight* 17kg; *magnification* x7; *field of view* 9°; *intensifier gain* x65,000; *range* 1,000m.

Cohu Surveillance Cameras

Designed and manufactured in the USA for over 40 years, Cohu Cameras are high resolution and extremely sensitive.

4710 and 4810 series: The 4710 and 4810 Series monochrome CCD camera provides high-resolution pictures with sensitivity as high as .07 lux. The blemish-free frame transfer image sensor provides pixel-to-pixel contrast variation of less than 5 per cent, with zero geometric distortion and no lag or image retention. Programmable jumpers select AGC on/off, auto black level, gamma, and a variety of synchronisation modes. Some available options include increased S/N to 60dB, spectrum coverage from 200nm to 1,050nm, long-term integrate for sensitivity increase to 0.005 lux, removal of imager faceplate for fibre-optic and laser applications, and painting with logo to client specifications.

Remote Head Cameras: Cohu's Monochrome Remote-Head CCD Cameras bring new flexibility to OEM design engineers and end users across a broad range of applications. The remote camera head is ideally suited for mounting on microscopes, robots, and other equipment with size and weight limitations. As with all Cohu CCD cameras, these cameras provide excellent resolution, sensitivity, and signal-to-noise characteristics. The $\frac{1}{2}$in format imager provides pixel-to-pixel contrast variation of less than 5 per cent, with zero geometric distortion and no lag or image retention. The 6500 Series Scientific Remote-Head Camera features front-panel control of gain, black level offset, auto black, gamma, sharpness, image polarity, shutter speed, and test pattern mode. This permits the user to extend dynamic range of the image (histogram stretch) before image acquisition by an image processor. The 6500 Series camera also provides an auxiliary connection to allow integration times to be varied between 1/30 second and 4 seconds.

Sure Fire Tactical Lights

A range of Sure-Fire Tactical Lights are available for fitting on to different weapon systems. The beam is aligned with the weapon, and by pointing the beam the weapon is automatically pointed at the target. The system is very light (0.15kg) and yet dazzlingly bright. Thus the target is blinded and unable to see the person pointing the light at him.

Employment: US Special Forces, Federal, State and local SWAT teams.

Sure Fire Tactical Lights

	Laser Products Sure Fire 6P Flashlight	Typical 5-cell Professional Flashlight
Size	4.9" x 1.25" dia.	15.5" x 2.25" dia
Weight	0.3lb.	2.5lb.
Construction	Aluminium	Aluminium
Lamp Type	Super Xenon	Krypton
Lamp Wattage Rating	6 W	4.4 W
Lamp Output Rating	11.5 MSCP	6.6 MSCP
Battery Type	Duracell Lithium	Alkaline
Battery No and Size	Two DL123A Cells	Five D-Cells
Battery Weight	0.08 lb	1.46 lb

7
Special Communications Equipment

Certain categories of IS equipment form an indispensable part of an anti-terrorist war. In particular, security forces are rarely in a position, particularly in an urban environment, to use conventional radio equipment; by and large it is too heavy, bulky and complex. Conventional military radio sets are not efficient in built-up areas, for they require line-of-sight or near-line-of-sight transmission paths for best results. Special radio equipment has therefore been developed for

IS and police work. In situations where security forces are operating from permanent bases, it is important that transmissions are scrambled or in cipher. This section of the book therefore includes some examples of portable scrambling and cipher equipment, in addition to examples of radio equipment suitable for use in IS situations. Anti-terrorist operations involve the detection of illicit transmitters, and some examples of transmitter detectors and direction-finding equip-

Below: Winkelmann Model 300 Counter-surveillance Receiver.

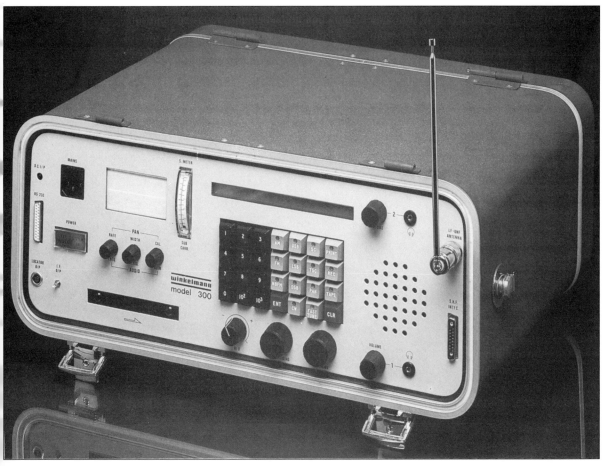

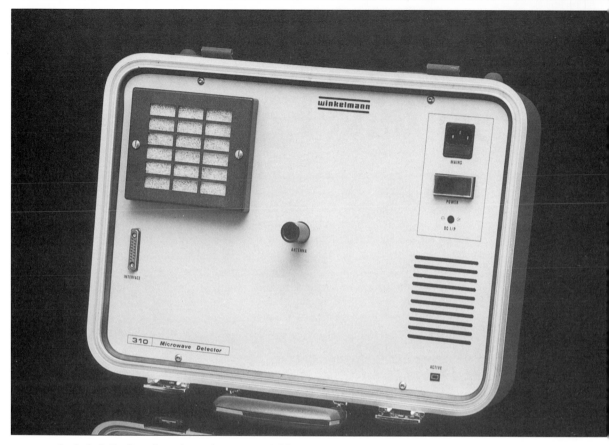

ment are included. Radio-microphone detection, surveillance tape recorders and other items of bugging equipment are more accurately categorised as espionage or anti-espionage equipment.

Brief mention must be made of automatic data processing (ADP) equipment in the context of IS operations. Increasing use is being made of ADP systems to speed the passage of information and for data logging. In particular it is possible to computerise vehicle data records, so that security forces can be alerted concerning lost, stolen or hijacked vehicles. Similarly, information and intelligence records previously handled by security forces on a card index system lend themselves to computerisation. But learning to live with ADP systems in the context of security has its problems. Many sections of the public, even in a terrorist situation, find it difficult to accept that private citizens' details are stored in an ADP system, viewing this as an erosion of individual liberty.

ADP systems also have problems for their user. The speed and spread of data dissemination means that the onus is on the *originator* of information to update his data constantly and not keep it in his head as 'background' if the system is to be valid for all the other users who have access to it. This could lead to a state of mind in which an incident or person that elicited no active response from an ADP record system is of no interest or significance. This chapter will not include photographs of ADP systems; pictures of 'black boxes' are not interesting or significant. However, it is important that the place of ADP systems in the fight against terrorism be appreciated.

Communications in an IS context can be considered in two main categories.

● Strategic Communications. Secure, reliable communications between the political leader responsible for committing the force and the commanders of the government agencies on the ground are extremely impor-

Above: Winkelmann Model 310 Microwave Detector.

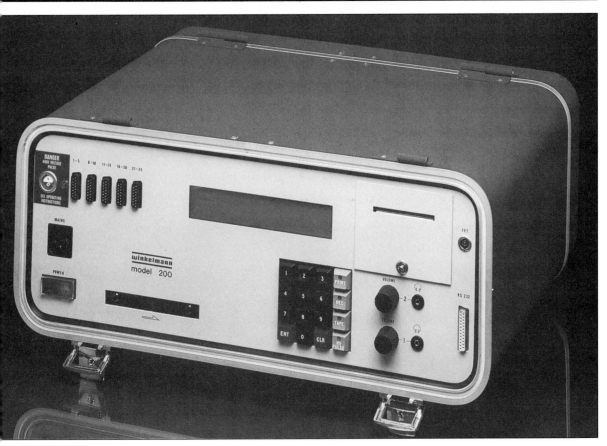

Above: Winkelmann Model 200 Telephone Line Analyzer.

tant. The political leadership requires up-to-date information on which to base decisions, and needs to be able to promulgate orders quickly. In practice this procedure usually involves a government crisis office manned by the responsible minister and his advisors (in secure communication with the head of state) and a tactical incident control centre; these communicate with one another by secure encrypted telephone.

● Force Tactical Communications. The force should be on one 'all-informed' radio net. This is essential if the all-important co-ordination between the different groups is to work. This net will ideally be encrypted, as terrorists are likely to be monitoring VHF and UHF frequencies. The net could be made up of the following elements:

1. Base station system in the force commander's HQ. This must provide the force commander with communications to his men throughout the likely area of operations and, at the same time, provide a link with the

police and the government official to whom he is responsible. He will therefore require at least two separate channels of communication, one to higher authority and one to his subordinate commander. That to higher authority will probably be a secure telephone link in most circumstances; that to his commanders will be a secure all-informed radio network. Both the force commander and his subordinate commanders may operate from vehicles or helicopters, so the force radio network must include sets suitable for use with foot patrols, vehicles and helicopters.

2. Company/team system. Similarly, the company or team commander will require communications upwards to the force commander and downwards to his sub-units or assault groups. His HQ will therefore be an outstation on the force commander's radio set, but will be the base station, or control, for communications with his sub-units or assault groups. In IS urban operations the platoon as a level or operational command will often be omitted; this may not be the case in rural operations. Thus the company commander is likely to have a large number of small sub-units (perhaps twelve or fifteen) under his command. These could be four to eight men strong and need to be in touch with company HQ at all times.

3. Individual hand-held receivers. Many of the small sub-units in a company (known in British Army parlance as 'bricks') will be operating in a sufficiently cohesive manner for radio contact between them to be neces-

sary. However, in some circumstances it may be appropriate for each member of a 'brick' to be in direct contact with the 'brick' commander by means of individual hand-held receivers. These should be small, compact and lightweight, and capable of withstanding exceptionally rough handling. They must be easily operated, bodyworn with a 'hands-off' operational capability to allow the user maximum freedom to use his weapons or other equipment. The system should be voice equipment in the VHF/UHF

Left: Winkelmann HR150 Hand-held Radio.

Above: Winkelmann MR150 Mobile Radio

frequency range, with a minimum of three switched channels, and it should contain built-in encryption. It should be able to be used with a covert earpiece: i.e. a condition that cuts off the loudspeaker (essential for sniper, bodyguard or covert roles). Similarly, it should be able to be used with discreet or covert microphones. Finally, it should be able to be used with throat microphones. This may, in certain circumstances, be useful for some members of a 'brick'; sometimes it may be necessary to limit this facility to

selected members to prevent congestion on the net during an operation.

An example of an unusually flexible and adaptable IS communications system is Cougarnet, manufactured by Racal, a British company specialising in military communications systems. A detailed specification of the Cougarnet concept will serve here as an example of the necessary parameters for an effective IS communications system. Cougarnet is not the only system of its kind, but it is one of the most effective, and one

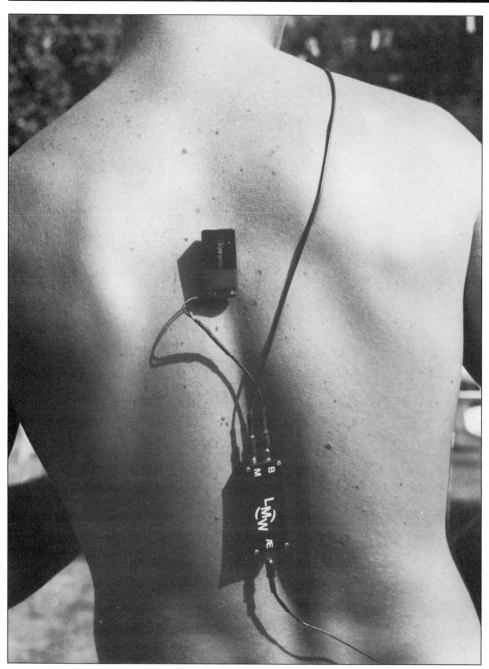

Left: LMW Covert Transmitter.

incorporating the latest technology. The British Army currently uses this equipment in Northern Ireland.

Cougarnet is a totally secure lightweight FM radio communications system, using a synthesizer-controlled hand-held radio – the very compact 'basic building block' of the modular system. This modular approach ensures that the system is easy to operate, and makes Cougarnet attractive to a wide range of military, paramilitary, security and emergency service units. The 2-watt personal radio can be converted easily into a high-powered radio by simple connection to an amplifier, and the unit can then be used as a static base station, or as a mobile or transportable manpack (depending on power supply). The radio can be changed from one role

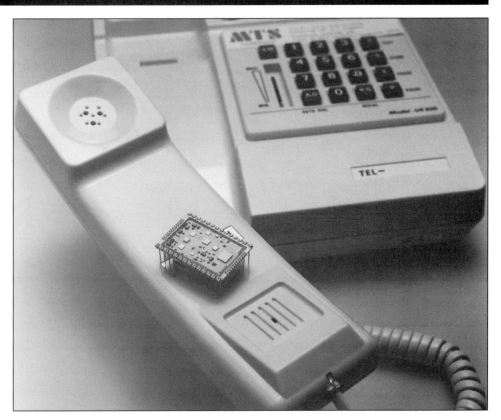

to another simply by altering the power supply. In the static role, power can be provided from an AC power supply; in the mobile role the vehicle supply will provide the power. A heavy-duty Ni-Cad battery is used for the transportable role.

The radio can be controlled remotely via an extended control unit, which allows the radio to be stored in a convenient place close to the antenna when being used in the mobile or static roles. At the same time, the radio is always easily available for use as a personal radio by removal from the amplifier and the connection of the battery, antenna and speaker/microphone. To ensure optimum flexibility in operation, the set has ten programmable channels to gain access to any of several networks. These may be single- or two-frequency simplex.

In operation, the Cougarnet system consists of a number of unattended talk-through stations linked together to allow users operating over different frequencies in different areas to communicate with each other. These links can be switched on or off from a central controller, allowing either independent operations or integration into a command net for combined operations. A station is equipped with two radios, and, in the event of the failure of one, the other is automatically activated. A method of continuous checking is built into the system during normal operation.

Although there has been a move towards push-button control in standard and mobile radio, it was felt that such controls, although perfect for normal environments, would not meet the demands likely to be placed upon them. For example, if an operator finds himself in the middle of an unruly crowd or in riot conditions, speed is vital, and rotary switches can be operated without looking at the radio, allowing him to concentrate on the real task in hand. The digital encryption modules built into Cougarnet allow two code settings to be used. This gives 'in net' privacy and security and is further enhanced by using a programmer or keyfill unit to change frequencies or codes. This technique eliminates errors and restricts the information to a 'need to know' basis.

Flexible and dependable communications are an indispensable part of all IS operations. In conventional war, operations are to some extent carried on by their own momentum – subordinate commanders are trained to continue to operate despite a break in radio communications, which may be the result of jamming, atmospheric conditions, mechanical failure, bad siting, nuclear effects or a number of other causes. IS operations require political direction, fine-tuning by operational commanders, the facility to negotiate with hijackers, for example, and instant reaction by assault forces. All of these demand totally reliable communications. This chapter includes a representative cross-section of the systems available.

ISRAEL

The Elbit Sniper Command, Control and Communication System

Elbit's SC-50505 is a sniper command, control and communication system designed to co-ordinate simultaneous firing by a group of five snipers by means of wireless transmission of each sniper's telescopic sight image in addition to a 'ready' indication mechanism. The system enables the operators to:

● Allocate targets to the snipers;
● Attain optimal setting of the moment of firing;
● Gain intelligence for planning;
● See the whole situation for the assaulting force, and for debriefing after combat.

Using continuous transmission of sight video imagery, the SC-50505 system provides the on-site commander with total control of the situation, and enables rescue/SWAT teams to take decisive action against terrorists while minimising the risk to hostages and law enforcement personnel. The capturing of each sniper's sight image (without degrading the sniper's optical channel) is achieved by means of a unique miniaturised unit containing mechanical interface to the telescope, an optical splitter and lens, a video camera head

Below: The Elbit Snipers co-ordination system.

and a light control mechanism.

Employment: Probably used by Israeli Security Services.

Data: *optical splitter* 100 x 55 x 45mm; *weight* 0.4kg; *splitter cable length* up to 2m; *wireless radio link operation range* in open area 5km, in urban area about 850m; *video transmitter power* up to 8W; *video transmission carrier frequency* around 800-950MHz; 150M of coaxial cable; *weight of loaded spool* 1.5kg; *displays* 4in CRT with brightness and contrast controls; *power supply* 12/24V DC, lithium batteries, 8hr operation.

SWITZERLAND

Riwosa Security Equipment
Mini Spy Detector

A portable electronic eavesdropping equipment detector, this consists of a transformer and circuit connected to a low-frequency generator and a frequency-scanning receiver. It allows security services to ensure that a room or vicinity is free of eavesdropping equipment or 'bugs'.

Data: *frequency range* 8-20MHz (scanning time 8sec), 6-1000MHz (scanning time 150sec); *temperature range* 0°C to 35°C; *operating time* 6-8hr; *battery charger* 220V; *dimensions* 42 x 31 x 8cm; *weight* 8kg.

Quick Alarm

This system enables security guards, policemen, or personnel of the armed forces to transmit a call for help invisibly to a central alarm centre. A switch-on insert located in the shoe enables the wearer to activate the emitter. The switch-on system is designed to permit its use with practically any type of 'walkie-talkie'. Not only is the alarm centre alerted, but all conversations are also transmitted, revealing the extent of the emergency.

Variants: For the security of particularly vulnerable personnel, a miniaturised emitter (rather than the 'walkie-talkie') can be attached by a suspender or wire holder to the individual to be protected.

Below: Riwosa Mini Spy Detector.

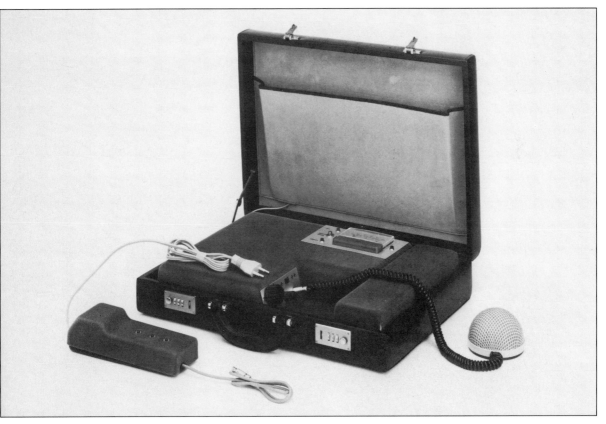

UNITED KINGDOM

Davies Industrial Communications Special Forces Assault Protection

CT100 Communications System: This is a personal communications system designed to overcome operational difficulties when using encrypted or digital personal radios. It provides good clear communications in high noise, electronic hearing protection, improved speech transmissions and improved signal reception in all situations. The Davies CT100 Assault Team Communication Harness comprises:

CT100E: An electronic ear defender headset type CT300/310 with an earphone for team radio and a lemo socket for connection to body harness CT100L. The electronic ear defender allows normal speech to pass at all times, with the ability to restrict, electronically, high-pressure sound from grenades and gunfire. Normal hearing levels are restored instantly after the loudest sound.

Above and left:
Davies Industrial Communications CT100 System

Right: Davies Industrial
Communications
CT100E System.

Reception from the assault team radio is reproduced in one side of the headset by a second earphone being incorporated into the earshell, providing good clear reception at all times.

CT100L: This body-worn microphone and switching unit has a large front-mounted 'Press To Talk' (PTT) button which can be operated by either hand. The unit has interconnect leads to body-worn radio and CT300/310 Electronic ear defenders, sockets for connection of the SF10 Respirator with integral microphone, and an additional PTT switch which may be worn on the wrist or on

237

a weapon. The body-worn microphone/ switching unit is fitted with an internal amplifier which can be set to the required radio transmission levels. When the SF10 Respirator is connected, the body-worn microphone is disabled. Both the body-worn or respirator microphones may be operated by depressing the PTT switch on the body or the secondary PTT switch on the wrist/weapon. All PTT switches are double-pole action.

CT100IM: A specially designed noise-cancelling microphone is housed within the SF10 Respirator, which only transmits speech from within the mask and excludes all external noise. When the SF10 Respirator is donned and the microphone connecting lead plugged in, the body-worn microphone is disabled.

4135 Firearms User Communications Harness: The 4135 Communications Harness is a flexible modular system designed to provide communications for armed officers in a variety of operational situations. Consisting of a junction box with sockets to accept a range of accessories, and fitted with a lanyard, it can be worn easily over or under

Above and left: Davies Industrial Communications 4135 Firearms User Communications Harness.

the clothing, and is clearly marked for ease of use. A covert microphone, earphone inductor and PTT switch can be connected, permitting the harness to be used in a discreet manner for undercover operations. The lapel microphone is particularly suited to use with low-level speech, and can be exchanged quickly for a respirator microphone. The audio output can be similarly changed from a covert inductor to a standard wired earphone, and the PTT switch can be changed from a covert type to a rifle-mounted or wrist-worn type. Unique colour-coded connectors and sockets on the junction box facilitate quick changes to suit the circumstances.

EMI Communications Security Devices
Bughound Concealed Transmitter Detection Device

The EMI Bughound radio-microphone detects and locates most 'bugs'– concealed transmitting electronic eavesdropping devices. It incorporates facilities for detecting devices using electrical mains wiring for carrier-borne signals, as well as those using

Right: EMI Bughound Concealed Transmitter Detection Device

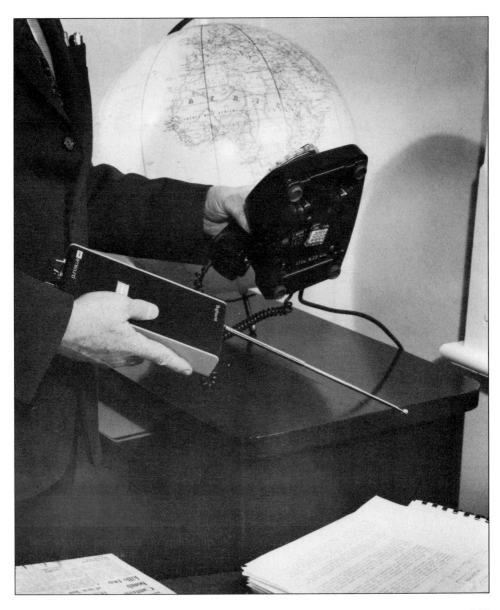

radio transmission techniques. The compact, portable unit provides audio and/or visual indication of the presence of 'bugs'. It is powered by self-contained batteries and has straightforward switch-operated self-test and search-mode controls. Detection of an eavesdropping transmitter device is registered by a red indication on the meter display, and a change in the tone heard in a small earphone monitor. Further verification of the presence of a device is possible in most cases by a second simple test routine, where its transmissions can be heard in clear audio through the earphone.

Telephone Scrambler Type 1313 Privateer

Developed by EMI Sound and Vision Equipment of Hayes, Privateer scrambles telephone conversations by inverting speech frequencies and producing a jumbled sound that can be understood only by a person at the other end of the line with a compatible unit. Privateer has commercial and military applications, and could be used at military or police static installations.

Variants: The portable version of Privateer, Type 1314, could have a police application, but is probably best suited to commercial use.

Left: EMI Telephone Scrambler Type 1313 Privateer

Employment: Numerous private companies in UK, Europe and the Middle East.
Data: *dimensions* 15.6 x 9.5 x 25.7cm; *weight* 4kg.

Lorraine Electronics TA 900 Telephone Line Monitor

One of the most serious threats to today's businessman is the possibility that his 'direct' telephone line is being listened to. Wire taps, series, parallel and infinity transmitters are readily available to those who wish to know more about private business affairs. The TA 900 offers a simple, cost-effective and reliable method of monitoring a telephone line and thereby improving the general level of security. This small desk-top unit will not only warn the user if conventional telephone surveillance equipment is in use, it will also help guard against the casual eavesdropper listening from an 'off-hook' extension.

Lorraine RFD Counter-Surveillance Protection

The RFD-X and RFD-XL have been designed to provide the individual with a simple and effective means of detecting and locating radio frequency surveillance devices. Radio signals are present in all areas, and the function of both detectors is to isolate and help identify transmissions that could represent a threat. The presence of a transmitter is indicated by a bar-graph display showing the degree of field strength, and thereby the relative proximity of the device. As the radio field strength increases, the detector also emits a faster audible 'bleep' to confirm direction. The detectors also provide a facility to listen to the offending transmitter (in crude form) through an inbuilt speaker. Each unit is supplied with a test module to simulate the environmental effect of being 'bugged' and also to give the user some practical experience in transmitter detection.

Below: Lorraine Electronics TA 900 Telephone Line Monitor.

Data: *size* 150 x 85 x 35mm (excluding detachable aerial); *power supply* self-contained PP3 battery (9V alkaline); *battery life* RFD-X 20hr, RFD-XL 12hr; *frequency range* RFD-X 10MHz, 1GHz; RFD-XL 10MHz, 2GHz; *detection* RFD-X FM, RFD-XL FM narrow, FM wide, AM; *sensitivity* 5mV at 100MHz; *display* progressive 10 digital bar-graph LED; *audio 1* progressive audible bleeper; *audio 2* speaker output

Left: Lorraine RFD Counter-Surveillance Protection

approximately 100mW, subject to acoustic feedback at close range.

Racal Communications Hunting Radio Direction Finding (RDF) Series 3200

The RDF3206 direction finding system has been specially designed for mobile operations in the VHF/UHF bands (25-512MHz). It is intended for use by internal security forces in 'hunting' illegal transmitters, and is well suited to operations in urban areas. The equipment can be installed in a variety of vehicles to fit the operational role, and there is full provision for concealment in the type of operation where secrecy is paramount. The system is based on Racal's well established RTA1470 series general-purpose DF equipment, but, by adapting the antenna design for mobile operations, a version has been produced that can be used in single station mode to home-in on a target transmission by taking successive bearings while on the move. It can also be used as part of a DF net in conjunction with other hunting vehicles or with a fixed DF site. By the addition of mast-mounted antennas (AE3020 series) the system can be quickly converted to fixed-location use with considerably enhanced performance.

Racal Cougarnet Communication System

The Cougarnet system has been designed to achieve area-wide coverage within the paramilitary environment. Maximum system flexibility is available to allow rapid deployment in the event of changing circumstances. All of the equipment has been designed, developed and produced to meet the exacting environmental conditions expected in the paramilitary area, particular attention being paid to ease of operation, often in difficult conditions. Coupled with this, well-proven technology, components and manufacturing techniques help to ensure high reliability and protection against EMP. The equipment throughout

Right: Racal Covert Personal Radio.

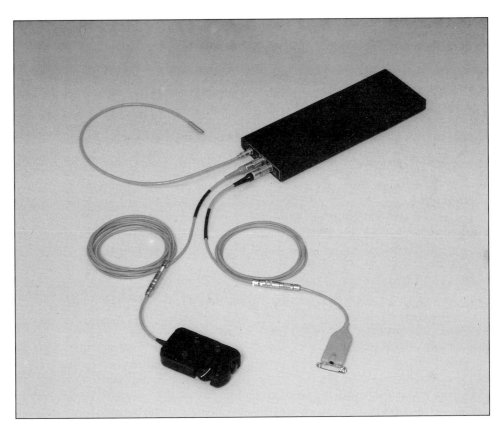

243

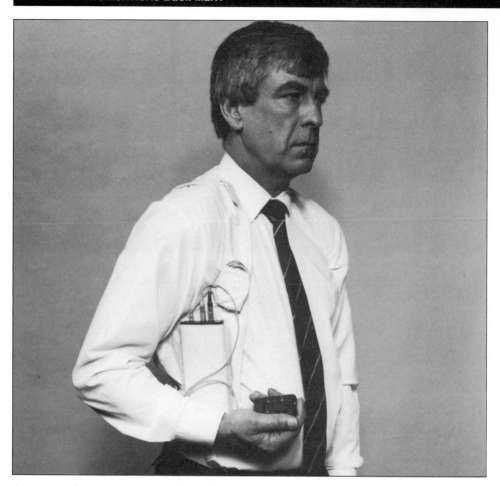

Left: Racal Covert
Personal Radio.

the system is synthesised, enabling simple reprogramming of channels, which could become necessary because of jamming, local interference or net redeployment. Both digitally encrypted and analogue speech can pass through the system. No engineering changes are necessary when passing either type of traffic, since the radios are designed to respond automatically to signals received and process them accordingly. To achieve full area-wide coverage both in rural and urban environments, VHF and UHF radios are available. The radio can be interlinked at will, to create an integrated and comprehensive net with complete area penetration over widely varying terrain. Strategically placed Talkthrough stations form the backbone of these nets. Often they will be sited in areas of high risk or inaccessibility, and to ensure continuity of operation all stations can be

equipped with hot standby systems. Full remote control and alarm facilities are available to monitor and control the system operators from a control location. For complex systems involving several networks, separate systems and operators' cells can be established.

System Control: The system is run from an Outstation Link Control Unit through which the system controller can address any Talkthrough site in the system and command changes or obtain status reports. Equally, any Talkthrough can radiate alarms which are fed back to the controller, who may take appropriate action.

Operations Control: When several individual networks are to be controlled from the same location, watchkeepers units are available for operational control of the system. These units allow an operator's watchkeeper to monitor the networks and, if the necessity

Right and below: Racal Cougarnet Area Communications System.

arises, to pass an individual network to an operations executive for control of a particular incident.

Internal Security Applications: The system provides an ideal communications network for internal security applications. Cougarnet's flexibility allows it be used for alerts where an incident has occurred. By deploying a Talkthrough station in the vicinity of the incident, an all-informed private communications network can quickly be established. If the optional digital security is used, no casual eavesdropper will be able to tell when communications are in progress, as the transmitted signal resembles white noise. Cougarnet outstations can be installed in vehicles, aircraft and boats or larger ships for offshore use. Different agencies can be equipped with their own networks and can operate independently of each other but, when the need arises, the systems can be linked to create an effective all-informed network to deal with specific incidents and then returned to normal when the incident is over.

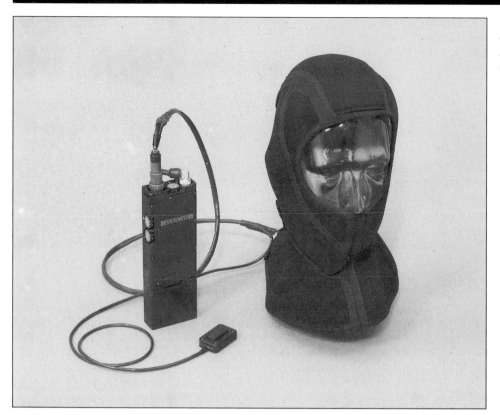

Left: Waterproof version of the Racal Cougarnet Area Communications System.

Left: Cougar Personal Radio.

Cougarnet Covert Personnel Radio PRM 4735

The PRM 4735 is an extremely compact radio specifically designed for covert applications. The basic radio consists of three units which are separated to give maximum flexibility in terms of distribution and configuration. The PRM 4735 Transceiver contains all the radio and cryptographic electronics in a compact slim unit which is ideal for carrying unobtrusively about the person. The MA 4736 rechargeable NiCad battery supplies the power for the transceiver, and can either be attached to the radio or remotely positioned. The MA 4737A Radio Control Unit (RCU) is designed to fit in the palm of the hand, giving control of on/off volume, channel setting, PH and voice. These controls have been designed to enable operation by touch alone. The A and B models provide four-channel selection, while the C model provides eight channels.

Employment: British Army and a range of police and military forces worldwide.

Data: *frequency range* PRM 4735L 76-8MHz, PRM 4735HA 138-156MHz; PRM 3745HB 154-172MHz; *channels* 10 programmable; *channel spacing* 25KHz; *supply* 7.2V nominal; *battery life* 3.7hr; *transceiver* 13 x 75 x 16.1mm, 350g; *battery* 69 x 75 x 16.6mm, 150g; *RCV* 70 x 40 x 20mm, 75g.

Security Research Helmet Receiver

Security Research developed the Helmet Receiver for emergency and riot communications. The receiver is compatible with commercial hand-held transmitters, and can be added to existing networks. It is available in low-band VHF and high-band VHF or UHF, and the frequency can be altered by a simple change of the crystal within the bandwidth. The sound is received via an acoustic transducer mounted inside the padding of the helmet, creating no hazard to the wearer. The antenna is spiralled round the acoustic tube, leaving no trailing wires. A rotary switch selects 'low', 'medium', or 'high' so that users can adjust the sound level to their environment. The receiver is powered by a disposable/rechargeable PP3 battery in a push-in holder, giving a minimum of eight hours of use.

Data: *dimensions* 110 x 105 x 35mm; *weight* 200g; *frequencies* 75-85MHz or 150-170MHz (VHF) and 420-520MHz (UHF).

Static/Mobile/Transportable System SRM 4515

The Static, Mobile and Transportable (SMT) unit is an integral part of the Racal Cougarnet system which can be configured as a base station, a vehicle station or as a manpack radio. The Cougar personal radio type PRM 4515 simply plugs into the SMT unit for instant conversion to a high-power radio sys-

Below: Security Research Helmet Receiver.

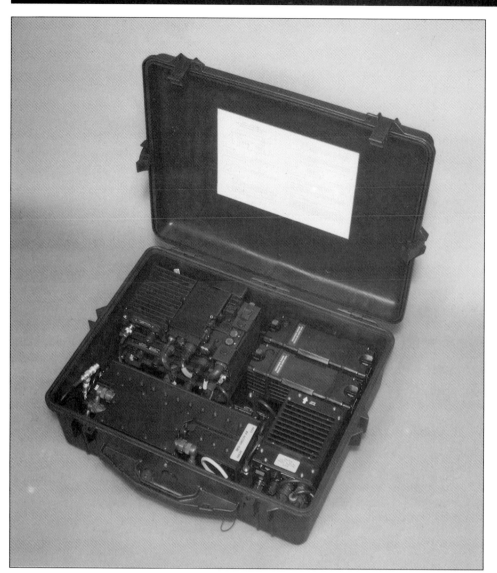

tem capable of multi-role operation dependant upon power supply. A quick-release mechanism allows an operator to remove the PRM 4515 at any time for use as a normal personal radio. Operating in the VHF and UHF personal frequency bands, the transmitter output may be 20W, 10W or 2W at VHF, or 10W, 5W or 2W at UHF. Ten pre-programmed operating channels are available, and channel frequencies are easily changed with a fill gun. Regardless of the role in which the SMT is used, any of the channels may be nominated for single- or two-frequency simplex operation. A minimum of external controls ensures easy operation and

thereby operator confidence. Secure speech operation is available by incorporating a personal radio fitted with digital encryption.

Employment: British Army and a range of military and police forces worldwide.

Data: *frequency range* TA 4523L 66-88MHz, TA 4523HA 132-156MHz, TA 4523HB 148-174MHz, TA 4523UA 380-440MHz, TA 4523UB 420-470MHz; *power supply* base station, mains PSU.MA4107C; mobile, 12V operates directly via 2-way connector, 24V operates via 24/12V vehicle adapter ST791750; manpack, rechargeable 12V battery MA4025D, optional 5-way battery charger MA4529A; *dimensions* (TA

Right: Cougarnet Static Base Station.

Below: The Cougar SMT Static/Mobile/Trans-portable) Power Amplifier and Transceiver installed on a motorcycle.

4523+PRM 4515) without battery, height 75mm, width 230mm, depth 150mm; with battery, height 75mm, width 230mm, depth 240mm; *weight* without battery 2.8kg, with battery 5.2kg.

Sonic Communications Equipment

Sonic Communications manufactures a range of covert communications equipment including radios (the SMC 517 L10 and SMC 545 L14), as well as ear devices and surveillance sports bags and handbags. The latter two incorporate covert listening equipment.

UNITED STATES

CSS Communications Control Inc

CSS manufactures wiretap detectors, telephone scramblers, tape recorder detectors, bomb detectors, kidnap tracking systems and infra-red viewers.

The Privacy Protector VL 33

Micro-miniaturised for portability, this system is actually of the same high quality as equipment used by professionals. In seconds, the VL 33 will scan a room for any bugs or transmitters hidden from view. As you approach the vicinity of a possible bug, a series of diodes will illuminate. As the searcher gets closer, more lights illuminate. It then verifies the eavesdropping device by letting you listen to the actual conversation.

Variants: The VL34 detects the presence of a hidden radio transmitter across the room. Then, with its 'phase lock loop circuitry', the VL34 even verifies that the transmitter has a microphone and that it is an actual bug. Only then will the panel of alarm lights be joined by a yellow verification light. This virtually rules out mistakes. A simple touch of the sensor pad resets the system for future use in an instant. Operation of the Privacy Protectors is almost totally automatic, and the retractable antennas steer the user right to the location of the bug. Since they are the size of a cigarette pack, both the VL33 and VL34 will perform a quick electronic sweep virtually any time, anywhere.

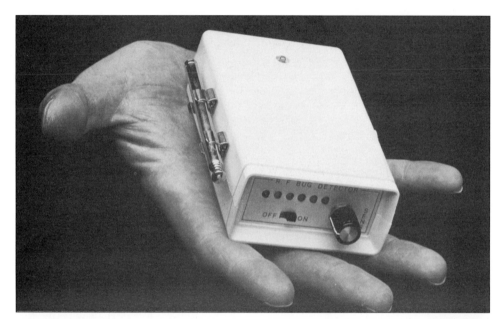

Left: The Privacy Protector VL 33

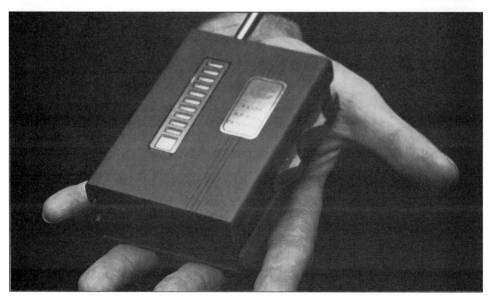

Left: The Privacy Protector VL 34

8

Assault Equipment

Assault equipment is used by counter-terrorist forces to gain quick entry into buildings occupied by terrorists. Perhaps the most famous incident of this kind was the SAS assault on the Iranian Embassy in London in May 1980, but there have been numerous other incidents around the world since that date. They have included kidnappers holding hostages, deranged gunmen threatening to blow up children in a school building, and aircraft hijackers threatening the lives of passengers and crew. In all of these cases specialist assault teams have been employed, using a range of equipment.

This equipment includes specially shaped explosive charges to blow holes in walls or blow in doors or windows, hydraulic equipment to force doors, listening and viewing equipment to monitor terrorists inside a building before an assault, abseiling (repelling) equipment to gain entry via windows and balconies from above, special lad-

ders to gain entry from below, and compressed-air mortars to fire grappling equipment on to a building. Stun grenades can also be used in an assault. They first came to the public's attention in the October 1977 Mogadishu hijack, when the SAS provided technical assistance (including stun grenades) to the German anti-terrorist force, GSG 9. They were also used by the SAS in May 1980 during the storming of the Iranian Embassy and by the French GIGN in the Christmas 1994 Marseilles aircraft assault. The purpose of the grenades is to shock the terrorists into temporary inactivity and to distract them .while entry is gained to the building or aircraft in which hostages are being held. The grenades produce one or more loud detonations and a blinding flash. The grenade body is usually made from card or rubber, and contains flash-powder of varying types.

Stun grenades are designed to be non-lethal, but the premature detonation of

Below: LEI Mk 2 Suppressed .22 pistol.

Left: Vz61 Skorpion 7.65mm machine pistol with disassembled suppressor.

Right: Mini Uzi 9mm SMG fitted with a suppressor.

Left: Vz61 Skorpion 7.65mm machine pistol with assembled suppressor.

Right: AMD-65 7.62 x 39mm SMG. Hungarian SMG version of the AK47.

Left: Makarov Wz63 9 x 18 machine pistol.

some types could severely injure the thrower. They are much like the British Army's training grenade, the Thunderflash, which can blow a hand off if the thrower does not get rid of the device the second he has ignited it. Many manufacturers in the UK, France, Germany and the USA now produce stun grenades. The British Army stun grenade used by the SAS is a classified item of equipment, and is therefore not illustrated in this volume. However, it is sometimes necessary to eliminate key terrorists either just before or during an assault, to protect the lives of innocent people. For this, super rifles can be used to target particularly dangerous individuals at long range. A representative cross-section is included in this chapter.

In recent years there has been an increase in assault situations, as terrorists become more determined to achieve their ends by any means necessary. Thus we have seen a series of aircraft hijackings in the former Soviet Union, a school siege in France, an assault on Kashmiri terrorists holding British hostages in Delhi, the Waco siege in the United States and a series of less dramatic police sieges in the UK. Assault equipment is suddenly more imortant for special forces, the police and SWAT teams.

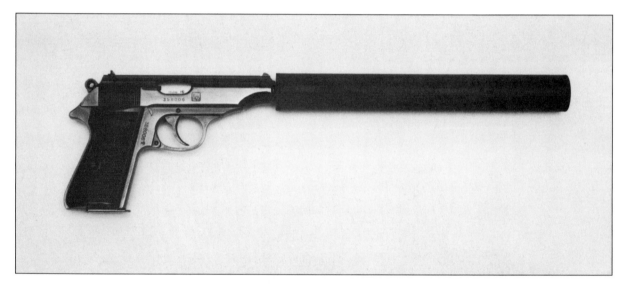

Below: Walther PP .38ACP pistol fitted with a suppressor.

Bottom: HK P7 9mm pistol fitted with a suppresor.

Right: Russian 5.45 x18mm PSM pistol.

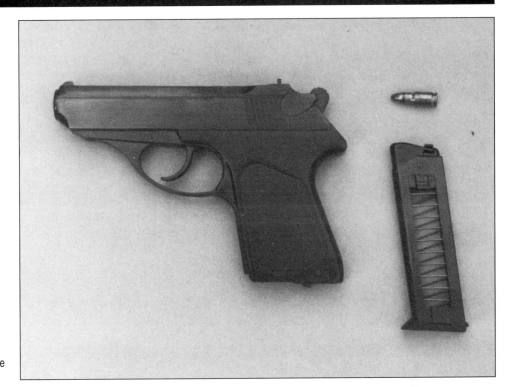

Below: Showing the difference in size between the Russian 9mm Makarov (lower left), the 5.45mm PSM (upper right) and the rare 9mm M Stechkin.

Right and below: The Chinese .22 knife pistol. The thumb rests on the trigger.

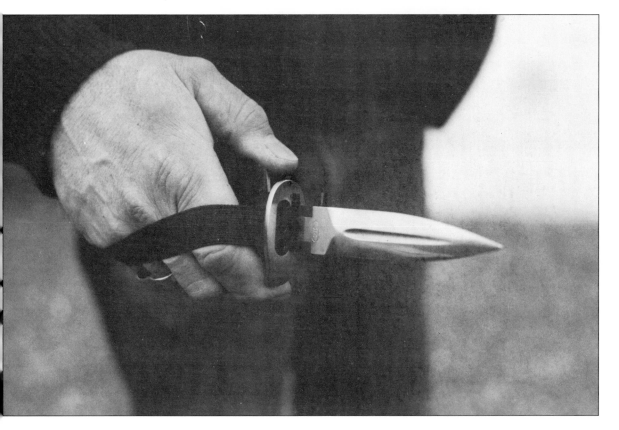

Opposite page: Security operatives fully equipped, showing machine pistol, automatic pistol, body armour, helmets, gas masks and radios.

AUSTRIA

Steyr Assault Weapons

The Steyr family of weapons are used by police and special forces the world over.

AUG/Police Calibre 5.56

This weapon is ideally suited for close-range assault operations. It is lightweight, accurate and has impressive stopping powers.

Data: *calibre* 5.56 x 45mm; *barrel length* 407mm; *overall length* 700mm; *overall height* 266mm; *weight without magazine* 3.3kg; *magazine capacity* 30 rounds; *operation* gas-operated; *firing mode* semi/automatic and automatic; *sighting* optical.

AUG 9mm Carbine

A highly accurate police weapon with an optical barrel adapter for CS and CN rifle grenades.

Data: *calibre* 9 x 19mm; *barrel length* 420mm; *overall length* 665mm; *overall height* 266mm; *weight without magazine* 3.3kg; *magazine capacity* 25 rounds; *operation* closed-bolt blowback; *firing mode* semi-automatic and automatic; *sighting* optical.

ISRAEL

Israel Military Industries Mini-UZI 9mm SMG:

Israel Military Industries, creator of the world-renowned UZI, has now produced a new, specially designed UZI, reduced in size and weight but retaining all the rugged reliability that has won the UZI the confidence of fighting men the world over. This new weapon is called the Mini-UZI. With stock folded, the Mini-UZI is just over 360mm long, permitting easy concealment under

Right: Steyr AUG/Police Calibre 5.56mm.

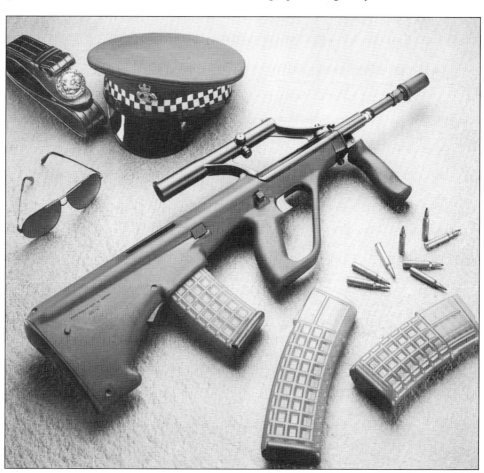

Left: The Mini-Uzi 9mm SMG.

ordinary clothing and carriage in minimal space in vehicles. It can be fired full or semi-automatic from the hip or, with stock extended, from the shoulder. Its perfect balance makes it easy to control during automatic fire, permitting sustained accuracy, even at a high rate of fire. Its simplicity makes it easy to clean and maintain. Fast, agile and completely dependable, the Mini-UZI is an ideal weapon for security and law-enforcement personnel and commando operations.

Data: *weight* complete submachine-gun 2.70kg, *magazine* 20 rounds, empty 160g, loaded 410g; 25 rounds, empty 200g, loaded 490g; 32 rounds, empty 220g, loaded 600g; *length* stock extended, 600mm, stock folded, 360mm; *length of barrel* 197mm; *rifling* R.H.4 grooves, 1 turn in 254mm; *method of operation* blowback; *breech mechanism* breechbolt; *feeding* box magazine; *ammunition* 9mm Parabellum; *sight line radius* 233mm; *front sight* post type, with protective battle sight guard; *rear sight* aperture 'L' flip type, set for 50 and 150m, with protective battle sight guard; *night sight* tritium (Beta) light; *muzzle velocity* 352m/sec; *rate of fire* 950 rounds/min; *effective range* 150m.

Stun Hand Grenade:

Originally designed for hostage rescue operations, the Stun Hand Grenade is particularly effective in an enclosed space, such as a room or the interior of an aeroplane. It will shock and immobilise the occupants for a few seconds, permitting entrance and prompt

Below: Stun Hand Grenades.

Above: The Franchi SPAS 15-Mil Shotgun.

reduction of hostile elements. The grenade stuns and immobilises by means of several temporarily blinding, extremely intense light flashes, accompanied by loud, paralysing noise. The Stun Hand Grenade is also effective in dispersing violent demonstrations and hostile crowds. Its principal effect is that of frightening and causing stampede.

Data: Grenade with fuze body, thin wall aluminium; *weight* 320g; *length* 162mm; *diameter* 63mm; *filler* 8 charges with a special pyrotechnic material; *fuse model* M489; *fuse type* pyrotechnic, delay; *fuse delay time* 2±¹/₂sec.

ITALY

Franchi SPAS 15-Mil

This Italian close-combat assault shotgun is ideal for close combat in built-up areas where there is a danger of ricochet from rifle rounds. It is also highly effective in ambushes and mopping-up operations, in which hit-

ting moving targets is problematical, and is particularly suitable in counter-terrorist assault operations.

Data: *gauge* 12 x 70mm smooth bore; *operation* manual pump action and semi-automatic; *aiming system* mechanical: with U rear sight and adjustable front sight; optical: scope on handle; *carrying handle* with mount according to stanag norms; *safety catch* on grip; *magazine capacity* 6 shots (+ 1 into chamber); *weight of unloaded weapon* 3.90kg; *weight of empty magazine* 0.45kg; *overall length* 915mm; *overall length with folded stock* 700mm; *barrel length* 406.4mm; *sight line length* 330mm; *overall height* 267mm; *overall width* 49mm.

Types of Ammunition: Split ammunition, including all types of 12 bore cartridges; slug ammunition, all types of slug; piercing ammunition, with steel slug; disabling ammunition, including plastic shot, 18 rubber shots or rubber single slug cartridges; launching ammunition, manufactured with propelling black powder, suitable for launching all kinds of grenades, CN, CS, smoke types etc. through muzzle device; CN/CS ammunition

UNITED KINGDOM

Accuracy International Sniper Rifles

The Model PM Sniper Rifle (L96 A1) was selected for service by the British Army after extensive trials, evaluation and endurance firings. The UK Special Forces needed one single weapon for counter-terrorist and covert operations to replace a number of weapons then in use. The

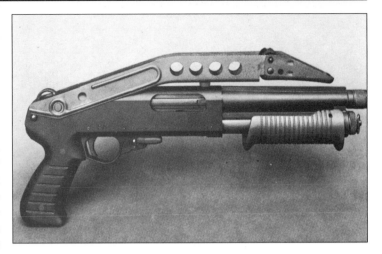

Left: The Franchi PA3/215 Pump Action Shotgun, the smallest gun in the Franchi range.

Right: Accuracy International Ltd. Left and right profiles of the assembled 'Covert' Model Sniper Rifle.

Left: Accuracy International Ltd 'Infantry' Model Sniper Rifle (L96 A1).

Bottom left: Accuracy International Ltd 'Moderated' Sniper Rifle.

Right and below: Accuracy International Ltd. The 'Covert' Model Sniper Rifle packed in its case.

British infantry needed a new sniper rifle. **Variants:** *moderated* sniper rifle (suppressed); *covert* sniper rifle.

Data: (suppressed version) the rifle is bolt-action, magazine fed and built to Build Standard MW32A/248; *weight* 6.2kg; *length* 1,200mm; *width* 90mm including bolt handle; *trigger* 12kg pull off, two-stage detachable; *sight* Schmidt & Bender 6 x 42 Military; *colour* olive drab/black; *suppresser material* aluminium alloy, stainless steel and hard chrome plated steel.

Performance (using A.I type SS 7.62mm ammunition) *velocity* 314m/sec to 330m/sec; *range* 200-300m; *adjustment of range in scope* 0 to beyond 330m; *suppression* better than .22 rimfire; *suppresser life* in excess of 5,000 rounds using subsonic ammunition; *portability* as for normal-length PM, or shorter by removing suppressor.

Armourshield
Special Forces Body Armour

This equipment stops most low-velocity attacks at 5m with front and back hard armour inserts with built-in trauma shield, protection is also provided against high-velocity attack.

Employment: British Army since 1986/7, and US Army since 1986.

Restricted-Entry Body Armour for Special Forces

This is designed for use by police or special forces where entry is of a restricted nature, such as aircraft or vehicle entry, or in abseil work from a building or helicopter. Protection is similar to Special Forces Body Armour.

Employment: British Army, major UK police forces, US military since 1987.

Left and right (top and bottom): Armourshield Body Armour in use.

Avon Industrial Polymers Ltd
Avon Dry Sacs

Special forces such as the British Special Boat Service or the US Seals operate from the sea. Avon inflatable personal equipment carriers are designed to keep contact equipment dry, being constructed from high-quality fabric reinforced rubber and having waterproof zips and nylon inflation/deflation valves. Avon Dry Sacs are used by the SBS.
Data: standard range (approx. sizes) *belt bag* 190mm dia. x 235mm; *radio/medical bag* 610 x 305 x 230mm; *rucksack bag* 750 x 560 x 290mm; other sizes to meet specific requirements can be produced on request.

Special Forces Assault Protection Equipment

The need for a high degree of protection against fire and heat in an assault has been recognised by security forces all over the world. As criminals and terrorists become more sophisticated in their methods of attack and increasingly make use of explosive blast and incendiary devices, the increased risk of serious injuries from flash, blast and heat becomes a matter of reality rather than a possibility. In combating this threat it is essential to use a cloth that is inherently flame-resistant, rather than one that has been treated with chemical flame retardants which are prone to deterioration and require regular and expensive dry-cleaning processes and retreatment. The GD Specialist Supplies suit is made from Nomex 3, which has been proved in operational use to provide a high level of protection. The suit incorporates flame barrier felt pads in the knees and elbows to give protection against impact on sharp objects and to allow the wearer to crawl across hot surfaces. To provide increased protection on high-fire-risk operations, in aircraft or high-rise buildings for example, the team member can increase the level of protection afforded him by wearing two layers of clothing. The assault underwear is made from carbonised viscose, which is inherently flame-retardant yet soft and comfortable against the skin. The outer suit is designed to give the maximum freedom of movement to the wearer, whether

Above: An Avon Dry Sac.

or not the underwear is worn. An abseil harness has also been specially designed, and is now available to interface with this system. The equipment offers the user an integrated personal protection package capable of withstanding the most severe and determined resistance in the course of anti-terrorist assaults and hostage retrieval. Key items of the equipment include:

SF10 Respirator, incorporating an internal microphone, anti-flash outserts, low-profile eyepieces and an entry for optional attachment of an air-escape bottle.

AC100/1 series Composite Helmet, with enhanced levels of ballistic protection and head coverage.

300CT Electronic Ear Defender and CT100 Communications Harness, incorporating a body-worn microphone with connectors for radio transmitter, respirator and ear defenders.

GPV 25 Body Armour, protecting the chest, groin and back from high- and low-velocity rifle and small-arms fire and fragmentation.

Fireproof Assault Suit, including overgarment, underwear, respirator balaclava and gloves, manufactured in inherently flame-retardant materials that combine high levels of protection against flash, blast and heat with comfort in use.

Abseil harness and assault waistcoat, made to a high standard and providing excellent assault capability and flexibility to the user.

Respirator NBC S10: This respirator was accepted into service by the UK MoD in 1985. It couples high levels of respiratory, gastro-intestinal and facial protection with continued operational effectiveness. The user is capable of tactical movement, weapons use and effective communications for long periods of time under threat.

Data: *protection* all warfare gases and aerosols, radioactive dust, etc.; *total leakage* <0.01%; *donning time* <9sec; *NBC hood interface* moulded face-piece rib for positive location; *breathing resistance:* inhalation 373 Pa at 80 litres/min, exhalation 108 Pa at 80 litres/min; *canister thread* STANAG 4155; *eyepieces* coated polycarbonate with high impact and scratch resistance; *communications* intelligible speech over half the distance of the unmasked head, plus additional audio communications interface; *drinking rate* >100 millilitres/min; *drink safety* three protective valves make safe drinking in contaminated environments possible; *total weight* <800g; *maintainability* can be maintained and repaired at unit level, using simple tools and minimal training; *life-cycle* 20 years.

Clow Assault Ladders

In close co-operation with the Police Firearms Division, Clow has designed and developed a range of assault ladders to suit most situations the modern force might encounter. The whole range of assault ladders are made from aluminium to BSS 1474, using large box-section stiles with serrations to front and rear to give better grip to hand and walls, etc. The heavy-duty rungs are securely set and deeply serrated for strength and extra grip. The ladders have an addition-

Below: A Clow Assault Ladder deployed from a Land Rover.

Left: Clow Assault Ladder.

Right: Three pictures of Dartcord Charge Linear Cutting (CLC)

al third centre stile for added strength and stability even when being used by several men simultaneously. The hollow aluminium sections allow maximum strength with lightness to aid speed of operation. Ladders vary in length from the Ground Floor Assault Ladder (120mm) to the multi-level Assault ladder (6,250mm). In addition, Clow produces vehicle-mounted assault systems on Range Rovers, Land Rovers and Mercedes 811D vans.

Haley and Weller Dartcord

Dartcord Charge Linear Cutting (CLC) consists of an explosive filling (TDX) contained in a continuous, shaped, lead sheath. As well as having underwater engineering applications, Dartcord can be used in rescue, security, terrorist and hostage situations. When the charge is detonated, the explosive shockwaves collapse and focus the lead sheath in the inverted 'V' into a fast-moving jet. When this jet reaches the target, it behaves in a

Dartcord Characteristics

Aluminium or Alloy

Product Code	CLC g/m (mm)	Straight Cut (mm)	Flat Curve (mm)	Tubular Curve
D102	10	3	3	2.5
D103	25	6	6	5
D104	40	10	10	9
D105	80	13	13	
D106	100	14	14	
D107	120	16	16	
D108	150	19	19	
D109	180	25	25	
D110	250	35	35	

Wood (Straight cut across grain)

Product Code	CLC g/m (mm)	Hardwood (mm)	Softwood (mm)	Blockboard/ Chipboard
D102	10	25	25	50
D103	25	50	38	75
D104	40	76	76	
D109	180	375		

Structural Materials

Material	Thickness (mm)	Product Code	CLC g/m
Single brick wall	115	D104	40
Double brick wall*	230	D109	180
Concrete**	50	D105	80
Concrete**	75	D107	120
Concrete**	100	D109	180
Concrete**	125	D110	250
Breeze block	75	D105	80
Breeze block	150	D108	150
Fibreglass (G.R.P.)	4	D12	10

* Assuming no cavity between double brick wall
** A second charge may be necessary to sever reinforcing bars in reinforced concrete.

manner similar to that of a high-pressure jet of water hitting soft earth. If the CLC is in contact with the target, another action assists the cutting effect. Shockwaves from the detonation travel through the target material, inducing compression and tension waves. These effects exceed the tensile strength of the material, causing development of a fracture below the jet cut. The cutting action of the jet can be further enhanced by artificially

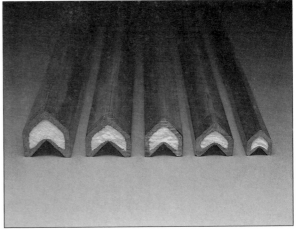

raising the shaped charge from the surface of the target material. This 'stand-off' allows more time for the jet to form before striking the target material, and consequently improves cutting performance. In this case the fracture generated by the shockwave is lost. The emphasis given to, and requirement for, the different cutting actions will depend upon the target material and configuration. The actual stand-off distance will be different for each size of Dartcord CLC, and may be affected by target constraints. If stand-off is considered desirable, the correct distances should be evaluated by trial firings.

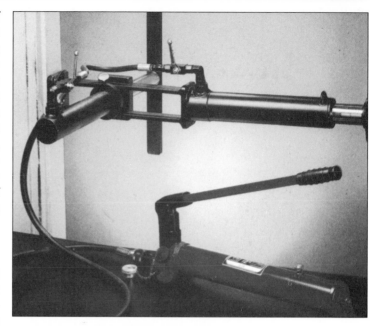

Hydro-Noa Doorbuster

There have been many instances in the past in which people have lost their lives as a result of being trapped in a burning apartment with no means of escape and no means for the rescue services to break in through the front door in time – especially when the door was a steel security door. The Door Buster Menny 1 has been developed to overcome this difficulty. It has proved itself during many rescue missions in which steel security doors have been forced open within seconds. The device is locked into the door frame, and a piston at the front of the apparatus is then operated, forcing the door open within a maximum of four seconds. It is available in five different versions, and has been sold to fire brigades, security services, rescue services, armed forces and police.

Law Enforcement International LEI-100 Laser Sight

This uses the latest electronic technology to incorporate many features not found in other laser sights, and is one of the most powerful 'red dot' laser sights currently available. The heart of the unit is a military grade 2mW* laser tube. This is mounted inside an aluminium casing which provides maximum shock resistance with minimum weight. Windage and elevation adjustments are independent of the laser tube, ensuring a constant zero even under heavy recoil. The LEI-100 can be fitted to most weapons, and is supplied with universal mounts.

Top left: Hydro-Noa Menny 1 Model A1 Door Buster.

Above: Menny 1 Model C3 Door Buster.

Above right: Menny 1 Model D4 Door Buster.

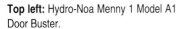

Left: Menny 1 Model H18 Door Buster.

Below: Law Enforcement International LEI-100 Laser Sight mounted on an MP5 SMG.

Data: *output power* 2mW (max); *dot size* 6cm (50m), 12cm (100m); *range* 600m (at night); *battery life* 100min (continuous); *weight* 0.65kg (including batteries); *length* 25cm; *temperature range* -10° to +60°C; *classification* Class IIIa laser product.

Parker-Hale M-85 7.62 Sniper Rifle

The M85 Sniper is a uniquely adaptable and robust high-precision rifle designed to give 100 per cent first-shot hit capability at all ranges up to 600m, and is sighted up to 900m. The specially designed action has a built-in aperture rear sight adjustable up to 900m for emergency use, or when use of optical sights would be impractical. The integral dovetail mounting is designed for rapid attachment and removal of telescopic or passive night-vision sights, and features positive return-to-zero and recoil stop.

Employment: British Army.

Data: *calibre* 7.62 x 51mm; *length* maximum overall 1,210mm, minimum overall 1,140mm; *stock* one-piece, composite material with choice of finishes; *weight* with telescopic sight and empty magazine 5.7kg;

Below: Parker-Hale M-85 Sniper Rifle. Complete sniper's kit in welded aluminium transit case.

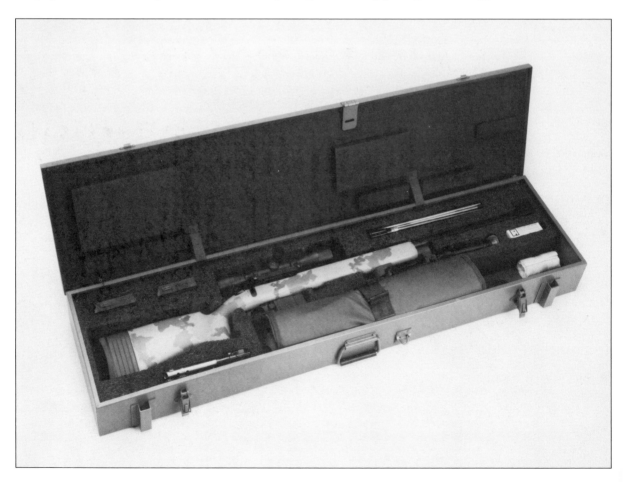

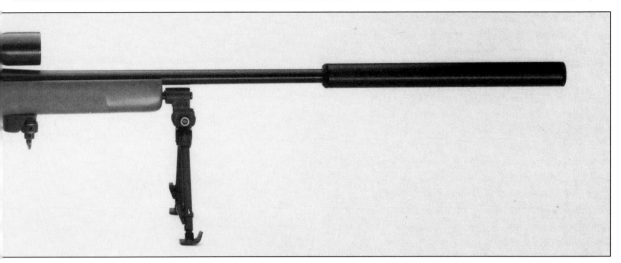

Above: Parker-Hale M-85 Sniper Rifle with Suppressor.

rifling twist RH 1 in 12in, number of grooves 4; *trigger pull* 0.9-2.25kg; *magazine* 10 shot.

Plumett Air Launchers
Plumett AL-50

This shoulder-fired air launcher stands at the top of Plumett's range of completely pneumatic launching equipment, and is designed for grapnel, line and projectile launching. The AL-50 is completely submersible and ideal for many covert military operations. Other applications include cliff or building rescue/retrieval and numerous other line-throwing applications.

Data: *range* using standard 8mm-diameter rope with grapnel fired at 60°, 45m horizon-

tal or 30m vertical; at 40°, 55m horizontal or 15m vertical; *grapnel* lightweight carbon fibre; fully loaded unit is submersible to a depth of 10m.

AL-51

This launcher provides an accurate and portable means of launching a rope or projectile in a wide range of environmental conditions. The system is particularly suited to use in maritime applications, including ship-to-ship, ship-to-shore and oil rig/tanker requirements.

Data: *range* 3mm rope, 100m; 25kg monofilament, 250m; *equipment* projectiles and stainless steel rope carrying rods; 3mm

Below: Plumett AL-50.

Below right: Plumett AL-51.

polyester rope; 0.5 litre air cylinder; spare seals, lubricant and tools; customised shock-proof carrying case; may be used with most air cylinders.

AL-52

Being base-mounted with adjustable bipods, the AL-52 is specifically designed for throwing higher payloads. This model is capable of accurately throwing a metal grapnel with rope, and permits access to buildings and structures where a heavier grapnel is required. The aluminium four-line grapnel penetrates glass and other fragile materials, and its hardened points secure into masonry and timber. The base mounting allows fine adjustment and repeatable accuracy.

Royal Ordnance Stun Grenade

Stun grenades are used in hostage or hijack situations where the aim is to dis-

Left: Plumett AL-52.

orientate and distract terrorists during an assault, but avoid injury to innocent hostages. The Royal Ordnance Stun Grenade is waterproof, and achieves silent ignition.

Data: *sound* 160dB; *diameter* 62mm; *length* 100mm; *weight* 200g.

UNITED STATES/UNITED KINGDOM

Left: Royal Ordnance Stun Grenade.

Law Enforcement International De Lisle Mk 4 Sniper Rifle

This is a fully-suppressed 7.62mm sniper rifle based on the Remington 700 action. Unlike most other weapons currently available, the De Lisle is designed to use both subsonic and standard ball ammunition. This capability is made possible by the extensive use of stainless steel in the suppresser assembly, which reduces maintenance and considerably increases suppresser life. The suppresser completely eliminates muzzle flash and, with subsonic ammunition, reduces firing signature to the minimum. It can be easily removed for routine maintenance without the use of tools. The De Lisle outperforms other weapons in its class, providing exceptional reliability and accuracy. The use of a heavy match-grade barrel permits the rifle to deliver outstanding accuracy at maximum range. With 7.62mm subsonic ammunition the effective range is over 200m. Using 7.62mm sniper-grade ammuni-

Below: Law Enforcement International De Lisle Mk 4 Sniper Rifle.

tion the effective range is increased, and targets can be successfully engaged at ranges in excess of 400m.

Data: *calibre* 7.62 x 51mm NATO; *action* bolt action; *magazine capacity* 4+1; *weight* 4.5kg (without sights); *length* 1,200mm; *barrel length* 355mm; *sights* optical and night sights available; *muzzle velocity* 320m/sec (subsonic), 760 m/sec (ball); *effective range* 200m (subsonic), 400m (ball).

UNITED STATES

Calico Light Weapon Systems

Calico manufactures a wide range of light weapon systems ideal for counter-terrorist situations. They are light, compact, have a high rate of fire and have magazines containing large numbers of rounds.

M-900S Semi-automatic Carbine

Data: *calibre* 9mm NATO/PARA; *capacity* 50 OR Operational 100 rounds helical-feed magazine; *action* retarded blowback, Cetme type, static cocking handle; *bolt* heat-treated A-2 tool steel with A-2 striker; *rate* semi-automatic; *barrel* 409mm heat-treated 4140; *weight* 2.868kg loaded with 50 vel magazine; *height* 175mm; *width* 78mm; *length* 876mm.

M-960-A Submachine-gun

Data: *weight* 2.83kg loaded with 50-round magazine; *length* 533mm with butt-stock

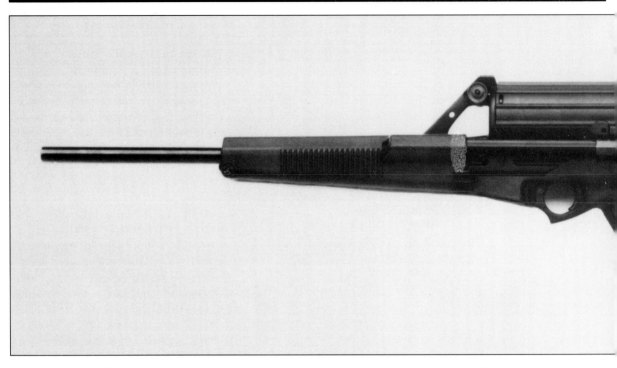

Above: Calico's M-900S Semi-Automatic Carbine. **Below:** Calico's M-960-A Submachine Gun.

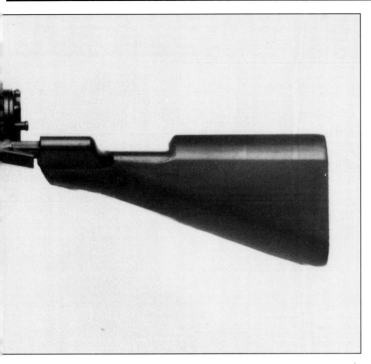

closed, 660mm with butt-stock extended.

M-950 Semi-automatic Pistol

Data: *calibre* 9mm NATO/PARA; *capacity* 50 OR Operational 100 rounds helical-feed magazine; *action* retarded blowback, Cetme-type, static cocking handle; *bolt* heat-treated A-2 tool steel with A-2 striker; *rate* semi-automatic; *barrel* 191mm heat-treated 4140; *weight* 1.968kg loaded with 50-round magazine; *width* 78mm; *length* 403mm.

Barrett Firearms Manufacturing
Barrett Light .50 Sniper Rifle

The Model 82 rifle is available in two configurations, to suit the needs of user groups with different tactical objectives. The original model, the 'Light 50', is configured for the long-range, high-accuracy, relatively low volume of fire role typical of use by sniper teams and outlined in the current US Army definition and requirement for the Special Application Sniper Rifle (SARS). This ver-

Below right: Calico's M-970 Shoulder Rig, including a M-950 High Capacity Pistol.

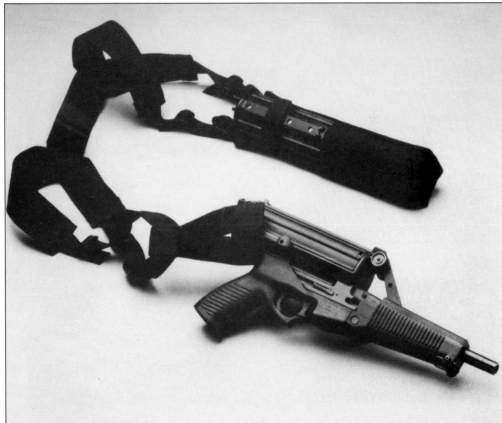

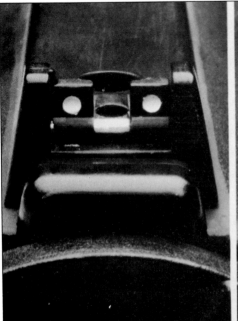

Above left: Calico's M-920 Cordura Brass Catcher

Above: Calico's M-905 Loader

Left: Calico's Flip Sight

Barrett Light .50 Sniper Rifle

Data

Specification	LSW	SASR
Calibre	50 BMG (12.7mm)	50 BMG (12.7mm)
Operation	Short recoil, semi automatic	Recoil, semi automatic
Overall Length	61 inches (154.9cm)	62 inches (157.5cm)
Barrel Length	33 inches (83.8cm)	33 inches (83.8cm)
Feed Device	11-round detachable box magazine	11-round detachable box magazine
Sights (quick detach)	4 x telescope	10 x telescope
Weight	32.5lb (14.7kg)	35.5lb (16.1kg)
Muzzle Velocity	2,848 fps (M2 Ball)	2,848 fps (M2 Ball)

sion is equipped with a 10-power telescope with a custom reticule that makes possible accuracy of 1 to 1.5 minutes of angle out to 2,000m with selected military ammunition. Special care has been taken to ensure the utmost accuracy. The second version of the Model 82, the 'Light Support Weapon', has features that permit a degree of sustained fire while still maintaining the accuracy for which the Model 82 has become famous. The light .50 is the most cost-effective means of disabling or destroying some of the most sophisticated threats. It has the ability to engage the enemy at ranges far beyond those at which small-arms can return fire.

When all of these factors are considered, it is obvious that the Model 82 can be the deciding factor in a critical engagement.

SF Firearms
MAC-10 Submachine-gun

The SF MAC-10 fires from an open bolt which is of overhung construction. This ensures that it is controllable even when bursts are fired with the stock retracted, and permits a barrel length of nearly six inches to be accommodated without detracting from the compactness/concealability of the weapon. The weapon has a fire selector on the left-hand side of the lower receiver which

Right: MAC-10 Submachine-gun with solid butt.

Left: MAC-10 Submachine gun with detachable butt detached.

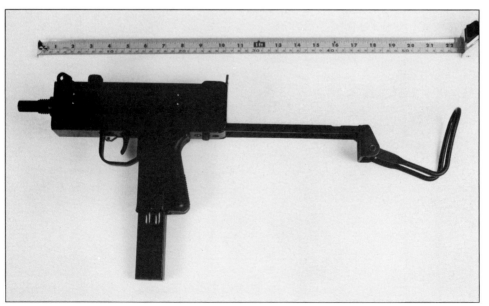

Left: MAC-10 Submachine gun with detachable butt extended.

enables it to discharge either a single round or on fully automatic. The SF MAC-10 is chambered for the standard NATO 9 x 19 Parabellum (Luger) round. The action can handle full-velocity SMG rounds, but will also cycle on subsonic rounds, for reducing signature, when a silencer is employed. The barrel is threaded as standard for a silencer. SF Firearms manufactures a silencer, similar to the Sionic, which has helictical spirals in place of conventional baffles, and can withstand fully automatic fire.

Data: dimensions, *length without stock* 267mm; *length of stock telescoped* 295mm; *length of stock extended* 548mm; *barrel length* 146mm; *maximum width* 50mm; *weight and capacity* gun without magazine 2.80kg; *loaded 32-round magazine* 0.62kg; *type of fire* selective (semi-automatic or fully automatic); *cyclic rate of fire* 950m rounds/min; *front sight* protected post; *rear sight* fixed aperture; *safety* manually operated safety system for locking bolt in open or closed position.

Below: MAC-10 Submachine gun with detachable butt folded.

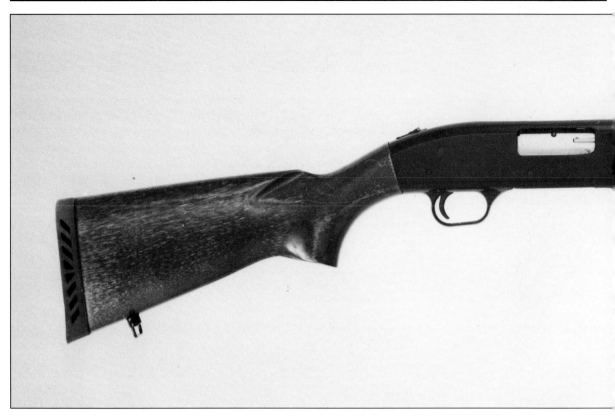

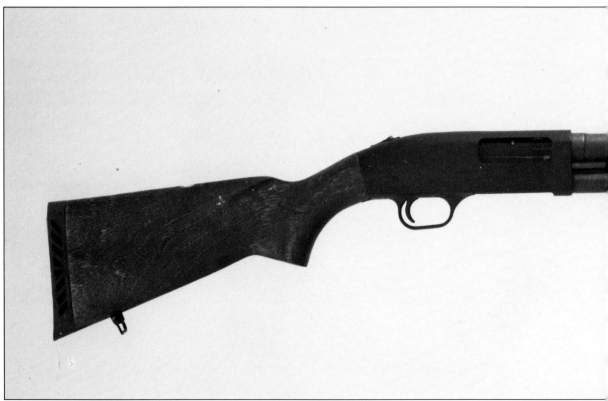

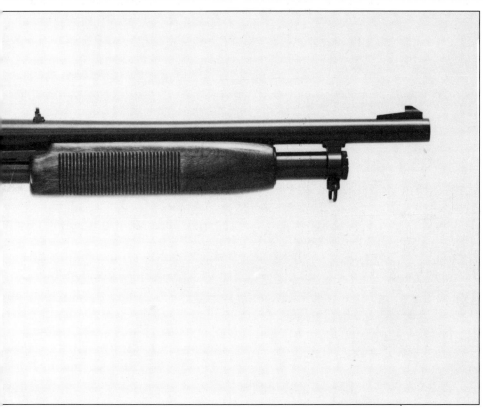

Mossberg Combat shotguns

Left: Mossberg 500-ATP-6S Enforcement 12 gauge, six-shot, pump action combat shotgun with an 18$\frac{1}{2}$-inch barrel.

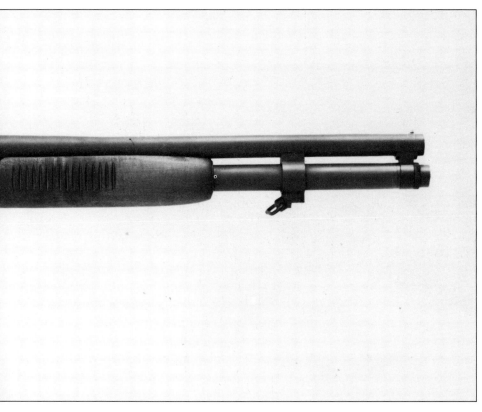

Left: Mossberg 500-ATP-6SP Enforcement 12 gauge, eight-shot, pump action combat shotgun with a 20-inch barrel fitted with a bayonet lug.

Left: Dragon 12 x 12 Shotgun

Below: F.R. Ordnance International Ltd MC51 7.62mm Submachine-gun.

Index